THE QUEER TURN IN FEMINISM

FORDHAM UNIVERSITY PRESS NEW YORK 2014

COMMONALITIES
Timothy C. Campbell, series editor

THE QUEER TURN IN FEMINISM

Identities, Sexualities, and the Theater of Gender

ANNE EMMANUELLE BERGER

Translated by Catherine Porter

Fordham University Press has no responsibility for the persistence or accuracy of URLs for external or third-party Internet websites referred to in this publication and does not guarantee that any content on such websites is, or will remain, accurate or appropriate.

Fordham University Press also publishes its books in a variety of electronic formats. Some content that appears in print may not be available in electronic books.

Library of Congress Cataloging-in-Publication Data is available from the publisher.

16 15 14   5 4 3 2 1

First edition

CONTENTS

ACKNOWLEDGMENTS

I was able to begin writing this book thanks to the one-semester research leave granted me by the Langue et Littérature Françaises section of the Conseil National des Universités in 2009; I would like to express my gratitude to the members serving on the Conseil at that time. The Institut National des Sciences Humaines et Sociales of the Centre National de la Recherche Scientifique allowed me to complete the work with the help of a grant in 2012; many thanks to its leadership team and to the jurors of the 35th section. I am grateful to the friends and colleagues at Paris 8 who supported me in this project (special thanks to Bruno, Denis, and Eleni!) and also to my graduate students in the Centre d'Études Féminines et d'Études de Genre at Paris 8; this book, a product of our classes and our exchanges, is dedicated, in part, to them. Heta Rundgren was of invaluable logistical help in juggling between the French and American "versions" of the texts I consulted. Catherine Porter, who translated the book into "American" English with patience, rigor, and talent, made it better by pointing out glitches and unclear or awkward phrasing. As the book had not yet appeared in French when she translated it, I was able to benefit from her questions and suggestions to make the necessary adjustments. To Cathy, all my gratitude! Let me take advantage of this exercise, more "American" than French, to let my friends Anne Deneys-Tunney, Hélène Merlin-Kajman, Catherine Nesci, and Isabelle Tournier know that, unwittingly and each in her own way, they contributed significantly to the impetus behind this book, as they did with earlier texts. The last word belongs to HC, my mother, since it was she who suggested the title.

Finally, I owe to my most strangely intimate reader, Jim Siegel, the gift of the "America" that propels my writing.

THE QUEER TURN IN FEMINISM

1

PARABASIS (BEFORE THE ACT)

POINTS OF VIEW

"But after all, who is interested, today, in sexual difference, gender roles and hierarchies, or even sexualities, in the United States of America—or, to be more precise, in 'theoretical America'? In her most recent work, at least the work she has been producing in the United States and for an American public, hasn't Judith Butler moved away from the divided field of feminist theory and queer theory? Hasn't she turned toward a more general theorization of the political, or to an attempt to reestablish moral philosophy on a 'poststructuralist' basis? Eve Kosovsky Sedgwick's last essays addressed the issue of 'affects' and 'feelings'; hadn't she stopped contributing to the field of queer theory several years before her untimely death in 2009, even if she continued thinking and writing 'in a queer fashion' to the end? Didn't well-known thinkers such as Janet Halley, a queer legal scholar at Harvard, and Andrew Parker, a queer literary critic, announce the end of queer theory as early as 2007, in a special issue of *South Atlantic Quarterly* titled *After Sex*?[1] Two years earlier, hadn't Janet Halley proclaimed the end of feminism—or rather the need to end it—in a book titled *Split Decisions: How and Why to Take a Break from Feminism*? In an article published in 2010, even the historian Joan Scott wondered about the 'usefulness' of the 'concept' of gender that she had helped develop and promote in the 1980s.[2] As for Wendy Brown, a well-known political theorist and (post)feminist, she has been playing Cassandra in the field of gender studies since 1997.

"This is all true, but still, gender studies and gender theory—or rather theories—are now well established in Europe. Long implanted in Northern Europe, they're now welcomed and recognized in France and Spain.

Universities are starting to make room for the questions they open up.[3] Publishing houses are creating collections featuring 'gender' and/or 'sexualities.'[4] American feminist and postfeminist thinkers are being translated. Judith Butler and Joan Scott, of course, but also Teresa de Lauretis, Donna Haraway, and all their predecessors: Carole Pateman, Carole Gilligan, and many others. And when Judith Butler comes to France, which she has been doing regularly for some time now, she speaks primarily about 'gender and sexuality,' after all.

"Let's think a little, finally, about the paradoxical way a certain Foucault has been received. For if it is true that Foucault conceived his *History of Sexuality* as a way to put an end to the modern myth of liberation of and through sex, isn't it also true that his work has played a major role in the emergence of gender and sexuality theory and politics in North America? Didn't he—in spite of himself—contribute to unleashing 'amazing revolutions of love' in the United States, first, and now in Europe?[5]

"So, all right, in the United States you can say that the theoretical scene of gender studies and queer studies is, for the most part, intro-retrospective. It is situated almost entirely under the sign of 'after,' as we see from the countless talks and publications that thematize 'after-ness' in various ways: the datedness, the posthumous character, but also the enduring if problematic legacy of women's studies, gender studies, and their queer posterity. But in France, these questions are quite current. While all definitions are being challenged in North America, efforts to consolidate them are underway in France. And then isn't the American 'intro-retrospective' discourse, as you put it, out of phase with the rest of the world, after all? On most of the continents of the planet, these 'amazing revolutions of love' haven't yet begun."

So I speculated and split myself in two as I began this book. For ever since I left France for the United States—more precisely, for Ithaca, New York—in 1984, I have been seeing double, and I have kept on doing so since my return to France, to Paris, in 2007. And this double vision functions, in particular, in the realms of gender and sexuality theory and politics.

I should explain that I arrived at Cornell University at a time when what has been called "French thought" was at the height of its ascendancy in the humanities. Now, this "thought," variously characterized as poststructuralist or postmodernist, was intimately concerned with the question of the feminine and the question of sexual differences, as Alice Jardine, herself an active participant in this history, showed in 1985 in *Gynesis: Configurations of Woman and Modernity*.[6] While Jardine used the term "modernity," as writers in France were doing in the 1970s, for what came to be called "postmodernity" soon afterward, her book sought to bring to light the role of the motifs of "the feminine" or "the woman" (Lacan, Lyotard), "sexual difference" (Lacan again, but even more importantly Derrida, Irigaray, Cixous, and Kristeva), "becoming-woman" (Deleuze), and "sexuality," in the constellation that became known as "French thought" in the United States. Jardine thus helped shed light on the intricate interconnections between this "French thought" and what gradually developed in the United States between 1980 and 1990, in contact with that thought, under the name of "gender theory" and then "queer theory."

Cornell has, in fact, been one of the privileged sites of "French thought" from the mid-1970s on. It was also one of the first American universities (thus one of the first in the world) to welcome a program of study devoted to questions of gender and sexuality, embryonically as a "female studies" program in 1969, then officially as a legitimate field of study and research in a women's studies program as of 1973. Most of the major players in the fragments of intellectual history I offer in this book also passed through Cornell, as students, faculty members, and/or visiting lecturers.[7]

And now it is "American thought," or what is being received under this name, that seems to be playing a central role in the rise of gender studies in France. And even if this so-called American thought is also penetrating French intellectual space in other forms (e.g., cognitive science, cognitivist or analytic philosophy), it is in the area of gender and sexuality and its interdisciplinary crossings with "postcolonial" analyses of "race" and "culture" that American thinkers are receiving particular attention and having a significant impact, which is at once intellectual, "popular" (via the media), and political.

In reality, the questions being raised in the field of gender studies today have constituted one of the main axes of Franco-American dialogue for almost seventy years. Since the publication of Simone de Beauvoir's *The Second Sex* after the author's return from America, then in the wake of the American reception of "French thought" in the domain of sexuality and gender, and right up to the recent translation in France of the principal American texts in this field (works that are themselves in many respects "digests" of "French thought"), "French" and "English" have been widely, perhaps predominantly, spoken when "speaking" sex(es), gender(s), and sexuality (sexualities) has been on the agenda.[8] What is designated as "gender theory" today is thus in more than one respect a "Franco-American" invention. In thinking about these questions, then, one cannot avoid reflecting on this "politico-cultural axis,"[9] and, more generally, on the relation between, on the one hand, a politics and a conception of genders and, on the other hand, the languages and cultures in which or from which this politics and this conception are being developed.

I certainly do not mean to limit the field of reflection to this "cultural axis" alone. The intellectual and political history of approaches to these questions clearly cannot be limited to these two geocultural zones, nor to their relations or intersections under precise historical conditions. I recognize and do not wish to minimize the contributions of other political and cultural continents, in particular those that do not belong to Western history, even though I should like to recall in passing that it was also in the United States, or rather in American universities, that postcolonial theory and postcolonial studies were born.[10] I am well aware that in this regard we are going to witness—we are already witnessing—major continental shifts bringing entirely new inflections.

No Western tropism on my part, then. I simply want to make clear, on the margins of this book, the reason for the "double vision" that affects my perspective. I lived through the "French" and Francophone moment in the United States, in the American university context. And now I am living through the "American" moment in France. Imagine my double good fortune and my redoubled astonishment when, after witnessing the fabrication of "French thought" in the United States, I came back to France in time to witness the "reinvention" of gender studies, presumed to have been imported from the United States.[11] A participant-observer, as social scientists would say, on both sides in succession and simultaneously, I find myself obliged to practice and to think, in a single movement, both retrospection and anticipation; I find myself caught between "already done" and "barely begun," between "there, it's over" and "we're finally there." To be sure, the experience is increasingly common today: All border-crossers know this dislocation of periods and places, through a telescoping of heterogeneous space-times, in this era of globalized material and symbolic exchanges, mass teletechnologies, and instantaneous transmission of information. Still, one must try to draw the complex intellectual and political lessons that such an experience imposes.

OBJECT CHOICE

A certain number of books and articles that have recently been published in France lay out a history, or rather elements of a history, of the constitution of the field of gender theory as feminist theory in the United States. For my part, without seeking to substitute an "origins narrative" of my own for the story that is beginning to circulate, and without making any claim whatsoever that my treatment of the questions that interest me will be exhaustive, I am attempting to bring different perspectives to bear and to bring to light other swatches of intellectual and cultural history that are harder to spot from Europe, by virtue of my own hybrid, "dislocated" vantage point. Far from seeking coherence and aiming at synthesis, I shall make a point along the way of noting the aporias, the dissonances, even the productive inconsistencies of the theoretical and political field of gender theory and queer theory as these have been constituted in the United States. Thus the four essays that follow are propelled by—and conceived as—certain questions that I am raising for myself, and that I am putting to gender theory and its queer variant. In particular, I shall observe the theoretical and political behavior of two "odd couples" following the emergence of feminist gender theory in the 1980s: one couple formed by "gender theory" and "performance theory," the other formed by "gender theory" and "queer theory"; obviously, these two couples are intimately connected.

In chapter 2, I ask myself how and why gender theory in the United States has developed as a theory of "performance," contributing to the "queering" of feminist thought and practices on the one hand, and the creative and mutually beneficial alliance of contemporary "performance" art with (post)feminist and queer thought on the other hand. By defining gender as an "act," a word that signifies both action and acting (in the theatrical sense), and by characterizing heterosexuality, understood as a cultural practice, as "an intrinsic comedy," Judith Butler conceptualizes gender as performance.[12] And she is not alone. Now, this conception does not stem solely, perhaps not even principally, as is too often suggested today, from a neo-Foucaldian analytics of power relations. It seems to me to have, in addition, at least two other identifiable though perhaps hard-to-reconcile "sources": on the one hand, what has been called in the United States the sociology of inter*action*, which stresses the theatricality of social relations, and which played an important role in the genesis of the notion of "gender" starting in the 1950s and, on the other hand, its "French" contemporary— the Lacanian analytics of desire—which, as we know, gives pride of place to masquerade, inviting us to read "feminine" and "masculine" identity formations as so many "displays" destined to support the play of sexual seduction. We understand, then, why cross-dressing, or "drag," has been a major object of interest and an anchor point for "American" gender theory and why the figure of the "drag queen" has imposed itself as the icon of a gender theory constituted from the outset as queer, even before being recognized as such.

In chapter 3, I take up the question of the centrality of the notion of performance in another way. Looking at the rhetoric and the politics of "visibility" in the political and theoretical field of "minority" identities and sexualities today, I reflect on a different mode of articulation and mobilization of the notion of "act." By way of this notion, which precedes and informs the more recent one of performance, several contemporary registers are conceptualized and connected: artistic action (for a certain artistic performance stems at once from "acting" and "acting out"), political action (it is no accident that one of the earliest movements of resistance to homophobia, which engaged in spectacular collective actions against the stigmatization of homosexuals suffering from AIDS, was called "Act Up"), and even sexual experience, since this is essentially envisaged, in a queer perspective, as a shift into enactment or an accomplishment of acts. The stress placed by a certain queer thought on sexual activity and even on the "sex act" itself, as the only pertinent object for "sexuality studies," aims to evade the questionable, reifying notion of "sexual identity," even while challenging the normative presuppositions and moral connotations that are usually attached to the description—or even the mere mention—of what is traditionally called sexual "behavior."

Envisaging here the question of "gender and sexuality performance" from a political perspective, I attempt once again to propose elements of the genealogy of this "call for visibility" that governs, in part, the discourse and the strategy of political struggles in this area. Once again, I stress the role played by the American sociology of interaction in the representation of social relationships; one could, of course, take the opposite tack and claim that this sociology merely formalizes the way in which social relations are thought and experienced in the United States. But I also try to show what the motif and the goal of "visibility" owe to the American civil rights movement, thus to the way in which the question of race has been raised in the United States.

In this sense, like gender theory and its queer avatar, a certain politics of gender(s) and sexualities seems to me to be inflected by the contexts of its original production, even if the differentiated places, modes, and times of its reception can, of course, always pull it or relaunch it in unprecedented directions.

In chapter 4, I start from a reflection on the way(s) in which language and linguistic practices register and precipitate movements of history and continental divides in order to analyze a certain "becoming-queer" of "sexual difference," a "becoming-queer" that participates in the contemporary "queering" of feminist thought, which interests me in several respects. By following the "travels" of the idiom "sexual difference,"[13] thus by stressing, against its partial or presumed reification, the instability of the uses of one of the key terms in thinking about gender and differences of sex from the time people began to take an interest in these questions, I am seeking to bring out the conceptual heterogeneity—in my eyes as irreducible as it is productive—of the theoretical field of gender studies. This semantic instability has to do, of course, with the constant modifications of the contexts in which the expression is used, thus also with the modes of "transport" of "concepts," with the vicissitudes of border crossings that are at once political, cultural, and idiomatic. Why do I say idiomatic rather than linguistic? Because, even while using the same natural language, thus the same lexicon, one can draw from it very disparate singular effects; and because it is precisely where we appear to be speaking the same language, sharing the same linguistic body, that differences are the least visible and consequently the most surprising. "Sexual difference" and *différence sexuelle* are false cognates—or false twins—of this sort, by virtue of their common Latin roots.[14] With and through these "differences," I am also interrogating the modes of constitution of the Franco-Anglo-American theoretical axis.

The earliest essays that can be characterized as "feminist," that is, those that denounce women's servitude through a critique of social institutions, can be traced to the late seventeenth century in the West. Simone de Beauvoir helped make Poullain de la Barre known in France,[15] but proto-feminist pamphlets of the sort he wrote, especially those criticizing the institution of marriage inasmuch as this institution organizes the legal, economic, and social dependency of women, were considerably more numerous in England during this period and throughout the eighteenth century. Contemporary feminist studies have brought the pioneering contributions of Mary Astell and Judith Drake and many others out of obscurity. Roxana, Daniel Defoe's "fortunate mistress," has been better known for some time: An extraordinary "business woman," a feminist before her time, she rejected marriage in favor of free-enterprise prostitution. Defoe, the son of a merchant and a merchant himself, was one of Mary Astell's readers. It is probably no accident that the beginnings of feminism—at the very least of feminist thought—are contemporaneous with the beginnings of capitalism in the West. The two are historically linked.

In chapter 5, I look at the forms and effects, remote but persistent, of this originary "debt" of Western feminism toward capitalism and bourgeois ideology. If "second-wave" feminism was indeed born in the wake of the challenge to capitalist society and the capitalist economy that characterized the liberation movements of the 1960s and '70s, the "crisis" of feminist thought attested by the rhetoric of "after-ness" and the "intro-retrospective" posture of gender theory evoked earlier is also perhaps in part, today, a crisis of the alliance forged between feminism and anti-capitalism.

And perhaps what I call "Roxana's legacy," that is, what a certain feminism and even more a certain postfeminism owe to the economic and social but also discursive and moral triumph of capitalism, plays a role in the formation of the two "odd couples" (gender theory/performance theory, gender theory/queer theory) whose tandem movements I follow throughout this book.

GLOSSARY

Readers will no doubt have noticed from the beginning of this preamble that I am multiplying designations and passing from one language to the other to evoke the places and objects that concern me: United States or America, *théorie du genre* or gender theory, feminism or postfeminism, and so on. This seeming fluctuation is intentional.

Here are some explanations, for more and less informed readers alike.

"AMERICA": I am well aware of the political critiques addressed to the everyday use of this name to designate the United States, an abusive practice that tends, if not to pass off the "United States" portion as the whole of America (North and South), then at least to obscure the fact that America cannot be reduced to its U.S. component (*sa composante "états-unienne"*). If I continue to use this term, it is not to signal approval of the "hegemonic" or "imperialist" gesture that consists in having the part stand in for the whole, in subsuming the south into the north, in denying or forgetting the diversity of a continent; it is because the "America" of which I am speaking is not always or not merely a territorial entity with precise boundaries. It is also a cultural zone whose contours do not simply coincide with the geopolitical entity "United States"; it is a phantasmatic territory, the one from which European "uncles" (and, today, also "aunts") continue to return. Finally, it is once again a question of vantage point: The adjective *états-unien* does not exist in English. One can use it only from outside the Anglo-American linguistic perimeter, even if one finds oneself in agreement with all or part of the critique of the sovereign position or the hegemonic tendency of the United States in the world today. Judith Butler, who has often criticized U.S. policies in her writings, calls herself—and can only call herself, in her own language, since she speaks "American"—an American. For my part, I write as I see, that is, double, or rather I write as a "Française" and an "Américaine," in a split but not contradictory affiliation with two geocultural continents.

GENDER THEORY, *THÉORIE(S) DU GENRE*: If the French noun phrase *théorie du genre* is a quasi-literal translation of "gender theory," the two expressions are not absolutely equivalent for me. When I use the English term, it is to indicate that I am speaking of the "theory of gender" in its "American," if not its original, version. And if I use the French expression sometimes in the plural, sometimes in the singular, it is because the so-called "theory of gender" has become plural and diverse in crossing borders. There is not, or there is no longer, today, a "theory of gender" in the singular, in either language. "Gender theory" underwent an initial and decisive mutation when it became in the 1970s what it was not at the outset: a "feminist theory." And "feminist theory" is anything but a unified theory.

POSTFEMINISM, (POST)FEMINISM: The term "postfeminism" rose to prominence following the model of other "posts" (postcolonialism, poststructuralism, and so on) in the early 1990s, coming to designate a set of self-critical positions within feminist theory itself. In the 1980s, voices had already been raised in the American feminist context calling into question the unity of the "subject of feminism," that is, "woman" as political subject and subject of the political. Suspecting that all or part of Western feminism, including the feminism(s) that came out of the anticapitalist movements or cultural protest movements of the 1960s, had white heterosexual women as their implicit models and that they were blind or insensitive to hierarchies of "race" and sexualities as well as to power relations among regions of the globe, this critical feminism came to be called postfeminism. In the United States, this postfeminism chiefly took the form of a critique of the hetero-sexist logic underlying a certain Western feminism. This is why it is often conflated with the thinking and tendencies known as queer.

For my part, I distinguish between two forms of postfeminism. First, a (post)feminism whose "immanent critique" aims less to discredit femi-nism than to refine its instruments of analysis: It is to this (post)feminism still faithful to the political and philosophical project of feminism—a word that really should be put in the plural—that I am adding parentheses: a way of signaling the productive instability of a "post" that does not merely signify a surpassing of, or an ideological break, with feminism. Second, a postfeminism (without parentheses) that, even as it assumes its genea-logical link with feminism, resolutely regards the latter as inadequate and outdated.

2

QUEENS AND QUEERS: THE THEATER OF GENDER IN "AMERICA"

PROLOGUE

A character has recently appeared on the French media scene.[1] "She" calls herself "Wendy Delorme." Wendy Delorme is a "woman of the stage" (as we would once have spoken of a "man of letters") of a new type, at least in France. She describes herself as a *performeuse*.[2] In her "one-woman shows," produced in geographical proximity to the steamy peep shows of Pigalle, she performs the spectacle of "femininity" with exaggerated mimicry: femininity as pantomime, following the example of the drag queens, flamboyant "women" of the male sex who played such an important role during the twentieth century in the formation of gay culture in America. A particular art of the spectacle is, in fact, the principal source and form of homosexual "gayness" in the modern Western history of sexuality.

Wendy Delorme accompanies her performances with a discourse that in itself reproduces the axiomatics of the "gender theory" developed in the United States between the 1950s and the end of the twentieth century. Femininity is not biological; it is a construction, Delorme repeats in the fall of 2007. Femininity is an ideal, and ideal femininity is never achieved. To be sure, such statements, endlessly reiterated in most of the courses and discourses on "gender" that are offered these days both in France and in the United States, are not exactly "made in America." The claim that femininity is a construction has been repeated endlessly since the difference between the sexes began to attract interest as a social phenomenon. From Freud through Joan Rivière, Simone de Beauvoir, and many others up to and including Judith Butler, who has not given his or her version of "femininity" as masquerade, pantomime, myth, travesty, comedy, performance? Who has not understood, given the advent of the so-called human sciences, that every social organization is a construction and that the relations between the sexes, being rule-governed, do not escape that rule? Who does not know, finally, in the wake of the convergent efforts of linguistics, psychoanalysis, and anthropology, that the universe of every speaking being is a fiction? "Construction" is the destiny of the social animal.

As for gender in general and the feminine gender in particular as "ideality," if Delorme borrows this concept from Butler, the latter presumably borrows it from Lacan, who defined the formation of sexual identity in 1958 as a process of identification with the "ideal type of [one's] sex."[3] One can always tend toward an ideal type by imitating it. But one can never embody it perfectly. It is on this condition that the ideal remains ideal and gender a lure. It is easy to see what the Lacanian formulation adopted by Butler owes to Plato. The ideal of gender, or more precisely gender as ideal, is a quasi-Platonic "idea": at once image and model, it produces copies, and only copies.[4]

So to what extent does the scene replayed by Wendy Delorme come from "America"? As we have seen, Delorme does not settle for acting, she "performs." She puts English on display, or more precisely a certain Anglo-American jargon, as the principal accessory of the character she portrays. "Wendy" is the given name of Peter Pan's playmate. To that eternal child (thus to the perverse par excellence, according to Freud), Marjorie Garber, a prominent figure in the "queer" version of American cultural studies, titled a chapter of her book on transvestism "Fear of Flying, or Why Is Peter Pan a Woman?"[5] As our *performeuse* surely knows, Wendy is also the name of Judith Butler's life partner. One journalist reported that Delorme presents herself on her business card not only as a "performer" but also as a "writer" (in English in the original), for she "writes" as well. Her performing language is American English. On stage, Delorme becomes "Wendy Babybitch." On her MySpace site, the list of her interests appears in English: "Girrlz that rock, Queer art and Litterature [sic],[6] Femmeness. Butches."

For Wendy is a "femme." In the Anglo-lesbian sociolect that grew up in the second half of the twentieth century in the United States, thanks to the development of homosexual communities in urban centers, a femme (pronounced and sometimes spelled "fem," rhyming with "gem") is a female homosexual who is trying to embody the "ideal feminine type." A femme thus imitates not "real" women but dreamed-up women, above all the ones dreamed of by "drag queens," men who reinvent themselves as "women" according to their fantasies and their desire for "femininity." In other terms, a "femme" is a travesty of a transvestite. Playing on the distance between the imaginary gender and the "real" sex, a femme brings out the fabricated character of femininity in its relation to masculinity, equally fabricated (both "made" and "made up") of her "butch" partner in the role-playing game, the latter representing the "ideal masculine type." But "femme," the word "femme," is also and initially a linguistic transvestite, a "translingual" idiom. In the American context, the distance that separates this "ideal woman" from this or that woman indexed according to her belonging to the female sex is marked by recourse to the French language, as if French connoted fiction and ideality in English. The role play (feminine/masculine) is translated and doubled in the linguistic play (English/French: "butch"/ "femme"). However, if the difference between a "femme" and a *femme*, a woman, can be played out in French, it is scarcely legible. Wendy and her peers have found a "French" translation of the "English" word "femme": Among themselves, they refer to themselves as *lesbiennes* "*lipstick*," "lipstick lesbians."[7]

Thus Wendy is not only an imitator of (feminine) perfection; she is above all a perfect imitator of the American scene of "gender trouble" from which she borrows her "identity," her language, her statements, in short all her theoretical and practical props. It must be said that between "perfection" and "performance," the relationship is more than narrowly lexical; we shall come back to this point.

This gesture of "imitation" is performative in more than one respect and to more than one degree; does it manifest "insubordination" with regard to social norms? Here I am alluding to Judith Butler's well-known essay, "Imitation and Gender Insubordination," published in the first American anthology of lesbian and gay studies in 1993.[8] Is Wendy Delorme "subversive," when her interventions respond to a particular cultural conjuncture (and thus to an injunction)? I am not sure.[9] But what this character does allow us to see at work, through the play of embedding, is a certain notion of "gender" as "role." Playing the role of the role that is gender, she displays the relation between "gender" and display, or, to use the language of Robert Stoller, a tutelary figure in American gender theory, between "gender" and "presentation of (the) self."[10] Thus for Delorme, there is no "gender" without a staging of gender, without a *theater of sexual identity*. Ordinary language hints at this, as it has us frequently talk about "roles" to evoke the positions and relations of sex. In contrast, relations of class or race are almost never conceptualized as rooted in dramaturgy; only in rarefied theoretical circles is the analysis of the performativity of social relationships occasionally pushed to such an extreme.

The theater exalts and fascinates. On stage, an actor is not only other than himself (if there is a "self"); he is, as the saying goes, "larger," thus more handsome, "than life": "ideal," in a sense. Without staging, there is no seduction. The "role" of gender, gender as role, is thus, properly speaking, seductive; a role seduces the one who plays it just as much as those who watch it being played. Its spectacularization eroticizes gender. To put it differently, in the double language of "gender theory" and "performance theory," it is in and through theatrics that gender and sexuality are articulated.

Is it because Wendy Delorme is "gay" or declares herself a "lesbian" (a self-appellation that also breaks with certain French cultural conventions in favor of "American" nomenclature[11]) that she has the ability and the desire to *act out* seduction scenes based on gender? The fact is that, from John Money's earliest formulations of the distinction between "sex" and "gender" (in the 1950s) to its feminist uses and developments by Gayle Rubin (1970s) and Judith Butler (1980s), thinking about gender in America has unfolded in particular proximity to what normative psychoanalysis and psychiatry have identified as sexual deviance: From the studies on hermaphroditism and transsexualism done by John Money and Robert Stoller to queer theory, and despite the quarrel that the latter started with its predecessor (gender theory), American gender theory has always been "queer." It may be consubstantially queer, unlike the reflections on sexual difference that were developed in France during the 1970s. The principal theorists of gender in the United States (Gayle Rubin, Judith Butler, Teresa de Lauretis, Biddy Martin, among others) may not all be self-proclaimed lesbians (Judith Butler, for her part, manifests suspicion toward any label functioning as an assignment), but they have assumed their identity as queer persons.

More or less intentionally, Wendy Delorme illustrates all this: the placement of questions of gender and sexuality on "gay" terrain; the liaison suggested and made between "deviance" and parody; and, finally, or rather first of all, the close relationship in the United States between gender theory and performance theory and thus between gender studies and performance studies—their parallel progress in the institutions that sustain them (universities, publishing houses, various cultural sites), their ongoing intersections and mutual influences.

In contemporary English, the language of publication (thus, today, of media dissemination) and that of "queer" self-proclamation are identical: A homosexual person "comes out" like a book or a recording and vice versa. Wendy Delorme came out in France at a moment when contemporary American theorists, and especially (female) theorists of gender and sexuality, were beginning to be translated on a very large scale.

It is thus time to think through the conjuncture and the *currency* of these phenomena. What interests me here is not simply the character of the role-playing, whether subversive or not; this question has been vigorously debated within gender theory, queer theory, and performance theory in terms that are renewing the language and the space but not necessarily the stakes of the old rhetorical debate about the status of "parody." Nor am I concerned here with the simultaneously close and ambiguous relations between American lesbianism and feminism, although it is important to think about these as well. I am interested in a broader question concerning the centrality of "theater" in the experience and the theory of gender as such.

What are the philosophical and political consequences,[12] and what are the cultural effects, of this at once practical and theoretical theatricalizing of gender?

THE "QUEENING" OF GENDER

> Gender role is the public expression of gender identity, and gender identity is the private experience of gender role.
>
> JOHN MONEY

In 1955, when John Money was a young pediatric endocrinologist specializing in problems of children's sexual identity in connection with what was then called anatomical and biological hermaphroditism (genital malformations, irregularities in chromosome markers, hormonal imbalances), he invented the notion of "gender roles."[13] Like his compatriot Robert Stoller but along a different dividing line, Money established the distinction between anatomico-biological sex and "gender."[14] This distinction became the basis for a particular strand of feminist theory, some twenty years later. Money—who attributes his views on the separation between sex and gender to Evelyn Hooker, a physician and psychologist of the previous generation who fought against the pathologizing of homosexuality—later assessed his own contribution to the development of feminist "gender theory," while noting the points of divergence, in *Gendermaps*, a work published toward the end of his career.[15]

The notion of "role" thus plays a crucial part in the elaboration of the epistemological difference between "sex" and "gender." According to Money, "gender role" designates "all those things that a person says or does to disclose himself or herself as having the status of boy or man, girl or woman."[16] It includes all the social aspects known as "adjunctive" (as opposed to those called "irreducible") that are involved in the binary classification of an individual as a masculine or feminine person: appearance (postures, gestures, clothing, makeup), erotic behavior, way of speaking, discursive positioning, but also interests, activities, education, and profession as well as legal, political, and economic status. In so doing, Money uses the term "role" both in its general sense as a function proper to a person in a society and in its more specialized sense as a role played on a stage by an actor, a sense that arose in the sixteenth century and that immediately took on a metonymic extension designating scenes played out in life as well as on stage.

For Money, the notion of "gender role" precedes and informs the later notion of "gender identity."[17] The primacy of role over identity can be read, moreover, in the definition of gender identity as "the private experience of gender role." The epigraph cited earlier is the conclusion of one of Money's definitions of "gender role," in a glossary prepared for a lay public in the early 1970s. In this same glossary, the article "gender identity" concludes as follows: "Gender identity is the private experience of gender role, and gender role is the public expression of gender identity."[18] The absolute circularity of these definitions is transparent, a circularity that is at once internal to each of the terms defined and characteristic of the relation between the two definitions. Although Money relies "naively" on a well-worn expressive model to explain these notions—the gender role is the public *expression* of the gender identity or the gender identity is the private *expression* of the gender role—the circularity of the paradigm belies the pertinence of recourse to such a model. If the gender identity "expresses" the gender role, which "expresses" the gender identity, which "expresses" the gender role, and so on, it is impossible to maintain the notion of an internal identity constituted in advance that would be "expressed" as it is externalized. John Money is already close, unwittingly, to a "performative" notion of gender. We shall come back to this point.

To indicate the consubstantial bond between gender "identity" and gender "role," Money later invented the composite notion of "gender-identity/role," designated in his writings by the acronym G-I/R. As he promoted the distinction between "sex" and "gender" and the conception of "gender" as a sociocultural encoding of personality, Money was led to refine behavioral and educational protocols designed to induce children of uncertain sex to adopt a well-defined gender identity. To this end, the child had to learn a gender role that conformed to the anatomical and hormonal shaping of the body decided on by the doctor with the parents' consent. In certain of Money's best-known cases, the process involved transforming into "girls" children who lacked penises, either owing to a congenital malformation or to a medical intervention (unsuccessful phimosis surgery, and even circumcision, which was widely practiced on American males in the twentieth century—as if to mark their masculinity from the outset with the seal of medico-social legitimacy[19]). Thus it was assumed, without reference to what psychoanalysis might have to say on the subject, that a child without a penis, a castrated boy, had to become the "girl" that he already was virtually, by accident, since the defining feature of a girl is to be castrated and to accept the fact, while castration is intolerable for a boy as such.

This practice of "sex and gender reassignment," intended to transform hermaphrodites into *normal* "men" or "women" according to an implacable binary logic (one can, and must, be only one or the other), was itself embedded within the more general context of treatment for "gender disfunction" in the United States. The 1950s saw the first medico-social definitions of "transsexualism," understood as a contradiction between the gender lived (or claimed) by the individual and the sex assigned at birth. The first medical congress devoted to transsexualism was held in New York in 1953.[20] As was the case with hermaphroditism or pseudo-hermaphroditism, transsexualism was first viewed as a problem affecting beings of the male sex. For almost twenty years, the cases studied and publicized were almost exclusively cases of conversion of individuals of the male sex to femininity; the greater frequency and visibility of this masculine "dysphoria" does not seem to have led doctors and sociologists working in harmony to reflect on the causes (psychological, but also historical and cultural causes) of this dissymmetry between the sexes in manifestations of gender trouble.[21]

In the absence of a thoroughgoing reflection on the nature of the unconscious wish that is expressed in the conscious wish to change sex, the American medical response generally consisted on the whole in acceding to the fantasy of transsexuals and proposing a technological solution based on surgery and hormone treatment.[22] This solution was all the more seductive in that it corresponded to the old "Frankensteinian" fantasy of a science eager to extend the boundaries of the possible and to fabricate new humans through its own means. It also corresponded to the founding "fantasy" of American culture, which is embodied in the figure of the "self-made man," against which no genealogical (and thus no genetic) determination can prevail. Every individual is free to make his or her own destiny and identity.[23] The technological response proceeded in this sense from the liberal ideology of gratification of individual desires denounced by Pierre-Henri Castel in his book on transsexualism. On another level, a refusal to interpret the symptom of gender inversion presented by certain "transsexuals" as a possible instance of unconscious homosexuality may also have been a factor. In fact, however liberal-individualist it may have been, American society pathologized and criminalized homosexuality to the point of making it literally unthinkable and unlivable. The transsexual manifestation and its spectacular gratification in the form of the simultaneous attribution-adoption of a new body and a new gender with reinforced contours would thus have had the "disguised" function of a "coming out" in which the "gender" put on display by metamorphosis was a metaphor for "sexual orientation."[24] The transsexual phenomenon, which was quite extensive for a time in the United States, has, in fact, diminished in scale since the cultural "coming out" of the homosexual movements in the early 1970s in the West. "Transsexuals," at least in the educated middle classes, are giving way to "transgenders," whose fantasies, identified and satisfied as such, can henceforth do without surgery. The theorization of the discontinuity between "sex(es)" and "gender(s)" has undoubtedly played a major role in the emergence of "transgender" identities, thanks to the successive efforts of "gender theory" and "queer theory." The transsexual body is not the body received at birth. The denaturalization of the sexed body by its "denaturing"[25] is now accompanied by a theoretical insistence on the non-unity of that body, which is conceived as "fantastic" rather than "organic," that is, both as the "external" projection of the subject's "internal" theater and as a cyborgian assemblage.

In an article titled "Sex and Gender Are Different" (2000), Milton Diamond, a psychosexologist and professor of reproductive biology at the University of Hawaii, seeks to clarify the terms used in human sexuality as a field of study. Critical of the reassignments of gender advocated and practiced by John Money, he takes up a position nevertheless in the territory marked out by Money and by Robert Stoller. Combining considerations borrowed from American medical psychology and perspectives opened up by gender theory, to which he alludes explicitly (as he does with Michel Foucault) or implicitly (as he does with sociologists of social interaction and with Judith Butler),[26] he establishes a double typology: that of the key concepts for studying human sexual behavior (sex, gender and gender role, sexual identity, gender identity), for which he recommends clear-cut, unproblematic distinctions, and that of the "dysphoric" profiles whose examination has led to the elaboration of these concepts, much as the study of neurotic patients had allowed Freud to understand the mechanisms of so-called "normal" psychosexuality. Among these profiles, and alongside the *transsexual*, the *intersexual* (and especially the unhappy intersexual—generally a male with hermaphroditic features who was brought up as a girl), the *transgender* (a category rightly described as the most recent and the most fluid), and the *transvestite*, there is also the *drag queen*, a character whose faded finery is borrowed from Elizabethan theater. In fact, while the figure of the "drag queen" appeared as such in England in the mid-nineteenth century, the word "drag," which was used to create the stage name, originally designated, by metonymy, female clothing with a train (cloak or skirt) worn by young actors—"boys"—who traditionally played the female roles in the theater.[27]

Camp style has always centered around the figure of the queen.

ESTHER NEWTON

What is a "drag queen"? What is signified at once by this character and by the interest in this character, to the point that he/she figures in an article on medical nosography alongside the more general category of "transvestite"? To answer this set of questions, I shall proceed obliquely.[28] I shall begin by evoking the work of an anthropologist who played a pioneering role in the joint development of queer studies and performance studies: I am referring to Esther Newton, the author of two books on the relation between gay culture or subculture and theater in the United States: *Mother Camp: Female Impersonators in America*, first published in 1972 and republished several times since; and *Cherry Grove, Fire Island: Sixty Years in America's First Gay and Lesbian Town*, published in 1993. Between these two dates, the whole American history of the theoretical and political grasp of gender trouble unfolded: the emergence and development of feminist "gender theory," which came about between 1975 and 1990 as feminists crossed the study of anomalies in sexual identity and behavior by American doctors and sociologists with "French thought" about "the feminine," sexuality, and social relations involving sex roles in society; the development of gay and lesbian studies starting in the late 1980s; and, finally, the critical reevaluation of the vexed questions and notions used in the divided field of feminist studies and gay and lesbian studies starting with the formulation of a queer perspective in the early 1990s.

Mother Camp was doubly noteworthy: Margaret Mead had opened the way to the ethnography of sexuality, to be sure, but Newton's was the first ethnographic study devoted to "gay" sexuality and culture—American, no less.[29] In this book, Newton studies the role of "drag queens," homosexual men who play at "doing women" on theatrical stages that are both marginal and popular, turning their self-assigned gender into a spectacle that is often continued off stage.[30] *Cherry Grove* explores the relation between gay culture and theater once again, proposing an ethnographic history of the cultural and artistic practices that prevailed in a New York summer resort area by that name: Cherry Grove served for a long time as a festive gathering place for the East Coast gay and lesbian community. Newton was particularly interested in the parallel evolution and reciprocal influences of the avant-garde American theater and the gay scene. On another level, her study of Cherry Grove allowed her to bring out the dissymmetry between the position of gays and that of lesbians, and their unequal status in the community, doing so at the very moment when the development of queer theory was in the process, as she saw it, of erasing the difference between male and female homosexuals; the term "queer" was now used for both groups without distinction, in the name of a nonbinary, even nongendered approach to relations of sex. In "Dick(less) Tracy and the Homecoming

Queen: Lesbian Power and Representation in Gay Male Cherry Grove," an essay from 1996 that pursues the reflection begun in *Cherry Grove*, Newton notes, "The tendency of some male and female queer theorists and writers to describe 'queers' . . . as if gender were no longer a relevant or important difference deletes just what, in my view, we should be highlighting: the appropriation of gay male practices and culture by lesbians."[31]

Newton occupies a paradoxical place in the intellectual history I am attempting to trace. On the one hand, she was one of the first in the American context to stress the relation between gender role, theatrical performance, and sexuality. On the other hand, from the 1990s on, she has opposed the theoretical developments that her own work had helped launch.

In a chapter of *Mother Camp* titled "Role Models" and reprinted in her intellectual autobiography, *Margaret Mead Made Me Gay*, Newton offers some of the reasons for the importance of the drag queen figure in gay subculture, through a series of remarks. (1) "There are relatively few ascribed roles in American culture and sex role is one of them" (p. 20). (2) "If sex-role behavior can be achieved by the 'wrong' sex, it logically follows that it is in reality also achieved, not inherited, by the 'right' sex" (p. 21). (3) "Homosexuality consists of sex-role deviation made up of two related but distinct parts: 'wrong' sexual object choices and 'wrong' sex-role presentation of self" (p. 22).

While in her 1972 text Newton does not use the lexicon of "gender" (which was still not very widespread during this period except among specialists in gender dysphorias), she nevertheless emphasizes the "theatrical" character of "sexual" (today one would say "gender") identity and behavior. These latter stem from role-playing at the outset (see her first remark); this is why they "naturally" lend themselves to exploitation on stage. And because role-playing is involved, any "actor" can play the role, whatever his or her sex (see the second remark). We know what Judith Butler will take from this description of the performance of gender: If a given gender role can be performed by a person whose sex does not necessarily match the gender on display, this means that sexual "expression" has nothing natural about it, thus that no particular model of sexuality and sexual identity is the "original" one. The femininity imitated by the drag queen on stage is already a role. And if homosexuality consists, as Newton asserts in her third remark, in a double inversion and thus a cumulation of roles—again: "Homosexuality consists of sex-role deviation made up of two related . . .

parts" [in the double sense of "components" and "roles," as in a play]—by taking at once the "wrong" gender and the wrong object, the theatrical structure of gender actually renders the opposition between the right," or "true" gender and the wrong or "false" one irrelevant.

But why does Newton privilege the feminine role on the scene of gender, at least in the way that drag queens (re)play it in the theater? First of all, Newton, who describes and presents herself as "butch," loves women, with and without quotation marks. At the end of her "butch" memoirs—in a short text titled "My Butch Career"—she tells how, during a performance by a middle-aged and not particularly attractive homosexual who had transformed himself into an impressive drag queen in Cherry Grove, she had been drawn onto the stage with him, or rather with "her," swept up by the stunning attraction of his character. The incident allows Newton to stress once again the consubstantial relation between the theatrical scene— here, more precisely, the theater of gender—and the scene of desire.[32]

More seriously, or, let us say, more generally, the drag queen illustrates the relation between theatricality and femininity by reenacting it: a historical relation, first of all, since from the start and for a long time playing a role in the theater in the West meant—for a man and for those men and women who watched "him"—being able (or being required) to play a woman.[33] The drag queen also symbolizes this relation, for if the task of theater is to "produce" femininity,[34] as if playing a role on stage—that is, playing at playing a role—were always, in a sense, playing at playing a woman, then "femininity" appears in exchange as a theatrical effect: an embodiment, or—in a reminder that a "person" is first of all a "mask"—an *impersonation* of a fantasy.

This is why, as Newton asserts on several occasions, a "butch" can be "campy"—that is, according to her 1972 definition of the term, "consciously stagy, specifically theatrical"—only if she becomes capable of imitating (thus of becoming in turn) a drag queen.

In "Dick(less) Tracy and the Homecoming Queen," Newton tells the story of Joan, a butch lesbian, who is elevated to the coveted distinction of (drag) queen of the year by the Cherry Grove community. This happened in 1994, and it was the first time a lesbian was "crowned." Joan's election gave rise to numerous debates and challenges. To get elected, according to Newton, she had to ask the local drag queens to help her transform herself. She also had to make it obvious that in her case, too, it was a matter of transvestism, thus of changing gender on stage, since a butch is first of all masculine in gender.

From this episode, Newton draws several conclusions about the analytics and politics of "gender roles." For her, above all, the story confirms the link between theatrical displays and the effect of "femininity." Disagreeing with certain "performance theorists" (including Sue-Ellen Case and Judith Butler), who emphasize the element of subversive play found every time someone adopts a gender in contradiction with his or her biological sex (e.g., when a female adopts the butch gender), she stresses what she calls "the lack of camp"—the absence of deliberate theatricality—of butches as butches.

The word "camp," with its numerous derivatives (campy, campiness, to camp up), which appeared between the 1930s and the 1960s, plays a key role in the description and evaluation of the cultural phenomenon I am attempting to analyze. "Camp" has virtually no equivalent in French apart from the verb *camper* in its transitive form, in the sense of "to portray" or "nail down" a character. The *Oxford English Dictionary* is reserved as to the etymological link between "camp" and the Latin *campus*, a noun that has given rise in both English and French to the lexicon of the camp as a military, sporting, academic, or touristic campus. The *OED* defines a "camp" or "campy" person as someone who is or who behaves like a homosexual; it also stresses the exaggerated gestures of "camp."[35] As we have seen, Newton for her part defines "camp" as a form of theatricality that is "conscious," deliberate, but also light and amusing, and she associates it chiefly with the performance of drag queens.[36] Newton thus sees Joan's election as the triumph of the "camp" version of homosexual culture and a confirmation of the association between "campiness" and feminine display. She is all the more delighted with this in that she has observed, starting in the late 1970s, a "masculinization" of homosexual culture, both among gays who exchanged their drag queen outfits and mannerisms for leather vests as if their political coming out,[37] thus their at least partial legitimization, led to their (re)phallicization,[38] and also among lesbians. Newton, in fact, shows in her series of essays that the lesbians' new cultural assertiveness, more recent than that of the gays, led them to imitate and thus reproduce the trends of gay culture.

And this is the second conclusion she draws from the Cherry Grove election. Joan's victory has an ambivalent political meaning and cultural impact. For if it consecrates the power of a theatrical femininity, it also confirms the subordination of lesbian culture to gay culture. To become "queen," Joan had to adopt the codes of gay culture and be "dubbed," as it were, by male homosexuals. The appropriation of gay practices by the lesbian community also marks the secondary status of the lesbian stance. And when the gay community deserts the stage of femininity, the lesbian community follows suit. This lesbian mimeticism then entails abandoning or denying any primordial identification with women (with and without quotation marks), thus "taking a break" from the defense of the cause of women known as the "feminist struggle." Gayle Rubin, another American lesbian anthropologist who devotes her work to the ethnography of sexuality, has developed a theory and a defense of this desertion of "the women's cause."

For Newton, this gradual distancing from "queen culture"[39] signifies not merely the most recent, and most insidious, defeat of a certain femininity. From her remarks on the conflation of all genders under the term "queer" and on the tendency of "queer theory" to subsume and supplant both "gender studies" and "gay and lesbian studies," we can see that, for her, abandoning the equation between theatricality and femininity means abandoning the category of gender as inscription or production of the feminine/masculine dichotomy.[40] Without femininity, there is no more masculinity, or, perhaps, nothing else but masculinity. Now, for Newton, there is no way to get around gender,[41] for no experience of desire can do without the theatrics of gender. This is how she accounts for the appearance on the Western cultural stage of the "mannish lesbian" (French *lesbienne hommasse*, later "butch" in America) at the beginning of the twentieth century. I shall come back to this point.

Finally, if Newton distinguishes the "campiness" of the (male or female) drag queen from the seriousness of the (female) butch, if she refuses to put the unconscious play of the "pre-theoretical" butch and the deliberate play of the drag queen or the post-theoretical butch on the same level, it is precisely because for her the play of gender "isn't a game," to speak like children who enact their lives in play.[42] If the butch plays a masculine role, if she is the "actor" of her own story, she is still not the master of her own play, but rather its plaything. This is why Newton resorts deliberately to the pre- or even anti-"theoretical" and paradoxically anti-"theatrical" vocabulary of "authenticity" to describe the position and the subjective experience of the "female" butch. The latter cannot escape, even if she wants to, from the binary division of the genders. This is also why even the drag queen is not only, not simply, "campy" in Newton's eyes but also tragic—tragic because comic, we might say, caught up as "she" is in her play and in her role. "I" am acting, thus I am what "I" am acting, Newton says in essence, offering a warning against the illusion of omnipotence—an effect of remote control—that is proffered by the intellectual possession (or the illusion of possession) of the keys to the game.

It is also, and this point must be stressed, a question of class. Theorists of gender, almost all middle-class women, reflect on their experiences in the comfort of the American academy. But the first "butches" in America appeared in working-class bars in large cities. The use of the word "butch" to designate these homosexual women who try to embody the "ideal masculine type" dates from the 1940s; it refers to the pseudonym adopted by a famous twentieth-century criminal, Butch Cassidy. The stereotype of a "tough kid" from the working classes of the American West, Butch Cassidy has become a legendary character. He supposedly earned his nickname because he had worked as a butcher, a low-status and somewhat troubling trade. It is easy to understand why butch dress has nothing in common with the elegance of a dandy: On the contrary, it is the exact replica of the "casual" blue-collar clothing worn by cowboys, men who have very little but are nevertheless intimidating. Similarly, the male and female drag queens studied by Newton, like the ones Jennie Livingston filmed later on,[43] were recruited not only from bourgeois seaside resorts but also from ethnic ghettos and other social substrata.

I have proposed to distinguish between pre- and post-theoretical "butches." Newton does not believe, as I have said, that lesbian gender play is, or has always been, deliberate, "consciously theatrical," except, precisely, as an effect—reflection and result—of a discourse that was developed starting in the 1990s at the intersection of queer theory and performance theory. By celebrating the campiness of lesbian gender play, Newton suggests, theorists such as Sue-Ellen Case and even Judith Butler brought this to the foreground, at least "in the eyes of the spectator" (male or female). If it is true, as Newton asserts, that the position of lesbians in gay subculture has always been secondary, and if this secondary status has prevented the development of an autonomous lesbian "aesthetic," can one not say that the theoretical stage constitutes for these "lesbians" the place of their triumph and their revenge? In the field and the game of theory, American lesbians have unquestionably gotten ahead of the gays. From this standpoint, it is as though the theory of performance—but also theory as performance—had supplanted the theater as the political and aesthetic expression of lesbians. And on the great virtual stage of theory, every sort of play is possible, even the impossible, since there is no reality test. In this sense, the stage of theory is properly speaking a perverse stage: I know perfectly well that playing is not playing, acting is not acting, but even so . . .

> Drag constitutes the mundane way in which genders are appropriated, theatricalized, worn, and done.
>
> JUDITH BUTLER

As is well known by now on both sides of the Atlantic: Judith Butler follows in the footsteps of Michel Foucault. He supplies a good portion of her lexicon and some of her conceptual tools (discipline, production, norm, regulatory ideals), and she shares with him certain of his most important objects of reflection (sexuality, the body, power). She is also indebted to Derrida—in a less visible way, to be sure, since she devotes very little analysis to his work[44]—for a certain intellectual caution toward the questions addressed, for procedures such as the systematic interrogation of binary constructions and for the suspicion that the closed nature of a system (whether cultural, political, or theoretical) can be described and conceptualized, if not penetrated, only by asking what its constitution excludes or represses. But it is perhaps especially to Newton that she owes her concept of gender as *performance and imitation of a normative ideal.* This less familiar aspect of the "genesis" of her thought is the one over which I would like to linger a moment here. Most of the essays that Butler has devoted to the problem of the constitution and the manifestation of "gender" over the past quarter-century refer to Newton. In one of her very first articles on the performance of gender, "Performative Acts and Gender Constitution: An Essay in Phenomenology and Feminist Theory," she cites Newton in a note.[45] In the last part of *Gender Trouble,* where she is attempting to provide a definition of "gender" as "performative," she again cites *Mother Camp* (pp. 186–187). She stresses her debt to Newton's "groundbreaking work on drag" in her preface to the second edition of *Gender Trouble* in 1999 (p. ix). Two essays included in Butler's *Bodies That Matter* are clearly inspired by Newton's work on the figure of the drag queen: "Gender Is Burning: Questions of Appropriation and Subversion" and "Critically Queer," which serves as the book's conclusion. Finally, she mentions Newton explicitly once again in "Imitation and Gender Insubordination," her contribution to the celebrated inaugural *Lesbian and Gay Studies Reader*. It is perhaps in this essay that she formulates most clearly what her conception of gender owes to her reading of Newton, a reading that she describes as a moment of intellectual epiphany. Here is the passage in question:

> I remember quite distinctly when I first read in Esther Newton's *Mother Camp: Female Impersonators in America* that drag is not an imitation or a copy of some prior and true gender; according to Newton, drag enacts the very structure of impersonation by which any gender is assumed. Drag is not the putting on of a gender that belongs properly to some other group, i.e., an act of expropriation or appropriation that assumes that gender is the rightful property of sex, that "masculine" belongs to "male" and "feminine" belongs to "female." There is no "proper" gender, a gender proper to one sex rather than another, which is in some sense that sex's cultural property. . . . Drag constitutes the mundane way in which genders are appropriated, theatricalized, worn, and done; it implies that all gendering is a kind of impersonation and approximation. If it is true, it seems, there is no original or primary gender that drag imitates, but gender is a kind of imitation that produces the very notion of the original as an effect and consequence of the imitation itself.[46]

"Drag," which I hesitate to render in French simply as *travestissement* (cross-dressing) for several reasons, some of which will become apparent later, is thus described by Butler, inspired by Newton, as the truth, or if I dare put it this way, the essence, of gender. Butler draws from this a certain number of effects and consequences.

If the drag queen's performance reveals the true nature of gender, if gender is above all "theatricalized, worn and done," this is because gender does not constitute an authentic "kernel" of subjectivity, given in advance by physiology or by the neo-natal environment: Like "drag," which is simultaneously, in today's language, a style of dress and a role, gender is in this view always already acted out, borrowed, and added. To grasp its forms and understand its wellsprings, it is thus necessary to focus both on the phenomenology of its manifestation, a study that itself requires a semiology and a typology of its "(re)presentation," its gestures and its utterances, and on the historical and cultural conditions of its "production," as one would do for any theatrical role. In modern, contemporary English, as I have already noted, the word "production" means not only "constitution," a term that Butler uses as well, but also "staging" or spectacle. Thus even when Butler situates herself explicitly on Foucaldian terrain, her conception of the "production" of gender finds itself inflected by the idiomatic connotations of the term in its original language. In the earliest texts she devotes to this subject, for example, in "Performative Acts and Gender Constitution," she indeed attempts, as her title indicates, a "phenomeno-logical" approach to gender. This approach relies principally on the way anthropologists have appropriated analyses first developed in the field of theater studies to try to interpret social life, in particular the highly symbolic and ostentatiously spectacular structuring phenomena called rituals.[47] But this "phenomenology" of gender, which focuses on the performance of its symbolic rituals in everyday social relations, is also very close to another line of analysis to which Butler doubtless owes her oldest and perhaps best-anchored conception of gender performance: in the case in point, the one shared by American sociologists of "interaction" such as Erving Goffman (mentioned in passing in "Performative Acts"); Harold Garfinkel, promoter of the American school of ethnomethodology; or Candace West and Don Zimmerman, who, in their "Doing Gender," traced American "role theory" back to the 1930s.

As we have seen, Newton describes the theatricality of gender, in partic-ular, through the culturally dated and connoted lexicon of "camp." Butler prefers the more abstract but also conceptually more complex language of "performance." The cultural history of this word, or rather of this family of words (perform, performance, performer; French has retained chiefly the substantive forms *performance, performeur, performeuse* and the adjectival *performant[e]*), resembles that of the word "gender" itself: Just as the old French word *genre* provided the English "gender" before going back into French with its Anglo-American sense, English borrowed the verb "to per-form" from the Old French *parfourmer,* in the sense of executing or carry-ing out an action. In English, the word took on the sense of "acting before a public" in the sixteenth century, and it is in this sense that French wel-comed it back into its lexicon. According to a historical dictionary of the French language, we find an isolated occurrence of the word "performance" in the sense of spectacle in Victor Hugo's *L'homme qui rit,* a novel with

Anglophone accents. But it is especially in our era that the word *performance* and its derivatives are taking hold in French in the sense these terms have taken on in performance theory and the theory of gender as performance. The fact remains that the lexicon of "performance" remains richer in meaning in English than in French. Among the uses of the verb "perform" listed in the *Oxford English Dictionary*, let us note, for the sheer pleasure of the language play, the sense of making love ("to have sexual intercourse, esp. satisfactorily"), to urinate or defecate (where children are involved), or to compensate for a lack ("to make up or supply what is wanting").[48]

Performance, the word performance, also expresses, as we have seen, a certain pull toward perfection, a kind of over-doing (from the Latin *perfectus* [*per*, "completely," + *facere*, "to make, do, perform"] via the Old French *parfit*). In this sense, performance is always already if not actually hyperbolic then at least hyperbolizing. Let us recall that the *OED* describes "camp" as a "use of exaggerated and over-acted movements and gestures." Similarly, Butler sees hyperbole as an index of theatricality.[49] Like Lacan, she identifies this tendency toward theatrical hyperbole not only in "camp" performance but also in the ordinary heterosexual relations that supply the model for, if not the key to, that performance.[50] She sees in it, in fact, the sign that what is aimed for, through mimicry, in gender performance (and gender as performance) is an unattainable ideal, a form or a type that is, if not "more true," then at least "more perfect" than nature. Hyperbole attests to the infinite distance that separates "performers" from their ideal even while serving as the instrument—the path and the trope—for spanning that distance.[51] Hyperbolic figuration thus signifies at one and the same time the success and the failure of gender performance. Hence its ambivalent character and the ambiguity of its effects. Magnification or caricature, the more manifest the hyperbole, the more visible it makes the dangerous and disconcerting proximity of the seeming contraries, idealization and abjection.[52] We know what use writers such as Jean Genet—after Marcel Proust—made of this ambiguity.[53] In any case, if femininity and masculinity are ideals that are at once inimitable and imitated (and imitated because they are inimitable), does this not imply that the "truest" women, if not the only true "women," those who most faithfully or most successfully imitate the ideal as ideal, are, precisely, drag queens? Seen in this light, all other women would be *femmes manquées*, "failures at being women" (because they fail to be sufficiently "hyperbolic"). If ordinary men and women are more or less failed, unsuccessful men and women, then the usual distinction between what is true and what is false, between reality and fiction, is radically affected: For, in the logic of a certain theater, the more something is false, the truer it is.

Between "Speech Acts" and "Bodily Acts"

> [It may seem] that there is a difference between the embodying or performing of gender norms and the performative use of discourse. Are they two different senses of "performativity" or do they converge as modes of citationality in which the compulsory character of certain social imperatives becomes subject to a more promising deregulation?
>
> JUDITH BUTLER, "CRITICALLY QUEER," 231

"My theory sometimes waffles between understanding performativity as linguistic and casting it as theatrical," Butler acknowledges in 1999.[54]

The last section of "Subversive Bodily Acts," titled "From Interiority to Gender Performatives," followed by the essay's overall conclusion, "From Parody to Theory," have earned *Gender Trouble* the harshest criticisms that have been levied against it. As Butler herself readily admits in her preface to the revised edition, it is the "occasional voluntarism" (p. xxvi) of her conception of gender that provoked reactions ranging from skepticism to indignation in feminist and poststructuralist theoretical circles.[55] Doesn't the idea that gender can be an "intentional act," the result of an individual decision by a sovereign subject, contradict the poststructuralist and more precisely Foucaldian conception of the subject—a conception defended by Butler, moreover? If an already-constituted "subject" is capable of "intentionally performing" his or her gender in a sort of deliberate after-effect, this also argues for an originary neutrality that would characterize the subject or the process of subjectification. Doesn't the secondary nature of gender traits in this process of subjectification reintroduce the ontological or onto-phenomenological gesture of secondarization of "sexual difference" made by Western metaphysics, a gesture analyzed by Derrida? Hasn't contemporary thought definitively invalidated the idea, supported by a certain existentialism, that the subject is free to choose his or her "masks," or in any case is meant to choose them? The critiques addressed to Butler thus led her to reformulate her theory of gender performance in the light of the Austinian theory of speech acts, revisited and deconstructed by Derrida in "Signature Event Context."[56]

If the language of "performance" indeed belongs to the theatrical register and invites us to relate the notion of gender performance to the old sociological notion of role as it is used in American role theory, Butler's preference, starting with the first edition of *Gender Trouble*, for the term "performativity" and its avatar, the "gender performative," prefigures the "linguistic" inflection of her reading of gender performance. However, neither Austin nor his Derridean deconstruction is explicitly invoked in *Gender Trouble*. And the definition of "performative" that Butler offers in that book does draw that term back toward a conception of the performance in question that is more "theatrical" than "linguistic": The word "performative," she writes, just after calling on us to "consider gender" as "an 'act,' as it were, which is both intentional and performative," "suggests a dramatic and contingent construction of meaning" (p. 190). Isn't it precisely because she is still conceiving of the "performative" here as a "dramatic and contingent construction of meaning" rather than as a "reiteration of norms"[57] that she slips for an instant into the "voluntarist" illusion for which she has been criticized? Doesn't the idea of "dramatic and contingent construction" presuppose, if not the existence of some "author" of the play that has been produced and performed, at least the distinctive persistence and permanence of the "actor" (at once "performer" and "agent") under the intermittent contingency of the "character"? To be sure, the motif of "repetition" as the constitutive feature of gender "performativity," a motif that prefigures the analysis of "reiteration" that Butler will later undertake in *Bodies That Matter*, is already quite insistent in *Gender Trouble*: "[T]he action of gender requires a performance that is *repeated*," she repeats over and over, stressing the verb "repeat" and its derivatives (p. 191). But in *Gender Trouble*, Butler compares and relates "gender performatives" to the phenomenon of "ritual" rather than to the structure of "iterability." If gender performance is repeated in a series of acts of continued (re)creation, if it has to be repeated to be sustained and if it is thus fundamentally "repetitive," this is because it belongs to the order of social rituals as a "theatrical ritual," just like "other ritual social dramas," as we see at the beginning of the statement cited: "As in other ritual social dramas, the action of gender requires a performance that is *repeated*" (p. 191). Not until the essays gathered in *Bodies That Matter*, then, does Butler achieve the conceptual "crossing" between performance and performativity, the "theatrical" and the "linguistic," ritual repetition and citational repetition.

I shall not linger over the well-known theses of J. L. Austin concerning the nature and function of the "speech acts" that the philosopher of language calls "performatives" so as to distinguish them, or rather try to distinguish them, from utterances he calls constative.[58] I shall simply say a few words about their Derridean reading because it is in the light of that reading that Butler reinterprets and appropriates the notion of "performative" in *Bodies That Matter*.

Derrida includes his at once friendly and amused critique of Austinian theory within the framework of a more general reflection on "communication." The communicational model, which informs the way "ordinary language" is ordinarily conceived and studied in analytic philosophy, presupposes, as Derrida reminds us, that meaning (or a meaning) is transmitted between a sender and a receiver and can really only be formed and transmitted in the space of interlocution. This model is thus based on the scene of speech, itself conceived "as the communication of consciousnesses or presences, and as the linguistic or semantic transport of meaning."[59] As Derrida emphasizes, following Austin, "Differing from the classical assertion, from the constative utterance, the performative's referent . . . is not outside it, or in any case preceding it or before it"[60]; it presents itself first of all as a *speech* act, in other words, as an act of language that has meaning and existence only within an interlocutory relation. Thus the act of "giving one's word" to someone stands as the exemplary performative, and this is why Austin also describes a performative utterance as a "perlocutionary act," a formula that characterizes the particular form and force of the linguistic relation established by the speech act between the sender of the utterance and its receiver. Austin insists on this on several occasions: A performative utterance that "does something with words" occurs only in the first person and in the present tense. And this is how it can be recognized at the grammatical level. A "performative" presupposes both the present of the utterance (verb tense) and the present of the enunciation (first person present tense), thus the presence of the speaker in the scene of speech. Consequently, it also implies the presence of a hearer, witness or receiver of the perlocutionary act, without whom the act would not have the efficacity that makes it a "performing" utterance. Derrida then focuses his effort on calling into question this value of "presence"—presence of the present and presence to self and to the other of the sender—attributed to performative utterances.

Austin excludes from the field of performatives worthy of the name any performative utterance that is *cited*. He recognizes, in fact, that an utterance that seemingly has all the grammatical and pragmatic features of a performative may appear in a play, for example, or in a novel. But in such contexts, it is only miming an "authentic" utterance; it only *represents* a situation of interlocution and more precisely of real perlocution, and it does not have the power to modify reality "for real." Thus the citation or the citational character of an utterance radically compromises its perlocutionary strength and value, hence its "performativity." Yet the same Austin includes among the performative speech acts those "that have the general character of ritual or ceremonial"; these he calls "conventional."[61] It is easy for Derrida to show that these so-called "conventional" acts—the words of commitment pronounced during a wedding ceremony, for example, or the words of a judge who condemns an accused person—are themselves citational acts. Far from constituting the manifestation of an absolutely personal intention in a pure linguistic present, the "conventional" act repeats a coded formula. Not only is a performative utterance always already a quotation, in such cases, but it draws its possibility and its efficacy from its very citationality. These "conventional acts" indeed are, or can be, "performative," but they "succeed" in actually accomplishing something—for Austin, the quality of a performative depends on its success—only because they invoke or cite formulas, and, with them, the whole system of conventions that authorize and legitimize these formulas. Thus, even in the moment of his apparently most deliberate and effective linguistic performance, the subject of an enunciation is not really the master of his words or intentions. "Could a performative utterance succeed if its formulation did not repeat a 'coded' or iterable statement, in other words, if the expressions I use to open a meeting, launch a ship or a marriage were not identifiable as *conforming* to an iterable model, and therefore if they were not identifiable in a way as 'citation'?" Derrida asks.[62] "'Ritual,'" he says again about these ritual performatives, "is not an eventuality, but, as iterability, is a structural characteristic of every mark."[63]

In "Signature Event Context," Derrida tries, in fact, to show that this structure of iterability, which undermines the notion of the subject's pure presence to self and to the other in discourse, affects not only what is ordinarily called writing, insofar as writing can "reproduce" or "imitate" a situation of "real communication," but the entire field of linguistic expression, even "all 'experience' in general, if it is granted that there is no experience of *pure* presence but only chains of differential marks," to the extent that experience "is not separated from the field of the mark" (p. 318).

However, iteration—of a statement or a behavior, since the structure of iterability concerns not only what we recognize under the name "language" but also what Derrida calls "the field of the mark" to which the experience of all animate beings belongs—then, is not mere repetition, not citation identical to an original. In fact, while the code as code can be, even must be, reproduced, and while reproduction of the code ensures the identification and the intelligibility of my statement or my behavior, at a certain level, iteration also includes in its structural possibility what Derrida calls "a force of rupture." As soon as the repetition of an utterance, or even a type of enunciation, breaks with the initial context of production of this utterance, that is, with "the set of presences which organize the moment of its inscription" (p. 317), then it is necessarily displaced, if not displacing. It is precisely this movement of displacing reinscription that Derrida names "iteration," recalling that *itara* means "other" in Sanskrit, according to "the logic which links repetition to alterity" (p. 315).

We can see how much Butler has been able to draw from Derrida's deconstruction of the Austinian performative. Because Derrida stresses the "ritual," coded, and repetitive dimension of every performative (Austin having already put his finger on the performative dimension of ritual), Butler can reinsert her analysis of theatrical ritual into this new theoretico-pragmatic framework. Radicalizing the analysis of the citational charge of performatives, she makes citationality the principal feature of the performative speech act: the Butlerian performative is citationality in action. As we know, she calls this citationality in action "reiteration." In his essay, Derrida shows how the "iterability of the mark" allows the mark to exceed the context of its inscription in advance, thus allowing it to be recontextualized subsequently without limits, thus without any direction for its reinscription that can be determined a priori. What Derrida says about the "mark" in general, and not only about speech acts, obviously applies to the marks with high semantic charges that we call "concepts." Butler thus proceeds to a reinscription, through citation and recontextualization, of the notion of the performative: The latter is henceforth pressed into service not for the analysis of the pragmatics of language but for the examination of the at once social and psychic deployment of the norms of gender and sexuality. Her analysis of the "performativity of gender" as an act entailing the "reiteration of norms" then allows her to clear up the theoretical misunderstanding provoked by some of her formulations in *Gender Trouble*. In Derrida's wake, she insists in "Critically Queer" on the fact that "acts of gender" are never—can never be—the manifestation of a sovereign and purely personal intention, no more than are the "conventional" language acts of a judge pronouncing a sentence:

> If *a performative provisionally succeeds . . . , it is not because an intention successfully governs the action of speech,* but only because that action echoes prior actions, and accumulates the force of authority through the repetition or citation of a prior, authoritative, set of practices. What this means, then, is that a performative works to the extent that it draws on and covers over the constitutive conventions by which it is mobilized. (pp. 226–227; emphasis added)

A little further on, she adds: "And one might construe repetition as precisely that which undermines the conceit of voluntarist mastery designated by the subject of language" (p. 231).

But if it is precisely because it repeats instituted or common practices that a performance can be effective, it is also by virtue of its iterability that it can "fail." More precisely, and here again following the Derridean analysis of "iterability," Butler tries to show that the "reiteration of norms" is at once the condition of their maintenance and the condition of possibility of their transformation, according to that "law" of alteration that affects every iteration (*itara*). The word "alteration," in French, points toward two modes of possible transformation, which can be combined: transformation by usage, as when a thing or a being is altered by the passage of time, and transformation by displaced and displacing reinscription. This is indeed the (double) "destiny" of norms, according to Butler.

While, in *Bodies That Matter*, Butler works to rethink the performance of gender as "drag" in the light of the Austinian-Derridean notion of performativity, in *Excitable Speech* she is also interested, conversely, in the intrinsic theatricality of illocutionary or perlocutionary acts such as hate speech, injurious speech, and harassing speech.[64]

The Butlerian problematics of the performative makes it possible to re-elaborate the notion of performance of gender by tying it to a less simplistic model of "gender role" than the one on which the sociology of social interaction and behavioral psychology or psychiatry implicitly or explicitly rely. But here I would like to evoke yet another way of complicating the analysis of the role and performance "of gender."

"Incorporation" of Gender, or "Gender Inc."

In *The Psychic Life of Power*, a collection of essays also published in 1997, Butler abandoned the "linguistic" model of gender performance[65] and returned to the spectacle offered by drag queens from a different angle, following a line of questioning that she had introduced in *Gender Trouble*. In that first work, Butler linked her analysis of the performance of gender with her challenge to any "substantialist" conception of gender. Gender, and consequently gender identity, manifests itself exclusively through a series of codified ritual "acts" that are at once speech acts and "bodily acts," since the repertory of bodily gestures itself functions as a language.[66] These reiterated "speech" acts obey the structure of citationality that characterizes the Butlerian performative. Because they cite codes and norms that precede the constitution of a subject of the enunciation and set conditions for the subject that is to emerge, they can in no case be interpreted as the expression of a primary psychic interiority. Gender performed and displayed is not the mirror of any sort of "soul." Asserting its "performative" character thus allows Butler to contest the notion that gender would belong to the internal space of the psyche. More radically, it is the very idea that there is such a thing as the interiority of the psyche, an "inside" distinguishable from the "outside," that Butler calls into question, following in Foucault's footsteps in the last section of "Subversive Bodily Acts," titled "From Interiority to Gender Performatives." In this section, Butler goes beyond challenging the idea that there could be an "internal truth" of gender, or even a "truth" of the (psychic) interior at all. Picking up on the analyses in *Discipline and Punish*, where Foucault describes the social fabrication of new "docile bodies" (the body of the soldier, the schoolboy, or the factory worker) in the nineteenth century,[67] Butler proposes to see the adoption of a gender not as the manifestation of an intra-psychic process, not even as the result of a mechanism for internalizing norms, but as the effect of what she calls "incorporation," to distinguish it from internaliza-tion.[68] To say that a given law, rule, or norm is "incorporated" rather than "internalized" is to say that its assimilation does not take place through its conversion into psychic features, but through its inscription on the body itself, an inscription or "corporalization" that the body signals by drama-tizing its submission to some particular "discipline."

In the final section of *Gender Trouble*, "incorporation," promoted to the rank of leading concept, belongs quite literally to the order of "embodi-ment," a term that could also be used to describe the work of an actor on stage. The interpretation of a character necessarily mobilizes the actor's body, and it always belongs simultaneously, therefore, to the order of *im-personation* and to that of *embodiment*. But while this embodiment may produce an illusion of truth, it does not imply the slightest correspondence between the role played and some internal truth, if there is any, on the part of its interpreter.

The notion of "incorporation" is nevertheless put to an entirely different use in the chapter titled "Prohibition, Psychoanalysis, and the Production of the Heterosexual Matrix" (pp. 45–100). In "Gender Complexity and the Limits of Identification," the section of this chapter that immediately follows the pages Butler devotes to Freud and the melancholia of gender, she defines "incorporation," after Nicolas Abraham and Maria Torok, as a process of phantasmatic identification with a lost or disavowed love object, through the assimilation of that object within the ego.[69] According to Abraham, To-rok, and Butler, "incorporation" characterizes the position and the proce-dures of melancholia.

To be sure, Butler gives a particular inflection to the psychoanalytic notion of melancholic incorporation, by making it the vector and the form of any embodiment of gender or of a gender. Her "theory" on this topic, as initially formulated in *Gender Trouble*, is well known. Taking advantage of the way in which, in *The Ego and the Id*, Freud extends the notion of melan-cholic identification that he had theorized for the first time in *Mourning and Melancholia*,[70] she makes this the originary mechanism of the adop-tion of a masculine or feminine gender by a given individual: By identifying with the love object that has been lost or disavowed—feminine or mascu-line, mother or father—and that it is obliged to renounce, the ego comes to "embody" the gender of that object. According to this model, the "feminine" girl would adopt the gender (presumed feminine) of the mother whom she has had to abandon as love object in favor of the father; the "masculine" boy assumes the features of the father (presumed masculine) whom he has had to renounce. In symmetrical fashion, the "masculine" girl assumes the features of the father (presumed masculine) whom she has had to renounce, and thus orients herself, like the loved and disavowed father, toward the love of women, and so on. Gender and sexual orientation thus find themselves linked in a chiasmic relation where masculinity and femininity (of the subject and of the object choice) intersect while maintaining their binary distinction. In fact, since, according to this logic, the subject "becomes" the (masculine or feminine) person that he or she cannot "have," the subject can love only the person he or she has not become: a person not of the other sex but of the other gender. In "Freud and the Melancholia of Gender," Butler takes much less interest in "feminine" melancholic identifications than in "masculine" ones. Unlike Luce Irigaray, who preceded her in analyzing a certain gender melancholia, Butler does not stress the identification of girls with their mothers; instead, she emphasizes the process of identification by heterosexual boys or homosexual girls with their fathers.[71] In "Critically Queer," she challenges, in part, this explanatory model, which has the masculine and feminine poles attracting one another according to a "heterogendered" binary logic.[72]

To the extent that an individual's gender is acknowledged and phenomenalized once again thanks to its corporeal "performance," melancholic incorporation would still belong to the order of "embodiment." But the performance in question here is no longer "simply" a matter of the inscription of a social discipline on and by the body. It is rather the effect and outcome of a complex process that opens up an "internal space" within the subject. Unconscious identification with the disavowed love object triggers a mechanism of phantasmatic internalization of the object, as we have seen. In "Freud and the Melancholia of Gender," Butler herself repeatedly insists on this work of internalization by the melancholic subject. Still according to Butler, who borrows her lexicon this time from Lacan, this work can be complemented by a mechanism of "forclusion," that is, of *internal* exclusion or expulsion, which concerns not the object but the orientation of the drive, when this latter attests to a homosexual inclination. This mechanism would deepen still further the encrypting that renders not only the subject's desire but his or her "sexual truth" undecipherable because it is literally "unperformable" as such.

In sum, if Butler upholds the notion of "incorporation" in "Subversive Bodily Acts" in order to demolish any idea of an interiority or psychic reality of gender, and if, as she writes in the final section of this chapter, the illusion of interiority produced by the performance of the body is "a function of a decidedly public and social discourse" (p. 185), it seems, quite to the contrary, that the notion of incorporation mobilized in "Prohibition, Psychoanalysis, and the Heterosexual Matrix" has to do with an "inside" that is, if not already constituted, at least carved in by the process of melancholic incorporation. And if it is, or rather if it is also, the force of something like a love, even a repudiated love, and not only the force of the norm, that provokes the melancholic pantomime, then it may be necessary to conceptualize further, or differently, than Butler does in *Gender Trouble*, the articulation between the social dimension of gender and its psychic dimension, and, more generally, the modes of coincidence or disjunction between the "psychic" and the "social."

In her 1999 preface, Butler clearly recognizes the existence and the import of such a tension: "The view that gender is performative sought to show that what we take to be an internal essence of gender is manufactured through a sustained set of acts," she writes (p. xv). And she adds, a little further on: "Does this mean that everything that is understood as 'internal' about the psyche is therefore evacuated, and that internality is a false metaphor? Although *Gender Trouble* clearly drew upon the metaphor of an internal psyche in its early discussion of gender melancholy, that emphasis was not brought forward into the thinking of performativity itself" (p. xvi).

As she herself notes in her preface, it is only in *The Psychic Life of Power* that she reached the point of proposing a coherent articulation of the two sources of gender pantomime: the "external" source according to which a given "morphological ideal" shaped by norms finds itself "incorporated" (in the primary sense of the term) by the subject during the process of "subjectification" and the "internal" source according to which a given libidinal position leads the ego to "incorporate" (in the second sense of the term) an object that is simultaneously loved and repudiated. And once again it is the theater of the drag queen that supplies Butler with the occasion for, and the possibility of, reconciling Freud and Foucault, or even Freud and Goffman.

The performance of drag queens orients several of the essays brought together in *Bodies That Matter*. But Butler again produces a reading divided along the fault line that separates the two conceptions of "incorporation" that we have just been examining. In "Gender Is Burning," an essay whose title points toward Jennie Livingston's documentary, "Paris Is Burning," on the Latina and Afro-American drag queens in Harlem,[73] "drag" performance is described as the spectacular display of the social process through which individuals internalize norms, a process condemned to a form of failure, as we have seen, by virtue of the structure of citationality in performance. The norms in question here are "morphological ideals" of gender, race, and class, whose "incorporation" is mimed or replayed by Latina or Afro-American drag queens: "The effect of 'realness' is the result of an embodiment of norms, a reiteration of norms, an impersonation of a racial and class norm, a norm which is at once a figure, a figure of a body, which is no particular body, but a morphological ideal that remains the standard which regulates the performance, but which no performance fully approximates."[74]

In "Critically Queer," however, Butler sketches an entirely different reading of the "performance" of these same Harlem drag queens: This time, as she sees it, "drag performance" allegorizes "some sort of melancholic incorporative fantasies that stabilize *gender*" (p. 235). According to the psychoanalytic logic redeployed here by Butler, the work done by the unconscious in the constitution and manifestation of gender is such that the signification of gender cannot be reduced to its appearance. The "repudiated identifications"—those that one does not see or that do not show— secretly inform those that are exhibited in performance.[75] By this token, as Butler again writes, "[W]hat is 'performed' works to conceal, if not to disavow, what remains opaque, unconscious, unperformable."[76] On the one hand, then, gender would be performable to the very extent that it consists in reproducing, by dramatizing them, normative representations and acknowledged ideals; the performance of gender would be no more than a ballet of perfectly identifiable figures. On the other hand, gender would be "performed" to the very extent that, and precisely in the place where, something resists or eludes representation; performance would then have, if not as its function, at least as its effect, that of masking something "unperformable."[77]

In any case, not until *The Psychic Life of Power* are these two lines of argumentation reconciled, in particular in the introduction and in the essay titled "Melancholy Gender/Refused Identifications." In a general way, the essays collected in this volume are presented in the introduction as so many contributions to the development of a theory of the subject, or more precisely of the process of subjectification. Butler is seeking here to rehabilitate—if not against Foucault then at least against an overly "mechanistic" reading of Foucault—the psyche and the role of "psychic life" in this process, the better to pinpoint the articulation between social constraints and psychic constraints.[78] A theory of the "formation of the subject" thus has to account for the process of "incorporation of norms," she writes.[79] And the notion of "incorporation" must not be used to reinforce the illusion that an already-constituted "inner sanctum" would precede the moment of internalization. At the same time, the "psychic operation of the norm,"[80] that is, the way(s) in which social constraints are manifested, transposed, and transformed by investing the subject, thus by "becoming psychic," does not stem from a simple mode of articulation between the social and the psychic: The psychic apparatus is not merely a recording device and must therefore not be conceived as the passive receptacle of such an "operation." Butler then appeals to psychoanalysis, and in particular to Freud's description of the relation between the ego, the id, and the superego, to try to show how the "operation of the norm" and the "operations" of the superego are conjugated. Thus, whereas, in *Gender Trouble*, melancholic identification was described by Butler as the "royal road" to the acquisition of a gender (feminine or masculine), and this was the case without regard to the sexual orientation of the subject that had been "gendered" in this way, in "Melancholy Gender," Butler reserves her analysis of gender melancholia for the heterosexual configuration alone: only this one, in fact, lends itself easily to the Butlerian analysis of the formation and action of the superego in this context.

Freud had already showed the role of the superego—indeed, he had even situated its genesis—in the process of melancholic identification. Unlike the "normally" grieving subject, the "ego" of the melancholic subject turns against itself by splitting into two agencies, one of which—the superego—incriminates the other—the ego. It is precisely this internal struggle within the ego that plunges the subject into melancholia. For Freud, the punitive action exercised against the ego by the superego reproduces in the psyche the former ambivalence of the ego toward its love object, an ambivalence that had, in fact, led to the disavowal of that object. So what is at stake is thus really a process of internalizing a situation that was first played out between the ego and an "external" object. Butler sees in this movement of self-punishing internalization, and consequently in the action of the superego, the psychic manifestation of the violence of norms. This normative violence would explain the initial ambivalence manifested by the individual toward the same-sex love object, an ambivalence that could go as far as the repudiation of that object. The amorous investment would survive in the subject without the subject's knowledge only in the form of a melancholic, thus self-punishing, identification with the repudiated or "refused" object. And this is why, in "Melancholy Gender/Refused Identifications," the drag queen's performance is interpreted not as a spectacular manifestation of homosexual melancholia or as a general allegory for the performance of gender, and still less, of course, as an exhibition of the homosexual's inner truth (his primary "femininity"), but rather as an allegory of "*heterosexual* melancholia."[81] "Drag exposes or allegorizes the mundane psychic and performative practices by which heterosexualized genders form themselves through renouncing the possibility of homosexuality, a foreclosure which produces both a field of heterosexual objects and a domain of those it would be impossible to love. Drag thus allegorizes *heterosexual melancholy* . . . ."[82]

The self-mockery of the drag performance—the way the drag queen "turns" and thereby incites her public to turn, even while laughing, against the character she is embodying—would thus mimic the self-punishing movement of heterosexual melancholia. But if the conjugation between the norm and the action of the superego makes it possible to explain the formation of gender identity under the "heterosexual" cultural regime, how can one explain the process of adopting a gender by a person who has not renounced the homosexual orientation? How, finally, can one explain that the heterosexual "tragicomedy" has been taken over and staged by these drag queens, who, unlike "mere" transvestites, are almost always homosexual in orientation?

To these questions, Butler does not offer either clear or direct answers. In the wake of her analysis of drag performance, she simply indicates that gender melancholia, as she has defined it, "can work . . . within homosexuality in specific ways that call for rethinking."[83] The privilege she grants to drag performance and to the conception of gender as drag nevertheless constitutes an indirect response to the two questions raised: If gender belongs to the order of drag, then, to the extent that drag performance functions exclusively with reference to the heterosexual scene of gender constitution, this makes homosexuality thus envisaged, and gender play in a homosexual context, not the expression of a primary sexual disposition or a primitive attachment but a *response to* and a *replica of* heterosexuality. Like the heterosexuality that she calls on the carpet, its homosexual counterpart, far from "unmasking" its "own" system of "refused" identifications— but does it have another besides the one it (re)plays?—would conceal it, and doubly so, even from the persons who "perform" it: a double dissimulation.

To be sure, such a conception of the performance of gender stems from a much more complex analytic model than the one that informs the "role theory" of the pre-Butlerian sociology of interaction. But it has a tendency to maintain the binary schema that presided over the earliest modern conceptions of homosexuality, those of the psychopathologists of the second half of the nineteenth century who saw homosexuality as a phenomenon of "gender inversion." With the difference that, in Butler's schema of gender melancholia, inversion is "inverted" in its turn: "Heterosexual" persons are the "inverted" ones since, according to the "melancholic" hypothesis, they have been compelled to reverse the trajectory of their libido by adopting a gender "opposed" to the presumed gender of the only love object to which they "legitimately" have access. Butler acknowledges on more than one occasion that other models besides gender inversion are possible for thinking sexual orientation: "[C]ross-gendered identification is not the only paradigm for thinking about homosexuality, merely one among others," she notes in "Melancholy Gender" (p. 146). On the following page, she suggests that the chiasmic crossing in which the two genders (masculine/feminine) and the two sexualities (hetero/homo) intersect like two pairs of opposite and inverted poles, may not be the only possible way of configuring the relation between gender and sexuality: "what constitutes the *sexually* unperformable may—*but need not*—be performed as gender identification" (p. 147; second emphasis added). Even so, she remains a thinker and supporter of "chiasmus," remaining reticent in the end toward more fluid or more frankly "plastic" conceptions of gender and sexuality.[84]

Finally, even if the "homosexual" parody of heterosexual gender melancholia exemplifies in its way the structure of performative citationality we examined earlier, we cannot fail to note that Butler continues, after *Gender Trouble*, to place the emphasis in her writings sometimes on the "linguistic" performative, as in *Excitable Speech*, and sometimes on "theatrical" performance, as in *The Psychic Life of Power*, published the same year; she never completely abandons either of these vectors of analysis, but she never brings them into complete coincidence, either.

"Black" Parody and Sham Marriages

Even though Butler hobnobs with psychoanalysis in a way that is both irresistible and ambiguous, the Butlerian theory of gender is not a hermeneutics. It has almost nothing to say about the reasons why the normative "ideal" takes any particular form in its feminine or masculine versions. Consequently, it says almost nothing, either, about the reasons for masculine domination or the abjection of femininity. And almost nothing, finally, about the structural or historical cause(s) of what is called—in a way that is perhaps naively pre-theoretical, but the observation is nonetheless accurate—the "inequality between the sexes." On what politics can such a perspective then rely? What critical promise can it make?[85] Since subjects are condemned to "perform" their gender, since one cannot distinguish rigorously between the hyperbolic performance of drag queens and the heterosexual comedy that these queens caricature as they enact it, what possibilities for transforming roles and norms does the parodic repetition of gender mimicry let us glimpse or hope for?

The question nags at Butler, who never ceases to raise it in the texts I have cited, while bringing to it once again a split response. Let us take, for example, "Gender Is Burning: Questions of Appropriation and Subversion," since this essay hinges entirely on that issue, as its subtitle indicates. On one page, we read that drag as parodic repetition of the staging of gender is indeed subversive: "[D]rag is subversive to the extent that it reflects on the imitative structure by which hegemonic gender is itself produced and disputes heterosexuality's claim on naturalness and originality" (p. 125), a formula that we find again in almost the same terms in "Imitation and Gender Insubordination" (p. 313). But on the same page of "Gender Is Burning," we also read that drag is not necessarily subversive, an assertion reinforced by the direct intervention of the speaking subject in the utterance: "*I want to underscore* that there is no necessary relation between drag and subversion, and that drag may well be used in the service of both the denaturalization and reidealization of hyperbolic heterosexual gender norms" (p. 125; emphasis added).

Butler oscillates. On the one hand, she sees the performative reiteration of norms as unavoidable, just as it seems to be for the (male or female) drag queens. She does not believe in what she calls, at the beginning of "Critically Queer," "the utopics of radical resignification" (p. 224). If there is any subversion, it does not operate through an exit[86] from, or a radical reconfiguration of, the normative staging of gender. There is no "off-stage," nothing beneath or beyond the "performative closure." To have an opportunity to transform something, it is thus necessary to repeat, that is, to reduplicate in order to "pass off" a repetition that has "always already" taken place. Irigaray's rewriting of Plato in *Speculum of the Other Woman*, the mobilization of the symbolics of the nuclear family by Harlem drag queens, and Butler's own reinscription of the Lacanian phallus all stem, according to the philosopher, from this work of reiteration: "Irigaray's critical mime of Plato, the fiction of the lesbian phallus and the rearticulation of kinship in *Paris is Burning* might be understood as repetitions of hegemonic forms of power which fail to repeat loyally, and, in that failure, open possibilities for resignifying."[87] She repeats this again toward the end: "This is not an appropriation of dominant culture in order to remain subordinated by its terms, but an appropriation that seeks to make over the terms of domination, a making over which is a kind of agency, a power in and as discourse, in and as performance, which repeats in order to remake—and sometimes succeeds."[88]

From infinite repetitions to minuscule variations of utterances, Butler's rhetoric mimes (unless, on the contrary, it supplies the model and the formula for) the process of repetition that *plays at displacement*. Playing at displacement, repetition displaces without (appearing to be) displacing. Thus the displaced reinscription of the "phallus" and its installation on the lesbian erotic stage amounts to a "remake" (a term used by Butler that signifies inextricably both "reprise" and "recreation") of its "signification."[89]

The risk, which Butler's hesitations about the drag queen's potential for theatrical subversion bring clearly to light, is that the parodic reiteration of norms may fail to transform these latter just as it "fails" structurally to reproduce them. In "Gender is Burning," Butler observes that the conjoined "denaturalization" of the norms of gender and race carried out by the Harlem drag queens filmed by Jennie Livingston in no way prevents the idealization of these same norms. Of what do these poor black transvestites or transsexuals dream?[90] They dream of the domestic comfort of a "sham" marriage.

Butler then turns her attention away from the spectacle of gender that these drag queens offer (themselves) to seek an answer to the political question in a different setting: that of the invention, by these same drag queens, of new forms of community. These individuals, in fact, gather together in (imaginary) "houses" presided over by "mothers" chosen from their group: "These men 'mother' one another, 'house' one another, 'rear' one another, and the resignification of the family through these terms is not a vain or useless imitation, but the social and discursive building of community, a community that binds, cares, and teaches, that shelters and enables," Butler exclaims enthusiastically.[91]

A certain effusive vehemence in tone—rare for Butler—betrays her affective investment in this evocation of a community that is at once abnormal and otherwise "ideal." And if Butler again sees in this new form of community a redeployment of family structure through "*resignification*" (i.e., as the prefix "re" indicates, a way of taking up again or repeating the family by giving it a different signification), this time she seems much more certain that this "resignification" is successful, that this "imitation" of a family is not "vain or useless," than she was regarding the spectacle of gender—subversive? not subversive?—offered by the drag queens.

There would be a great deal more to say about this dream of a mothering, quasi-familial community whose motifs come up again in the numerous essays Butler devotes to the problem of kinship as a site where the social bond might be reformulated. Butler's enthusiasm is all the more striking in that she is intent everywhere else on contesting the exorbitant role granted, according to her, to the figure of the mother by a certain feminist discourse. But let us not dwell on this; for the moment, I shall simply emphasize that Butler seems to have espoused one of the lessons Newton disseminated through her ethnographic history of Cherry Grove: No, the denaturalization of gender does not suffice to shift norms and the positions of the subjects who embody them, nor does the unbridled "proliferation" of genders that begins when gender no longer refers exclusively to the dividing line between men and women.[92] The men of Cherry Grove may well be "queens" (or perhaps, on the contrary, "male butches" or even "bears"[93]) and the women "butches" (or even "stone-butches," or, on the contrary, "femmes" [fems]); the power relation between the two is scarcely modified.

The gay subversion of the heterosexist gender division probably does not suffice to change the status quo between men and women.

DRAG AND *DRAGUE*: THEATER OF GENDER
AND SEXUAL DISPLAY

The Scene of Lesbian Desire: Elements of a Genealogy

For Esther Newton, the theatricality of gender has an erotic function and value above all else. I have already evoked the episode in her "butch memoirs" in which she relates with delight the erotic transport she experienced thanks to the gripping theatrical performance of a male drag queen. Similarly, she ties the cultural invention of the "butch" gender in the early twentieth century to the new sexualization of relations among women.

In "The Mythic Mannish Lesbian: Radclyffe Hall and the New Woman," Newton draws on the reading of a famous English "lesbian" novel by Radclyffe Hall, *The Well of Loneliness*, featuring a character named Stephen Gordon, a homosexual woman of the masculine gender, to propose an analytic genealogy of the butch figure.[94] *The Well of Loneliness*, published in 1928, immediately became if not a best-seller at least a media phenomenon in the Anglo-Saxon world, like its French predecessor and near-contemporary, Victor Margueritte's *La Garçonne*. For Newton, the "mannish lesbian" emerged in the context of a sexualization of the demand for autonomy formulated by those whom she calls the "new women."[95] During the nineteenth and early twentieth centuries, female "romantic friendships" may have begun to constitute an alternative to heterosexual marriage, but these friendships were conceived in a language that was both idealizing and desexualized. The eruption of the figure of the "invert" (a masculine woman who desired women) in the 1920s corresponded, according to Newton, not only to the vulgarization of the psycho-sexological and psychoanalytical doctrines describing homosexuality as an "inversion" of genders (or of "sexual identities") and objects; it also bore witness to the eroticization of the scene of relations among women, an eroticization that was part of the "modernist" reaction to conservative Victorian moral values. "For many women of Radclyffe Hall's generation, sexuality—for itself and as a symbol of female autonomy—became a preoccupation. These women were, after all, the sisters of D. H. Lawrence and James Joyce. For male novelists, sexologists, and artists rebelling against Victorian values, sexual freedom became the cutting edge of modernism," Newton writes.[96] In so doing, she explicitly links the formation of what she calls elsewhere "gay genders" ("butch," "femme," "drag queen," and so on, genders that result from the displacement and redeployment of feminine and masculine attributes on the terrain of homosexual relations) to the sexualization of relations among women. According to her, the scene of desire needs gender play, as she explains later in her essay: "Thus, along with their desire to be modern, our bourgeois lesbian ancestors had another powerful reason to embrace change. Before they could find one another in the twentieth-century urban landscape, they had to become visible, at least to each other. They needed a new vocabulary built on the radical idea that women apart from men could have autonomous sexual feelings."[97]

The new lesbians had to make themselves *visible* to one another. The outward "visibility" of their "mannish" gender was at once the condition and the form taken by sexual display. Finally, because sexual desire was not considered at the time to be "inherent in women," as Newton indicates, to the extent that it was not a correct or acceptable feminine expression (an axiom that Freud translated in the same period by stating that "there is only one libido," which could not be termed feminine),[98] the active desire of a woman for another woman could only be figured as such through its masculinization: "Because sexual desire was not considered inherent in women, the lesbian was endowed with a trapped male soul that phallicized her, giving her active lust."[99]

The creation of the butch as a phallic woman desiring another woman led to that of the "femme" (fem) as a figure for the butch's object of desire. "Hall's vision of lesbianism as sexual difference and as masculinity is inimical to lesbian-feminist ideology," Newton concludes[100]; here she contrasts the relation of identificatory solidarity among women that is the basis for feminism with the desiring relation based on what she calls "sexual difference," understood as the inextricable difference of genders and sexualities.[101] In "Critically Queer," Butler invites us to "theorize" "sexual difference" within homosexuality in terms that once again recall Newton's reflections.[102]

Butler is not far from Newton when she remarks in *Gender Trouble* that butch and femme "identities" have an erotic power of attraction.[103] This is also the case when she interprets the white lesbian filmmaker Jennie Livingston's exclamation of admiration before the performance of a Latina drag queen, Octavia Saint-Laurent, as a moment of "transsexualization of lesbian desire,"[104] and once again when she raises questions, at the end of "Critically Queer," about the meaning and the theoretical and political effects of the analytic separation between the realm of gender and that of sexuality.

This interrogation became a systematic critique in a 1994 essay titled "Against Proper Objects."[105] This essay was published for the first time in a special issue of the journal *differences* devoted to the (partly failed) encounter between feminism and queer theory, a schism that resulted from (or was attributed to) the theoretical distinction between studying gender and studying sexuality. In so doing, Butler stood up against an entire sector of the queer movement, which, starting from a challenge to the heterosexual partitioning of genders, claimed to think and experience sexuality, following Foucault's example, in a radical or principial indifference to stagings of gender and the questions that these raised. Butler's intervention in this regard takes, in particular, the form of a critical interpellation of Gayle Rubin, another lesbian anthropologist dealing with questions of gender and sexuality whose work has played an important role in the formation and formulation of Butler's conception of gender.

Genders of Sexuality

Gayle Rubin is still not very well known in France, but she is read in all the programs in gender studies, gay, lesbian, bisexual, and transgender studies, and queer studies in the United States. Two of her essays stand as milestones in the intellectual and political history of American feminism and postfeminism: "The Traffic in Women: Notes on the 'Political Economy' of Sex" (1975) and "Thinking Sex: Notes for a Radical Theory of the Politics of Sexuality" (first published in 1984).[106]

"The Traffic in Women" constitutes one of the earliest attempts to formulate a feminist epistemology that relies chiefly on structural anthropology and psychoanalysis to conceptualize the specificity of women's oppression. In this essay, Rubin also formulates one of the first feminist theories of gender oppression, supplying theoretical bases for the distinction between sex and gender as this distinction functions in the field of feminist theory in the United States. Here again, Judith Butler points out on several occasions how much her own conception of gender in *Gender Trouble* owes to "The Traffic in Women."[107] Finally, the essay is one of the earliest examples of active importation of "French thought" in the service of a political and theoretical project. (I include Freud in "French thought" because it was through the reading of Lacan that a rereading of Freud was launched in the American academic context.)

The "Rubinian" conception of gender does not stem from the American psycho-sociology of "self (re)presentation" whose genealogy I have sketched in part. Relying on the theses formulated by Claude Lévi-Strauss in *The Elementary Structures of Kinship*, she conceives of gender as the translation on the social and symbolic level of the dissymmetrical positions of men and women in the system of exchange described by Lévi-Strauss. According to the anthropologist, the exchange of women, which results from the prohibition of incest, is the foundation for the *socius* (be it solidary or agonistic) through the play of kinship bonds—among clans, families, tribes, communities—that are conditioned by this exchange. The distribution of men and women by gender thus has no basis in nature; it results on the one hand from the dissymmetrical structure of this exchange, since men are the agents and beneficiaries of the exchange, while women are at once its objects and its means, and on the other hand, from the sexual division of labor within the family, a division also analyzed by Lévi-Strauss in a later essay, "The Family."[108] In this latter text, the anthropologist hypothesizes that it is precisely this sexual division of labor within the family that makes heterosexuality "obligatory," by making men and women dependent on one another for subsistence. According to Rubin, the Oedipus complex "discovered" by psychoanalysis only translates onto the level of the individual psyche the double rule prohibiting incest and imposing heterosexual alliance, ordering men's and women's destinies in a dissymmetrical way.

Rubin's second major essay, "Thinking Sex: Notes for a Radical Theory of the Politics of Sexuality," was very quickly viewed as both a queer manifesto and a postfeminist manifesto. It played a foundational role in the emergence and the political justification of the field of lesbian and gay studies, as this field came to be constituted in the late 1980s before its queer reformulation in the 1990s. Reproduced a number of times in various anthologies, "Thinking Sex" is the opening text in *The Lesbian and Gay Studies Reader*, a copious collection of "gay" and "lesbian" theoretical texts published in 1993 at a point when gay and lesbian studies programs were beginning to multiply on the American university landscape.[109]

Written in the triple context of the emerging AIDS epidemic that was mainly affecting male homosexuals at that point, the conservative turn marked by Ronald Reagan's election, and the climate of homophobia that was currently dominant in the United States, this text calls for the elaboration of a theory and a politics of sexuality that would study and defend what Rubin calls "sexual dissidents,"[110] that is, all those—homosexuals, transsexuals, sadomasochists, fetishists, sex workers (male or female), and practitioners of "intergenerational" sexuality—whose sexual practices are stigmatized or even criminalized. In this essay, Rubin distances herself from feminism, whose inability or reluctance to deal with these problems she stresses. She denounces even the alliance of certain feminists with what she considers a repressive politics.[111]

On the theoretical level, Rubin advocates the heuristic separation of the two meanings of the word "sex" in English: "Sex," she states, means both "gender" and "gender identity," referring thus to men and women as sexed beings, and "sexual activity," "sexual relations." According to her, the fusion of these two meanings gives rise to the erroneous idea that sexuality (understood as sexual activity) derives from the "sex" of its practitioner and that it is more specifically a function of the relations between men and women.[112] She contests both the treatment of sexuality as deriving from gender or from belonging to a sex *and* the implicit heterosexism of this logic. She rejects the idea that feminism is the best political and theoretical tool to conceptualize and denounce sexual oppression, to the extent that it understands the latter as the oppression of one sex by another, and thus pays no attention to the oppression of which queers and "perverts" of all genders are also the object, by virtue not of a gender politics but of an axiologics of sexuality. Thus she calls for the formulation of a "radical theory of sexual oppression" that would be distinct from the feminist analysis of sexual hierarchies.[113] In the process, she also formalizes the distinction, if not the break, between a certain lesbianism and the feminism with which it was once associated, if not confused.[114]

Between "The Traffic in Women" and "Thinking Sex," Rubin had read Foucault. In "The Traffic in Women," Rubin was already dreaming, in the manner of Monique Wittig (whom she had presumably just read), of a society freed from the "straightjacket" [sic] of gender, thanks to a revolution in the organization of what Lévi-Strauss calls "kinship structures."[115] But it is the Foucaldian notion of "sexuality," and the idea that we might pass—that we have already passed—historically, in the West, from a cultural system dominated by a "deployment of alliance" (the name Foucault gives to the organization of kinship) to a system dominated by a "deployment of sexuality," which allows Rubin to formulate the necessity for an epistemological break between "gender" and "sexuality." In so doing, Rubin rejects psychoanalysis, upon which she had called in her analysis of the formation of genders, and she refuses henceforth, following Foucault's example, to submit the analysis of sexuality or sexualities to any hermeneutic procedure whatsoever.[116] Sexuality as a social phenomenon is no longer anchored in the "gendered subject" but rather in the "body and its pleasures." Let us note nevertheless that, in "Thinking Sex," Rubin gives a rather literal and restrictive interpretation of Foucaldian "sexuality." For if, under the term "sexuality," Foucault subsumes a set of discursive, institutional, and cognitive arrangements having to do with "sex," Rubin tends to use this term to designate the quite varied gamut of sexual practices, licit or not.

Supported by Rubin's analyses (the position of "Thinking Sex" as the opening essay in the book indicates its seminal value), the editors of the *Lesbian and Gay Studies Reader* thus made "sexuality" the "proper" object of their inquiry and thereby consecrated the separation between gender studies and sexuality studies, although in more prudent and nuanced terms than Rubin's. Their introduction includes the following statement: "Lesbian/Gay Studies does for *sex* and *sexuality* approximately what women's studies does for gender." And a little further on: "Without attempting to anticipate the outcome of that process, we can still describe lesbian/gay studies by saying that it intends to establish the analytical centrality of sex and sexuality within many different fields of inquiry . . ." (pp. xv–xvi).

It is in response to this gesture of methodological separation between "gender" on the one hand and sex-and-sexuality on the other, and thereby also to the "perverse" effects of a certain reading of "sex" inspired by Foucault, that Butler formulates her critique in "Against Proper Objects." Her approach is at once methodological, philosophical, and political. She contests the analogic binarism and the temporalization of the distinction between gender studies and gay and lesbian studies, as the latter is formulated in the first statement cited previously: From this point on, lesbian-gay studies are to be for sexuality what women's studies have been for gender.

In the name of a certain conception of language as a foyer of at-once incompressible and unmasterable significations, she speaks out against the operation that consists in depriving the word "sex" of its ambiguity in English by excluding from the field of its definition, by a simple methodological decision, those aspects of "sex" that refer, or may refer, to the question of sexual difference, thereby tying this question to that of sexuality and vice versa in a way that is as irreducible as it is equivocal. She stresses that the deliberate exclusion of gender from the field of reflection of lesbian and gay studies threatens to render the latter incapable of accounting for transgender and transsexual fantasies, which both mobilize phantasms and performances of gender; finally, following the analyses by Biddy Martin that appear in the same volume, Butler expresses the fear that a theoretico-political field that neutralizes any suspicion of dissymmetry between "lesbian" and "gay" in its presentation (lesbian/gay studies), and sees itself as freed from gender, thus from the feminism that would take gender as its object, would play into the hands of phallocentrism.[117] Toward the end of her essay, she thus writes:

> It seems clear that the methodological separation of questions of sexuality from questions either of sexual difference or of gender within lesbian and gay studies reintroduces the problem of the feminine—and feminism—as a site of the irrepresentable.
>
> . . . If sexuality is conceived as liberated from gender then the sexuality that is "liberated" from feminism will be one which suspends the reference to masculine and feminine, reinforcing the refusal to mark that difference, which is the conventional way in which the masculine has achieved the status of the "sex" which is one.[118]

The political and theoretical quarrel between Gayle Rubin and Judith Butler bears witness to the internal tensions in the queer movement, split as it is among contradictory identifications, even as it strives to call into question the relation between sexuality (or sexualities) and identity (or identities).

And yet even Rubin herself does not manage to maintain a radical separation between "gender" and "sexuality." In an interview with Judith Butler that the latter titled "Sexual Traffic," in a reference to the anthropologist's two major articles, Rubin discusses at length her new skepticism, if not toward feminist theory as a whole, at least toward a certain American feminist politics; she describes her political, ethnographic, and theoretical interest in what she calls not sexual difference but sexual differences;[119] she affirms her solidarity with gay sexual politics; she looks back on her distaste for psychoanalytic hermeneutics and its treatment of perversions; in short, she sums up everything that has led her to challenge the paradigm of "gender" as a tool for analyzing sexual manifestations and sexual oppression. Now, at the end of the conversation, just when she is evoking for Butler the object and stakes of her latest ethnographic study (focused on the gay male "leather" community in San Francisco[120]), the "gender" motif that she had banished comes back in irresistibly to haunt her remarks. The last three pages of the interview deserve to be cited at length:

> Leather is a broader category that includes gay men who do SM, gay men who are into fisting, gay men who are fetishists, and *gay men who are masculine and prefer masculine partners*. . . . Among gay men, leather and its *idioms of masculinity* have been the main framework for gay male SM since the last 1940s. . . . Among gay men, the *adoption of masculinity* is complicated, and has a lot to do with rejecting the traditional equations of male homosexual desire with *effeminacy*. . . . *A masculine homosexual (like a feminine lesbian) was once considered an oxymoron*; such persons . . . were unthinkable in terms of the hegemonic models of sexuality and gender. The development of the leather community is part of a long process in which *masculinity* has been claimed, asserted, or reappropriated by male homosexuals. . . . Gay male leather, including gay male SM, codes *both desiring/desired subjects and desired/desiring objects as masculine*. . . . There are also *symbolics of effeminate homosexual SM* . . . Straight SM was not territorial, and, if anything, *the dominant stylistic idioms were feminine*.
>
> The imagery of heterosexual SM and fetishism draws a lot on *feminine symbolism*. SM erotica aimed at male heterosexuals often has mostly female characters, and the few *male characters are often effeminized*. . . .
>
> I do not mean to imply that there are no "masculine" heterosexual male masochists or sadists. Moreover, *this feminine imagery* is not as hegemonic for heterosexual SM as is masculine *imagery* for gay male SM. But a visible and common style of heterosexual SM involves a *feminine woman and an effeminized man*, a sort of fantasy "lesbian" couple.

Meanwhile, among actual lesbian sadomasochists, there seems to be a pretty even distribution of *masculine and feminine styles, genders*, and symbolism.[121]

Masculine/masculine, masculine/feminine, feminine/feminine, feminine/masculine . . . The erotic theater of the sexual differences that Rubin would like to offer up to conceptualization and experience without the aid, or rather the "straightjacket" [*sic*], of gender, is described entirely through the prism of gender. To be sure, "masculine" and "feminine" are deterritorialized, denaturalized, even parodic, but that does not keep them from being convoked, quite the contrary. The hyperbolic performance of gender in these erotic relations (and in their evocation) attests to a kind of overinvestment in gender. It is as though the sexual scene, in Rubin's sense, could only be a "scene" and could only make sense if one were to begin (again) with the play of gender. Butler, who cannot fail to have perceived the objective irony of these remarks, probes one last time: "I'd like to bring us back to gender." But Rubin evades the invitation, and the conversation ends with these words: "I think I will leave any further comments on gender to you, in your capacity as the reigning 'Queen' of gender!"[122]

How are we to understand the role of gender in the phantasmatics of the erotic encounter—as if without gender the sexual scene were if not inconceivable then at least unplayable?

While Butler may owe her conception of gender as "drag" to Newton, most of those who view gender as stylized performance have been able to find a way to conceptualize the relation between drag and flirtation (French *drague*) by drawing on the work of Jacques Lacan. The contemporary French verb *draguer*, meaning "to flirt, to approach, to attempt to seduce a potential sexual partner," clearly comes from the English "to drag," which can be translated by the French *tirer*, meaning literally "to pull," and particularly to pull toward oneself an object that offers resistance, as a fisherman tries to drag in a fish he has caught in a net. The English verb can also be translated by the French *traîner*, meaning to pull (something) behind oneself, as in the heavy "train" of the type of dress worn by transvestite actors (and from which "drag queens" take their name). In order to emphasize the consubstantiality of *drague* and "drag," that is, of a certain seductive pantomime aimed at catching the object of desire in one's nets *and* of "gender" as cross-dressing, thus as essentially "queer," I prefer to use the English term "drag" rather than the French term *travesti*.[123] No *drague* without "drag"!

Lacan and the "Comedy of the Sexes"

But let us look at Lacan. The rediscovery of Joan Rivière's text "Womanliness as Masquerade" and the queer reflection on masquerades were mediated by a reading of Lacan. Butler devotes an entire section of the second chapter of *Gender Trouble* to a reading of "The Signification of the Phallus," and, through this "writing" by Lacan, to the question of the masquerade in Rivière. She returned to "the meaning of the phallus" in her essay on the "lesbian phallus," published in *Bodies That Matter* in 1993. A volume of essays edited by Sue-Ellen Case, which was published the same year as *Gender Trouble* and which sought to conceptualize the articulation between the two emerging fields of gender theory and performance theory, also devotes a good deal of attention to Lacan.[124] Two contributions to the special issue of *differences* that included the friendly dispute between Judith Butler and Gayle Rubin also invoked Lacan (especially *The Four Fundamental Concepts of Psychoanalysis*) in dealing once again with the problem of the masquerade.[125]

In "The Signification of the Phallus," as I have already mentioned, Lacan describes "the instating in the subject of an unconscious position," masculine or feminine, as a process of identification "with the ideal type of his [sic] sex" (p. 575). Like Butler after him, Lacan connects the notion of ideal on the one hand with the image of the ego (and the ego as image),[126] and on the other hand with the notion of regulatory model, thus with the "registers" of the imaginary and the symbolic.

In the various essays he devotes to the "mirror stage," Lacan elaborates on the relations between what Freud calls the bodily ego, the first "form" of the ego, and the ideal ego. Mirrors give back to very young children a unified image of a body that children still perceive piecemeal and as uncoordinated. The image of the body—the prototype of the ego, since children grasp it and recognize themselves in it—thus has an idealizing function. The "self" that the child can point to is from the outset an "ideal" ego. The child's narcissistic investment in the image is related to this process of idealization. From this standpoint, the imaginary grasp that establishes the love of self as ideal ego functions as a prototype for sex-based identification, conceived as an identification with a narcissistic thrust.

But if sex-based identification as identification with an "ideal type" draws the thinking about sexual or gender identity that results from it toward a problematic of the lure (as narcissistic illusion and trap, for both the self and the other[127]) right from the start, for Lacan the "unconscious castration complex" is what generates these at-once stereotyped and differentiated identifications and transforms them into role plays. These role plays make sexual relations both possible and impossible, according to an irreducible aporia noted repeatedly by Lacan.

At the outset, the "castration complex" is described as a dramatic springboard. According to Lacan, it "functions as a knot . . . in regulating the development that gives its *ratio* to this first role: namely, the instating in the subject of an unconscious position," masculine or feminine. To be sure, the word "role" may simply mean "function" here. The function of "identification with the ideal type of [one's] sex," this time as a regulatory model, is to make the procreation of children possible in heterosexual relations, Lacan says in effect.[128] (He thus suggests, as did Freud before him, that neither sexual identity nor heterosexuality is decided in advance by some "nature of things.") But the mention of this "first role" also serves to propel the sexual relation understood as relation between subjects identified as masculine or feminine onto a theater where the puppeteer is none other than the operation of castration. The adoption of a masculine or feminine position, as the "first role" played by the subject, marks the latter's first appearance on the scene of desire.

The problematics that emerges from Lacan's reading of Freud is very well known: The "discovery" of sexual difference in early childhood is interpreted as a discovery of the "reality" of castration (conceived essentially as castration of the mother) by the little boy *and* by the little girl. The girl thus agrees to see herself as the boy sees her. If she doesn't have a penis, it's because she has lost hers. From this point on, the boy will try to protect himself against the threat of castration that he perceives hanging over him owing to the "avowed" castration of the girl. And the girl will try to repair the injury done to her by making up for the lack. Thus both "sexes," in their difference and in their relation, would have a connection with this lack of a penis. Lacan makes the "phallus" the representative of this lack, the signifier of castration.

For Lacan, it is the lack—what he also calls the experience of privation ("real" or not: this is of no importance as long as the lack is experienced as such)—that introduces the subject into the order of desire. And since the phallus is the signifier of what is lacking or what may come to be lacking, it becomes, in Lacanian logic, the "ratio [reason] of desire." "This seals the conjunction of desire, insofar as the phallic signifier is its mark, with the threat of or nostalgia based on not-having [*manque à avoir*]," Lacan writes.[129]

Because the phallus is at once the signifier of a lack that must be masked and the cause of a desire that proceeds masked because it cannot recognize its own structure and object, it precipitates the relations between "the sexes," which depend on it (this is what Lacan calls "sticking to" the phallic function), into the realm of comedy: "This is brought about by the intervention of a seeming [*paraître*] that replaces the having in order to protect it, in one case, and to mask the lack thereof, in the other, and whose effect is to completely project the ideal or typical manifestation of each of the sexes' behavior, including the act of copulation itself, into the realm of comedy."[130]

In Joan Rivière's famous case study, "Womanliness as Masquerade," it is a woman who wears a mask. This woman, an intellectual, was in the habit of acting out "femininity" whenever she ended a public lecture in which she had, in contrast, demonstrated her phallic capacity. After her scholarly performance, she sought to attract the sexual good graces of the men in the audience by "playing at being woman." At one point in her analysis, Rivière states the well-known hypothesis according to which there is no difference between authentic femininity and femininity as masquerade[131]: femininity remains authentically a mask, thus a secondary formation, a woman's defensive reaction against her own "phallic" drive. Rivière is strictly Freudian here. Her patient, as described in this text, illustrates in an exemplary manner the theory of Rivière's master, according to whom femininity is a complicated arrangement between a woman and her own originary phallicity, a phallicity that survives, moreover, in the masked penis envy which characterizes the "feminine" attitude. Remove the mask and you will see the original "little man" who *is hiding* beneath the woman.[132]

Lacan, read carefully, does not say this. To be sure, he pays due respect to the Freudian logic deployed by Rivière, formulating the hypothesis "that it is in order to be the phallus—that is, the signifier of the Other's desire—that a woman rejects an essential part of femininity, namely, all its attributes, in the masquerade."[133] She does this in order to *be* the phallus, thus in order to hide the fact that she *has* it or would really like to have it, in the case reported by Rivière. But on the Lacanian stage, the mask is not the prerogative of women or of "femininity." "Seeming" (*paraître*) plays a role in both "cases" (it "replaces the having in order to protect it, *in one case*, and to mask the lack thereof *in the other*").[134] The phallus itself, Lacan writes, "can play its role only when veiled."[135] Thus one will see it only as a signifier and no one will be inclined to confuse it with the organ that it "symbolizes." On another level, as Lacan adds at the end of his text, is "the fact that femininity finds refuge in this mask, by virtue of the *Verdrängung* inherent in desire's phallic mark."[136] A way of saying that desire hides its game and its goal, just as a woman plays with a veil, moving between display and modesty, making modesty itself a weapon of seduction. The notion of *Verdrängung* is usually translated in French as *refoulement*, repression. In the case of phallic veil play, it would be more a matter of "holding back" a desire that does not know (or does not want to know) its ends.

The consequence of this generalized comedy is that "in human beings virile display itself [appears] feminine." "Man as such" imitates "woman as such." The mask of the "second sex" makes it the *first of the genders*, the one after which virile comedy is modeled, as a dance of seduction and a display of, as well as a shield from, castration.[137]

In order to "*draguer*" (flirt), one thus has to "get in drag" (put on a veil as one "puts on" formal manners), by virtue of this "*Verdrängung* inherent in desire's phallic mark" that I have just evoked. Does this mean that sexual scenes of the queer type reenact the play of castration, thus of phallocentrism, since it is the symbolic operation of castration that fosters the assumption of the phallus? This is indeed what Judith Butler suggests in "The Lesbian Phallus."[138]

Lacan himself, however, nuances his statements in *The Four Fundamental Concepts of Psychoanalysis*, a collection of lectures from his 1964 seminar.

During this seminar, which was focused in part on the gaze, appearance, and the status of representation, and always on the question of what is called love, Lacan reasserted the asymptotic relation of desire to love, if by "love" is meant attachment to the "being" of some particular object. Already, in "The Signification of the Phallus," he was making fun of the naïve illusion of anyone who wanted to be loved "for himself," that is, for what he "is" and not for what he "signifies" for the other: "[T]he subject," Lacan writes, "*designates his being only by barring everything it signifies*, as it is seen in the fact that he wants to be loved for himself, a mirage that is not at all dispelled by simply pointing out that it is grammatical (since it abolishes discourse)."[139] Thus "I" can only elicit "love" by *appearing* to be precisely what I *am* not. During the thirteenth session of his seminar, Lacan insists once again on the non-being or the non-reality of the object of desire as such: "The phantasy is the support of desire; *it is not the object that is the support of desire*."[140] Finally, in the fourteenth session he concedes that, in the framework of amorous "representation," "there may well be a representation of the objects of the external world, choice and discernment, the possibility of knowledge," in short, appreciation up to a certain point of the reality of the other. Nevertheless, he adds, "[N]othing represents in it the Other, the radical Other, the Other as such."[141] In other words, only the desire that is supported by the fantasy (and not the reality) of the object puts us into relation with "the Other as such." And this setting into relation takes place by means of a masquerade, as a spectacular deployment of the fantasy:

> This representation of the Other is lacking, specifically, between the two opposed worlds that sexuality designates for us in the masculine and the feminine. Carrying things as far as they will go, one might even say that the masculine ideal and the feminine ideal are represented in the psyche by something other than this activity/passivity opposition of which I spoke earlier. Strictly speaking, they spring from a term that I have not introduced, but of which one female psycho-analyst has pinpointed the feminine sexual attitude—the term *masquerade*.[142]

Masquerade—which is not the exclusive privilege of the "feminine sexual attitude," as Lacan reaffirms once again here, in opposition to Rivière—compensates for the lack of such a "representation of the Other" between the sexes. It is what allows each sex to apprehend the other as "feminine" or "masculine," ensuring the (phantasmatic) passage from other to Other. This entry into the dimension of the Other as installation on the scene of desire provokes the assumption of the feminine ideal and the virile ideal, by substitution of the "feminine ideal" for woman or rather for a particular woman, and the masculine ideal for a particular man: in a word, by the substitution of "gender" for "being."

We see clearly here the relation between the gender ideal (and gender as ideal) and the Other, *l'Autre* with a capital *A*, through which Lacan also designates the dimension of the Symbolic as unconscious operator and regulator of all relationships. But if Lacan, like Freud in his later writings, distinguishes the constitution of the feminine and masculine genders from the opposition between activity and passivity, he does not seem to relate it here to a problematics of castration, as he did, still in Freud's wake, in "The Signification of the Phallus." At this point, his discourse on "masquerade" as a spectacular putting into play of the genders stems less from psychoanalysis, properly speaking, than from general anthropology or even zoo-anthropology. In fact, if Lacan takes care to distinguish the "human" masquerade from animal displays at the very moment when he is establishing a relation between them,[143] he explains the function of masquerade in a way that dispenses with the dramatic knot of castration, opening up a different perspective on the scene of genders, one that might give rise— who knows?—to other futures. "I set out," he says during the ninth session, "from the fact that there is something that establishes a fracture, a bipartition, a splitting of the being to which the being accommodates itself, even in the natural world."[144] This "splitting of the being" foreshadows the "*Spaltung* of the subject" that follows upon the subject's entrance into the symbolic. Lacan then goes on to develop a general theory of masquerade, "under the general heading of mimicry":

> It is this that comes into play, quite obviously, both in sexual union and in the struggle to the death. In both situations, the being breaks up, in an extraordinary way, between its being and its semblance, between itself and that paper tiger it shows to the other. . . . [T]he being gives of himself, or receives from the other, something that is like a mask, a double, an envelope, a thrown-off skin, thrown off in order to cover the frame of a shield. It is through this separated form of himself that the being comes into play in his effects of life and death, and it might be said that it is with the help of this doubling of the other or of oneself, that is realized, the conjunction from which proceeds the renewal of beings in reproduction.[145]

Lacan's discourse is equivocal. He plays on the classic distinction between being and appearance and seems to relate this distinction, following Lévi-Strauss, to a simultaneously chronological and epistemological break between nature and culture, a break that he reaffirms at the end of this paragraph in the name of the essential heterogeneity between human beings and animals: "Only the subject—the human subject, *the subject of the desire that is the essence of man*—is not, *unlike the animal*, entirely caught up in this imaginary capture. . . . Man, in effect, knows how to play with the mask . . . ."[146] Humans know that they are playing (with the mask) and thus remain masters of their game, whereas animals play without knowing it: These are postulates that Derrida will call into question in his analysis of Lacanian anthropocentrism.[147] And yet the same Lacan seems to designate "under the general heading of mimeticism" a phenomenon "of nature" as well as of culture ("a splitting of the being to which the being accommodates itself, even in the natural world"); he goes on to subsume "animal" and "human" under a single term—"the being"—in the paragraph I have just cited, in such a way that he seems to be offering, this time, a simultaneously naturalizing and teleological explanation of masquerades. A sort of behavioral "shield" that protects "the being" (animal or human) from the threat of disintegration inherent in any encounter with the other, the latter facilitates "the renewal of beings in reproduction," just as, in "The Signification of the Phallus," "the instating of the subject in an unconscious position" appropriate to the "ideal type of his sex" allowed the subject "to answer the needs of his partner in sexual relations" and even "meet the needs of the child who may be produced thereby" (p. 575). Is this yet another way of justifying the heterosexual biological "program"? The following paragraph prevents us from limiting ourselves to that reading. "The lure," Lacan continues, "plays an essential function therefore":

> [i]t is not something else that seizes us at the very level of clinical experience, when, in relation to what one might imagine of the attraction to the other pole as conjoining masculine and feminine, we apprehend the prevalence of that which is presented as *travesty*. It is no doubt through the mediation of masks that the masculine, . . . the feminine meet in the most acute, most intense way.[148]

Who or what meet(s) in the final analysis "through the mediation of masks"? Not the "beings" in their indistinctiveness as living humans or animals; not men or women as beings of flesh and culture combined, either. It is "the masculine" and "the feminine" that meet as "such," that is, as "lures"; conjunction of the masculine with the feminine, as Lacan says, but also, perhaps, as is suggested furtively by the wording of his last sentence, which uncouples the two genders—attraction between the feminine and the feminine, the masculine and the masculine[149]: pure play of genders, in any case, consecrated by the figure of the *travesty* (or transvestite, in French), raised to prominence by the italics, and whose function as an erotic multiplier rather than as an aid to reproduction Lacan emphasizes this time (it is "through the mediation of masks that the masculine and the feminine meet").

On this basis, one might be able to theorize "sexual difference" as the erotic (and non-hierarchical?) difference between genders that Butler calls for in "Critically Queer" and in "The End of Sexual Difference?"[150]

Lacan takes up this line of analysis again in his 1971 seminar (*The Seminar of Jacques Lacan, Book XVIII*), published in translation in 2000 as *On a Discourse that Might Not Be a Semblance*.[151] Here again he insists on the "dimension of semblance" as a constitutive dimension of the "sexual relationship." This time he is determined to distinguish more clearly between human "sexual display" and animal displays, recalling that the "semblance" that characterizes "human sexual behavior" is "conveyed in a discourse."[152] But this distinction between human and animal as a distinction between the symbolic level and the imaginary level of masquerade remains nevertheless unstable. The "ethological level" at which Lacan situates his analysis explicitly here tends, in spite of everything, to bring men and animals closer together, even though this kind of behavioral analysis, whether of one group or the other, does not have to be buttressed by physiological considerations, as Lacan is careful to point out.[153]

The belated publication of this seminar made it unavailable to American queer theory or performance theory as these were being elaborated in the 1990s. Both would have found resources there, however, to further justify their intersection. Would the Butlerian "doing gender" not benefit from being juxtaposed with the Lacanian "doing-man" (*faire homme*) toward which "the behaviour of the child can be interpreted as oriented" and which "constitutes the relation to the other party"?[154] Of this doing-man, Lacan writes after offering some remarks about the distinction between "sex" and "gender" inspired by his reading of Robert Stoller's *Sex and Gender*,[155] "one of the essential correlates . . . is to indicate to the girl that one is so, . . . we find ourselves, in a word, put right away into the dimension of the semblance."[156] What distinguishes the Lacanian and Butlerian "doing-man" and "doing gender" from West and Zimmerman's "doing gender," and also from the comedy of the sexes according to Goffman, is precisely the fundamental articulation, in the first case, between gender(s) and sexuality: The masculine or feminine masquerade, "semblance," and "gendered" behaviors do not consist merely in "embodying" or "interpreting" "morphological ideals" and stereotypical behaviors; they are at once the condition and the—theatrical—form of the "sexual relation" (as an impossible relation).

"Gender" and "Sexual Difference"

My way of convoking "gender" in my reading of Lacan and "sexual difference" in my commentary on Butler may have been surprising. In the field of American gender theory, as it has developed since the 1980s, there is a distinction between "the paradigm of sexual difference" and "the paradigm of gender," not so much to oppose them, since they are often brought up together or in succession, as to indicate the diverse origins of an intellectually composite theory. Patrick Garlinger, who summarizes for his own part a long line of commentaries on the question in an article on Leo Bersani, defines the difference between the two paradigms this way: Femininity as "gender" would refer to a set of cultural images and attributes arbitrarily associated with the category "woman" as a sexed being. For Anglo-American proponents of a theory of "sexual difference" based on arguments for the most part imported from Freudo-Lacanian psychoanalysis rather than from the deconstructions of that theory offered, for example, by Cixous, Irigaray, and Derrida, femininity would have nothing to do with images and attributes but would result from the adoption of an unconscious position: that of the "lack" (or the lacking) that would make femininity the place of the unrepresentable as such.[157] The two positions seem hard to reconcile. The first is linked to a problematics of social "visibility" emphasizing the "spectacular" character of the masculine/feminine duality; the second, in contrast, raises the question of what eludes representation.[158] And yet slippages from one "paradigm" to the other are extremely frequent among the practicians of *gender theory* and its *queer* avatar (or modification), as Garlinger himself notes in connection with Bersani. These slippages, which sometimes take the form of abrupt changes in analytic register, are not necessarily identified as such by those who carry them out. In this respect, they probably signal a theoretical difficulty. In fact, the two paradigms already coexist in Lacan. What are those "essential attributes" of femininity that are "rejected in masquerade" if not the "visible" or identifiable elements that constitute femininity as a socially recognizable gender? As for the "masquerade," as Lacan describes it, there are good reasons to view it, as Butler and other theorists of gender do, as a prototype of "gender performance." The Butlerian conception of "gender performance" is divided, as we have seen, along two axes that evoke this double paradigm. Lacan himself loses sight of the properly psychoanalytical interpretation of sexual difference (as dissymmetry of the symbolic positions linked to the castration knot) in favor of a zoo-anthropological or "ethological" reading of the play of genders in *The Four Fundamental Concepts*. Does this mean that one viewpoint invalidates the other? Not necessarily. Let us say, rather, that their uneasy combination attests to the fact that none of these paradigms suffices to account all by itself for the differential, if not oppositional and hierarchical, constitution of the feminine and the masculine.

POWERS OF GENDER TYPES AND TYPES OF POWER

My friends, I want her to be a queen! 'I want to be a queen!' And they were kings for one whole morning.[159]

ARTHUR RIMBAUD

In her book *Power and Intimacy in the Christian Philippines*, the British anthropologist Fenella Cannell inquires into the fascination of contemporary Filipinos with the beauty contests organized in certain provincial cities by male transvestites. She devotes a chapter titled "Beauty and the Idea of America" to this phenomenon. In her analyses, Cannell maintains a prudent distance from the considerations of "gender theory" regarding this type of performance. What interests her are the cultural and political implications of the phantasmatic relation to America manifested on these occasions. America is the last power to have occupied the Philippines on the pretext of liberating them from Spanish colonization. "Beauty contests," whose references and canons are borrowed from Hollywood, are explicitly presented in this context as stagings of an "American dream" that is overdetermined by the recent colonial relationship between the two countries. But the "idea of America" at work in these "queer" contests actually functions quite like the "gender ideal" in the "gender performances" analyzed by Newton and Butler. Not only does queer performance represent, here too, a certain "idea" of America but in both cases—whether the "idea" of America or the "idea" of femininity is at issue (and the two are fused, moreover, in a certain "idea" of "glamour")—the "imitator" or impersonator of the idea/ideal feels invested with *power*, and sees himself/"herself" in that light. "Power" is the term that comes up most often in Cannell's text when she is trying to define the effect and principal benefit of these "performances" of a new type in this cultural sphere. The *bakla* themselves (*bakla* is the Tagalog name for drag queens)—attribute their "charismatic power to seduce" to their way of "exposing" or "exhibiting" themselves in public.[160] According to Cannell, the participants in these competitions become the "receptacles of a power" that they appropriate for themselves by adorning themselves with its emblems.[161] Finally, what gratifies the *bakla* most in these performances is not only being seen by the public as the (ideal) "women" they take themselves to be but becoming "stars" before (and through) the eyes of the public by becoming "women."[162] The "star" is, of course, the "democratic" and Hollywoodian equivalent of the "queen." If, through cross-dressing, the drag queen achieves not only the status of "woman" but also and in the same move, as the name s/he adopts indicates, that of "queen," is there not, in fact, in these scenes, a claim to power? But what type of "power" is involved?

Newton, Butler, and Lacan, in their own ways, have already put us on the trail of a certain masculine or feminine "gender power," as the power to "drag" the other, to draw the other into one's net by constituting oneself as an object of desire; in other words, by *masking oneself*. A mask confers power on the one who wears it. Thus the living animal that "decomposes itself, in a sensational fashion, between its being and its semblance," becomes "a paper tiger," in Lacan's formula, as soon as it puts forward its "semblance" in order to preserve itself or to carry itself off in the context of an erotic conquest or a death struggle.[163] The "paper tiger" would be, to the animal, what the "queen" is to the "man": its elevated image, the representation of a power as fragile as paper, but perhaps just as strong in its ability to constitute a symbolic weapon, a support and instrument for writing.[164]

Some will contend that there is a big difference between ordinary gender play and queer beauty contests. But perhaps the difference is not all that great. If we are to believe Lacan, the "identification with the ideal type of a sex" through which a given "being" lines up under the banner of a "gender" (masculine or feminine) stems from the same process as the scene of *queer* dressing. In both cases, it is a matter of masking oneself in order to appear to "be" what one does not "have," or what one is not. In this sense, as we have seen, the logic of gender and the logic of drag are the same. And for Lacan, as we have also noted, the seduction scene that proceeds via masks to the threshold of copulation is not played out simply between two individuals. As masks, and owing to masks, the actors in this "comedy" are already on an invisible stage, before an invisible public, since they do not merely have a relation to another actor but, through and beyond that other, to the Other. Similarly, Butler sees in the Harlem drag queens' performance an allegorization of "the incorporative fantasy of melancholia" that leads subjects to adopt a given "gender."[165] Just as Greek theater—a theater of masks—brought into view a certain hidden reality of the Greek city-state, so queer theater, from this perspective, would reveal the nature of gender in the West, would unmask (by way of) the mask. Finally, if the simple fact of disguising oneself already makes the "dragger" (in the French sense) the "queen" he wants to be by virtue of the "power" of the mask, the competitive structure of this queer theater—which takes the form, in Cherry Grove or Harlem, of a contest for the best impersonation of the feminine "ideal"—would make manifest the claim to power at work in every attempt to embody a gender: Through the "wanting to appear as a woman" (or "man"), we would always be witnessing a "wanting to be (chosen) as queen" (or "king").

But I return to my question: Of what power are we speaking here? Does a "queen" rule over the "hearts and minds" of her subjects the way a "king" rules over his subjects and his country? By putting the question this way, I am trying to put my finger on what strikes me as a difficulty in the field of (American) "gender theory," but also in its "French" forebears and in its contemporary "French" translation, regarding the way the motif of power is handled. "Power" is everywhere, both the word and the thing itself, especially, of course, ever since Foucault, making his history of sexuality no more and no less than a treatise on power in the West, designated "sexuality" not just as one field among others where power is exercised but as the field par excellence of its manifestations and its constitution. "Power" is everywhere, yes, and above all everywhere where sex and sexuality are concerned; but is it everywhere the same?

"Power, power," whispers Esther Newton in "My Butch Career," high-lighting by this doubled utterance the attraction exercised by the word it-self: "Power, power: butch dykes had it, Gertrude Stein had it. Not power over femmes, who were as likely to be the seducers or to make more money or to lay down the law. And not worldly power, of course . . . Butches had the confidence to take space from the straight world where none had ex-isted, and the power of artists to make new forms out of cultural clay . . ."[166]

But if butch dykes and Gertrude Stein "had" the power that Newton wants to possess, Newton tells us almost nothing about the nature of that power. She expounds at length, however, on what it is not: It belongs nei-ther to the order of "domination" of one gender over another ("not power over femmes") nor to the conventionally political order ("not worldly power"). How then are we to understand another statement by Newton, from a 1984 essay titled "The Misunderstanding: Toward a More Precise Sexual Vocabulary"? "Power and sexual desire are deeply, perhaps intrinsi-cally connected in ways we do not fully understand and just can't abolish. Masculinity and femininity are entrenched, enduring aspects of personal-ity, not just changeable styles."[167]

Isn't Newton implicitly associating "power" here with the exercise of an inextricably erotic and symbolic domination of one gender over the other, suggesting that the relation between power and desire is as funda-mental as the interplay between masculine and feminine to which it appears to be tied? The notion of "power" invoked at this point does not dispel the misunderstandings, as Newton herself recognizes ("Power and desire are . . . intrinsically connected *in ways we do not fully understand*" [emphasis added]).

Butler in turn postulates an "intrinsic" relation between power and sexu-ality in *Gender Trouble*, in terms that, while they are clearly Foucaldian in inspiration, do not do away with the difficulties: "*If* sexuality and power are coextensive, and *if* lesbian sexuality is no more nor less constructed than other modes of sexuality, *then* there is no promise of limitless pleasure after the shackles of the category of sex have been thrown off."[168]

The difficulties have to do in part precisely with the reference to Fou-cault. The Foucaldian conception of "power" is presumed to be known and understood and thus not to be in need of explanation or questioning. As for the consubstantial relation between "sexuality" and "power," which is the specifically Foucaldian element of the hypothesis, it is not demonstrated, but simply, or rather categorically, postulated. Anyone familiar with Butler's writing knows the countless sentences that begin, like the one I have just cited, with "if." As we learn from classical grammar, which reproduces in its formula the rhetoric-logical structure it is itself seeking to describe, "*if* the protasis is posited, *then* the apodosis follows." In other words, the condition stated is not "hypothetical" in the sense that it would remain uncertain and would still have to be demonstrated: It is, as in a mathematical formula, the basis for the demonstration. Thus the co-extensivity of sexuality and power needs no demonstration. On the contrary, presented as irrefutable, it confirms in advance the thesis stated in the apodosis. Some will say that the hypothesis in question has been sufficiently tested and verified elsewhere—for example, earlier in *Gender Trouble*, and, of course, in Foucault's *History of Sexuality*. The trouble is, though, that such a postulate, in its massive generality, bears a misleading resemblance to various statements by Catharine MacKinnon, another American feminist of the first rank, who is known not to be a Foucaldian, and who does not conceive of either "sexuality" or "power" (the word or the thing in both cases) the way Butler does.[169] What to do when quasi-identical statements about the consubstantial link between "sexuality" and "power" have divergent meanings and political import? Shouldn't that lead us to handle words more carefully? Shouldn't we consider, for example, that the word "power" raises a problem (a crucial problem that is important to address) before we adopt it as a solution? This is indeed what is at stake in the essay Wendy Brown devoted, in *Politics Out of History*, to the "contradictory" uses and conceptions of the notion of "power" in contemporary political theory.[170] We would then have to pursue more precisely in—and for—the field of thought called "feminist" what Brown did for a certain theoretical continent, to which gender theory belongs at least in part, and which she identifies as "contemporary left political thought."

In texts of a Foucaldian persuasion, and especially in the area called "gender," the word "power" sometimes exercises power today in such a way that it escapes, like all sovereigns, the law of critical vigilance that is applied to the subjects it concerns or that concern it. In a feminist and Foucaldian contribution to a 1994 volume titled *Power/Gender: Social Relations in Theory and Practice*,[171] Karlene Faith rightly insists on the need to qualify and problematize the key terms she uses (such as "woman," "feminism," and "patriarchy"), but she does not deem it useful to do the same thing for the word "power" and its Anglo-American derivatives (in particular, the word "empowerment," which is widely used and highly charged in this theoretical space). In *The Psychic Life of Power*, Judith Butler studies the role of "power" in the formation of subjectivity. "Power" is a matrix of subjection *and* subjectification; the subject is both governed and governor by virtue of the "power" that gives it place and form, and it is this constitutive ambivalence that interests our philosopher. But once again, "power" is not treated as the—or a—problem, but as a given, or the "datum" of the problem.

Yet the same Butler reminds us, in "Critically Queer," that "neither power nor discourse are rendered anew at every moment; they are not as weightless as the utopics of radical resignification might imply."[172] This means not only that "power" has a history that continues to haunt and weigh on its contemporary forms but also that discourse—and consequently the discursive treatment of power—also has a history, one that produces effects whether we like it or not, and that must be taken into account.

What do we call "power"? The problem of the translation of thoughts, of systems of logic, even of different idioms by means of a single conceptual language is obviously not a new one. Western reflections on power (the word and the phenomenon or phenomena it designates) go back at least to Aristotle, or rather to French and English translations of Aristotle. In a sense, one might say that Aristotle was the first Western philosopher to connect something like "power" with something like "sexuality" (conceived as a social phenomenon) in his *Politics*. We know that Aristotle distinguished between the political sphere as the realm belonging to the community of free men and the domestic sphere in which the power of the *despotes* was exercised, properly speaking, over his wives, his children, and his slaves. Émile Benveniste, and Derrida after him, worked on the root *potis* and its derivatives in Greek (*despotes*, *despotikos*), which have given us all the words in the family of the French *pouvoir* and *puissance*, and the English equivalents "power" and "potency."[173] *Potis* is related to a Sanskrit root, *patih*, which means spouse, head of the family. The word *despotes* gives the English word "spouse" and the French *époux*. In short, the despot, or the one who exercises *power as such*, is the spouse (*époux*) or head of the family, the master of the household. And we must not forget that "domination," another term that is commonly used as a synonym for "power" today, refers literally to the power exercised over the household, in the house (*domus*), thus, culturally and historically, over the women, children, and "domestics" confined in this space. To designate the form and the exercise of "power" in the public sphere, Aristotle drew on a different family of words. The elected head of the political community was the *basileus*, and the "power" manifested and exercised in that sphere is not of the order of the *potis* but of the *dunamis*, which has given other derivatives ("dynamic," but also "dynasty," from the verb *dunasthai*, of the same lexical family). And yet it is true that most English and French translations of Aristotle render *potis* and *dunamis* and their derivatives with a single word or a single family of words, that of "power." In these translations, then, "power" as the exercise of domestic domination (if I may be allowed the pleonasm) connected with the hierarchical organization of the relations between the sexes is confused with "power" as *dunamis*, both "productive" force and *action*, closer to the contemporary notion of "empowerment" developed by Foucault and Butler. To be sure, power left "home" (*domus*) in the West a long time ago, and has been deterritorialized. We have thus forgotten that the despot is by definition someone who treats his subjects as (his) women or (his) children, someone who "domesticates" the public sphere. The fact remains that the notion of "power" in its origin raises the question of the relation between the genders, and the term remains difficult to conceptualize simultaneously under the headings of "domination" and "production," "subordination," and "dynamics."

In her second preface to *Gender Trouble*, Butler asks us to avoid reducing "power" to "hierarchy" too quickly, thus asking us to adopt a conception of "power" that is more Foucaldian than Aristotelian. The request is understandable, but it may be tenable, and with it the distinction between power and hierarchy, only if we do precisely what Butler warns us against on several occasions: Forget history, misread the effects of language that attests to history and preserves (thus reactivates) its traces unbeknownst to us in such a way that we can do nothing but repeat by displacing, and displace by repeating.[174]

Then what are the relations between the power of the mask, and gender as mask, and "relations of domination"? What are the relations between the logic of the fetish deployed by Lacan[175] and the analyses of the "gendered" expression of relations of domination in "authoritarian" or "democratic" regimes proposed by Joan Scott in her famous article "Gender as a Useful Category of Historical Analysis"? If I evoke this article in particular, it is because it defines gender as "a primary way of signifying relationships of power," and it calls for an elaboration of a theory of gender on the basis of this definition. It is also because the translation of Scott's article in France by a group of female historians in the late 1980s and its wide reception among French feminist scholars signaled a political, cultural, and theoretical turning point in the Franco-American history of the formulation and treatment of these questions.[176] According to a hypothesis that is shared by those who have recently undertaken to produce the intellectual history of this field, the dissemination of Scott's essay marks the true foundation of "gender studies" in France; this foundation thus coincides with a reversal of direction of the intellectual currents circulating between France and the United States: After having exported theories of "sexual difference" to the United States, France began to import American theory or theories of "gender." The hypothesis has its place, but the situation is perhaps more complicated than it appears. Joan Scott is a historian of France, and her university career coincided with the extraordinary career of "French thought" in the United States between 1975 and 2005. Her theoretical and political positions and propositions were nourished by her reading of Foucault but also of Derrida; she read Bourdieu but also Lacan. When Scott wrote this essay, Judith Butler had not yet intervened in the emerging field of gender theory. In contrast, Scott had read the "first" Gayle Rubin on the one hand, representatives of "French feminism" on the other. As I have already noted, in the United States the idiom of "sexual difference" and the idiom of "gender" are not construed simply as opposites, as they are in France, where these two languages continue their course of mutual exclusion and referral to a distribution believed to be clear between divergent theoretical and political perspectives. In the American context, the terms are not necessarily opposed; most importantly, they are put to different uses.[177]

What does Scott mean, then, or rather what is she saying, when she defines gender as "a primary way of signifying relationships of power"[178] and spells out her thinking in the following terms: "It might be better to say, gender is a primary field within which or by means of which power is articulated. Gender is not the only field, but it seems to have been a persistent and recurrent way of enabling the signification of power in the West, in Judeo-Christian as well as Islamic traditions."[179]

Is this a Foucaldian statement? The motifs and the language may lead us to think so. In a recent article, Scott herself revisits and questions her own earlier statements on gender as a "useful category of analysis"; she asserts that she did indeed write this seminal essay under "the influence of Michel Foucault."[180] However, the historian distances herself clearly from Foucault when she substitutes "gender" for "sexuality," and when she advocates the development of a theory of gender rather than of sexuality. In the United States, as we have seen, the appropriation of Foucault by certain representatives of the queer movement was accompanied in the 1980s by a rejection of the problematics of gender in favor of a more strictly Foucaldian theory and politics of sexuality. Similarly, when Scott seeks to show how the use of gender as an analytic category could not only enrich classical historiography but also transform the discipline of history by calling into question the traditional distribution of its investigations and its knowledge (e.g., between "political history," "cultural history," and "history of mentalities"), the examples she gives of the sites and modes of "gender" analysis attest to a not-very-Foucaldian conception of "history" and "power." At the end of her essay, she does propose to revisit "political history" or the history of war—traditionally masculine realms—in the light of gender, but she continues to envisage politics, or the political, in a non-Foucaldian way, from the angle of regimes of sovereignty.[181] In short, no clear or unified conception of power can be gleaned from this essay, even though it aims at theorizing gender as a "signifier of power relations."

I return then to my question: Is Scott's definition of gender as a "field of articulation of power" compatible with the analysis of a certain power of gender as "drag" proposed, in the wake of Lacan but also of Newton, by the whole current within gender theory that merges with—or emanates from—performance theory? It can always be argued that this question is badly formulated because it wrongly confuses "gender" as a concept aiming to account for the mode of regulation or binary distribution of sexed individuals and "the genders" as "masks," likenesses, or identity-asserting performances. From this perspective, Scott's analyses would belong to the first understanding and use of the word "gender," whereas Newton's would belong to the second. But if I maintain my question, it is because it seems to me that the distinction between "gender" in the singular and "genders" in the plural—and I am not unaware of the connotations and the political and theoretic stakes involved—remains profoundly unstable. It would be easy to show, for example—and I hope to have helped do so by my remarks on the subject—that Butler slips constantly from one sense or pole to the other, and that her theory of *gender* is at the same time a theory of *the genders* and vice versa. If "gender" as "drag" refers at first glance to the sense of "identity marker" rather than to the sense of "system of hierarchy-establishing relationships," it remains as difficult to keep these senses separate as it is to separate the different senses of the word "sex" in English, and now also in French, as Rubin would like to do.

The analysis of the scenes and figures of what is called "power" thus requires differentiated approaches. But it is equally important to study the modes and sites of intersection of its "significations" and of the systems of logic that mobilize the concept. Isn't it the intersection of logics of desire and logics of domination that theorists are trying, for example, to think through under the heading of "phallocentrism," a term born within psychoanalytic theory but to which certain strands of feminist theory have given a political extension? Similarly, a purely anthropological approach to the power of the mask, and to gender as mask, does not suffice to account for the adoption and the symbolics of a given "mask," which have been historically determined by very concrete power relations. Thus if one wants to "have," that is, *appear to have* "power" in the twentieth century or even today, one has to wear an "American" mask. This is true of the *bakla* in the Philippines, who attain "stardom" phantasmatically only by dressing as American queens, and it is also true of Wendy Delorme, whose American panoply has the effect, if not the goal, of forcing the French media to pay attention.

The fact remains that, if the analytics of power from Aristotle to Foucault requires an examination of the ways in which the masculine/feminine differential has been used, and if it belongs in this sense quite rightfully to a theory of gender, just as the theories about "gender roles" developed from Money to Newton, or from Lacan to Butler, do, gender theory remains in tension between an analytics of desire (and of the theater of gender as an erotic machine) and an analytics of domination—even if the latter is now deterritorialized, even if, like the new forms of economic "power," it is "dematerialized."[182] If there is no unity in the field of gender theory today, thus no unity of "gender" as object of and tool for analysis, there is no unity, either, in the concept of "power" and its use.

EPILOGUE

I shall draw at least three "lessons" from this inquiry. The first has to do with the relation that I have repeatedly stressed between the theater of gender (or genders) and the stage of desire. The second involves the history of the relation between gender theory and queer theory in America. The last bears upon the meaning and form of a certain cultural history today.

1. "Sexuality in this sense, perhaps, can *only* mean queer sexuality" (Eve Kosofsky Sedgwick).[183]

What does the spotlight focused on "drag" allow us to theorize? Without drag, as drag queens, their fans, and their observer-analysts have pointed out many times, there is no "sexuality"; without gender roles, no "power(s)" of the subject as subject-of-desire, thus no possibility of "dragging" (in the French sense), no erotic relations between one "side" and another.[184] And if, as Lacan writes, there is no heterosexual copulation without preliminary play-acting (and playful preliminaries), if, as Butler repeats, heterosexuality is in itself a comedy and a constant self-parody;[185] if heterosexuality is therefore also or above all a game of drag, then can one not say that heterosexuality, inasmuch as it produces a certain scene of desire, is always already "queer"? Here again, does Lacan's insistence on the fundamentally "deviant" character of human desire (deviant because it has been deviated in order to "resolve" the Oedipal crisis) not go in the direction of a "queer" reading of heterosexuality? But we should no doubt avoid generalizing. Just as there is no such thing as "homosexuality in general" but rather there are homosexualities, as evidenced both by the great diversity of discourses on the subject from within its "perimeter" and by the proliferation of gay and lesbian genders, we must recognize that there is no possibility of unifying the so-called field of "heterosexuality."

Finally, when in the epigraph cited previously Eve Sedgwick suggests in a provocative and deliberately ambiguous way that only "queer" sexuality can be qualified as sexuality, precisely because sexuality as such is "queer," she is indirectly pointing to an interesting contemporary phenomenon. In tandem with the growing blendedness of Western societies, a certain social neutralization of the difference between the sexes as an erotic difference seems to have opened the way to a desexualization of the heterosexual relation. Masks are falling and the stage of erotic theater is being deserted. It is as if, at the moment when, in the West, the relations between the sexes in their so-called heterosexual modality no longer seem to rely on that comedy of appearances, thus on the distribution between "masculine" (as appearing "to have the phallus") and "feminine" (as appearing "to be the phallus") with which Lacan enjoyed playing, comedy, and thus in a sense "sexuality," is taking refuge elsewhere, is being restaged in the theater of so-called queer or transgender relations. A parodic repetition of the "masculine" and the "feminine," masquerade, seductions, transgressions, and inversions, all these mobilize the binary panoply of the genders the better to play with them and thus to derive ultimate pleasure from them. This is proof that desire is nourished by fictions of gender rather than by "realities" of sex. Thus queer sexuality, because it recuperates the erotico-phantasmatic charge abandoned by a heterosexuality that has, in part, stopped playing the game, now exercises a much higher power of attraction than so-called normal sexuality. This is why the rumor is flourishing in queer circles (especially of the *cuir*—leather—variety) that heterosexuality, which is no longer in play or playful, is not, or is no longer, a "sexuality." [186]

2. What is called queer theory in the United States appeared in the wake of gender theory and was presented as its "immanent critique." Queer theory's origins are generally linked to the simultaneous publication, in 1990, of Judith Butler's *Gender Trouble* and Eve Kosofsky Sedgwick's *Epistemology of the Closet*. The two works offer critiques of the binary division between genders and consequently of gender theory as a theory of the constitution of the masculine and the feminine and of the relations between the two. Each in her own way, Butler and Sedgwick seek to demonstrate that the binary conception of genders is a "heteronormative" construction, and each thus challenges a certain heterosexist bias at work in feminist theory as gender theory.

And yet, American gender theory and queer theory are much more mutually entangled than one might be led to believe by the apparent chronology of their succession and the posture of queer theory as a deconstructive follow-up to gender theory. It all began, as we have seen, with the destabilization of the reference of gender to sex, a move that was induced by the study of hermaphroditism and transsexualism, and through these, the study of deviations of sexual identity and behavior. In this sense, American gender theory was constituted at the outset as a theory of gender trouble. It is thus no accident, as I suggested at the beginning of this study, that its principal representatives have been (and still are) "queer." From Money to Butler, "gender" has, of course, never referred to "anatomical sex," whose unity, identity, and naturalness have all been questioned in various ways by intersexualism and transsexualism. But the term does not simply designate social sex, either (i.e., men and women as social categories), since its conceptual determination depends precisely on a breakdown in the logic of that reference ("masculine" does not necessarily refer to "man," or "feminine" to "woman"). Gender theory, in this sense, is not reducible to, or even always precisely compatible with, a sociology of domination that studies the distribution of men and women between the categories of dominant and dominated.

Finally, because from the start gender theory has stressed gender as role, thus as "drag," it has borne the seeds of its own "queer" development. Conversely, while certain proponents of queer theory have been determined to reject gender as a binary construction, this view of gender unfailingly comes back into their own discourse, if not as an analytical tool then at least as a category as unavoidable as it is problematic. The denaturalization of genders and the deconstruction of their binary structure do not necessarily signify the disappearance of the deconstructed categories. These approaches do not exhaust the erotic, psychic, social, or political experience of the differences between genders and/or between sexualities. While these differences are not "given" but "constructed," they are nonetheless marked: labile at certain levels, ready to be reconstituted at others. Queer theory may offer some space to gender theory; it may not, however, be able to do without it.

3. In 1955 the lesbian essayist and novelist Ann Aldrich published *We Walk Alone*, a proto-ethnographic work that describes the emergence of the lesbian as a social type in America in the mid-twentieth century. She devoted a chapter of the book to comparing the cultural manifestations of lesbianism in New York and Paris. For that purpose, she looked at two lesbian bars: Both are in Paris, but one, in Montparnasse, draws American tourists and tries to reproduce the atmosphere of a lesbian bar in New York, while the other remains "purely" Parisian. In the first, which advertises itself as a dance cabaret, English is spoken. Some creatures of the female sex play the role of "butches"; others play "femmes." They sit at tables together.

There is flirting (*de la drague*). At the end, the (female) American consumers have to pay for the comedy that is played out at their expense. The affable lesbians who have welcomed them and gotten them to drink and dance are employees of the bar. The other site, a very French lesbian café, is literally underground, in a basement, in an area of Paris that draws few visitors. What Aldrich notices here is that there is nothing to notice. The Parisian lesbians do not seem to split into "butch" and "femme" categories. Blurring the genders or indifferent to their distribution, they wear trousers and lipstick. Discretion is the rule; soft music; no exaggerated gestures or facial expressions; no "dramatic" costumes; no extravagant demonstrations of "affection."[187] Peace and quiet in the maternal comfort of an unobtrusive wine bar, protected from onlookers inside and out. Aldrich notes that, unlike the bars frequented by male and female homosexuals in New York, this one has no mirrors. People cannot see themselves or others, and they cannot watch themselves playing their roles. Nothing specular, nothing spectacular, therefore, in all senses of the term. Forty years later, in *Vested Interests*, Marjorie Garber qualifies the earliest historical manifestations of "French" lesbianism in terms that recall Aldrich's observation: virtually no role play, virtually no gender roles. If Gertrude Stein and Alice Toklas played at being husband and wife, one wearing long coats and Greek sandals while the other wore flowery print dresses, it was because they were "Americans." "True" French women wore "Sapphic" garb, which connoted a cultural particularity but did not necessarily refer to the masculine/feminine divide. "The lesbianism of Paris," Garber concludes, "was neither exclusively 'male' nor exclusively 'female.'"[188] In this sense, it did not grow out of the "American" problematic of queer cross-dressing that I have evoked here.

Does this mean that "gender" as drag is and remains an "American" invention? Not exactly, since this "American-ness" is being deterritorialized, since cultural history and national history can no longer coincide straightforwardly, since "cultural phenomena" are now "exported" almost as quickly as capital circulates. But it means nevertheless that gender theory is not a pure conceptual construction, that it is also a cultural artifact, and that it has to be treated as such, that we have to raise the question of its contexts of production and reception, its modes of existence, and its rhythms of circulation.

Today, in France, there is "Wendy Delorme" and there are lipstick lesbians. These are the ones we see, or who show themselves, the ones who are talked about on the new scene of gender trouble. There are also, of course, Marie-Hélène Bourcier and Beatriz Preciado—but if these latter are better known and have been around longer on a certain "queer" theoretical scene, they are perhaps less "visible," by virtue of the extra attention granted even today to gender play on the feminine side, that is, to "femininity" as spectacle.[189]

The "Wendy Delorme" phenomenon is inscribed both in a particular "French" context and in a broader system of model formation and "information" transfer.

What has been called "French thought" irrigated the American intellectual continent for more than forty years. Recently, the flow has been reversed. France has stopped being a major exporter of ideas and theory. And it has started to import its "intellectual" nourishment avidly from the United States. Judith Butler's and Eve Sedgwick's books are translated; so are those of Teresa de Lauretis and Donna Haraway.[190] Publishing houses, colloquia, and media are abuzz with echoes produced by queer and transgender thematics. One can read this "about-face," whose earliest signs coincided with the premature disappearance of Derrida in 2004, as a symptom of collective melancholia. This massive intellectual (counter)transference onto an ideal "American" ego is accompanied by a concerted forgetting or misremembering of what the "new American thought" owes to the (late) "French thought. Thus buried, or rather encrypted, "French thought" finds itself at once explicitly disavowed and unconsciously preserved thanks to this transference, just as is the object of melancholic affection for the grieving subject according to Freud.

By overplaying the "American" provenance of her discourse and her performances, Wendy Delorme places herself squarely in that context. But her way of transcribing an axiomatics, to which Judith Butler gave the most complete form, in "tableaux" that could be converted, in turn, into video clips or magazine photos, and, similarly, her fetishist indexation of "femininity," with the panoply of fishnet stockings, a corset, and a bracelet made of nails, call for additional remarks.

According to Freud, fetishists (male and female alike) put to work, or at least put on stage, a "denial" of "sexual difference." Similarly, a certain queer stance is rooted in a challenge to the meaning and presumed effects of that difference. Isn't it paradoxical, then, to emphasize "gender difference" as some queer activists and thinkers tend to do? Isn't "(over)doing the 'femme [fem]' gender" still a way of nodding toward sexual duality by stressing the feminine-masculine opposition ("femme" being contrasted both with "butch" and with "male")? Jean Baudrillard's analyses of the contemporary forms of "sexuality" aim precisely to decode this paradoxical phenomenon, which the socio-semiologist spotted as a cultural trend as early as 1987. To this exaltation of the "signs of sex" in the fetishist display, against a background of indifference to (the) sex(es), and even to sexual pleasure, Baudrillard gives the name "transsexuality." In "We Are All Transsexuals Now," he writes: "[T]he transsexual is both a play on non-differentiation (of the two poles of sexuality) and a form of indifference to *jouissance*, to sex as *jouissance*. The sexual has *jouissance* as its focus (*jouissance* is the leitmotif of sexual liberation), whereas the transsexual tends toward artifice— both the anatomical artifice of changing sex and the play on vestimentary, morphological and gestural signs characteristic of cross-dressers." And a little further on, he adds: "After the orgy, desire and sexual difference, we have here the flourishing of erotic simulacra of all kinds and transsexual kitsch in all its glory."[191]

A certain "kitsch," or taste for "kitsch," indeed characterizes contemporary Western queer culture. Just think of the "kitsch" shops of the gay neighborhoods in Chicago or San Francisco. "Kitsch" is at once a mixing and troubling of styles—mirroring gender trouble—and a proliferation of non-utilitarian objects. In other terms, it is the fetishism of merchandise, insofar as the desire aroused by merchandise no longer has any connection with its use value but is linked, quite to the contrary, with the suspension or annulment of use value. In "Sexual Traffic," Gayle Rubin, who seeks to offer a non-Freudian reading—and a defense—of fetishist eroticism, thus stresses its "objective complicity" with industrial capitalism. "I do not see how one can talk about fetishism, or sadomasochism, without thinking about the production of rubber, the techniques and gear used for controlling and riding horses, the high polished gleam of military footwear, the history of silk stockings, the cold authoritative qualities of medical equipment, or the allure of motorcycles . . ." (p. 85).[192]

Fetishist and sado-masochistic "perversions" are nourished by the production of manufactured objects. By gesturing playfully toward them, by manipulating the accessories of a certain pornographic imaginary, the character Delorme creates reminds us, in turn, that a certain sexual display indeed has something to do with the eroticism of merchandise. After all, the word *pornè*, source of the modern word "pornography," comes from the Greek *pernenai*, which means "to sell." "Pornography" thus designates the inscription of sexuality in the market register. To be sure, the linkage between fetishism—the imaginary hold of manufactured objects—and merchandise is not a new idea: it dates back some one hundred fifty years. But this idea is undergoing a particular revitalization among queer thinkers, male and female—of the *cuir* persuasion, of course.

In "Thinking Sex" and in her ethnographic work, Gayle Rubin attempts to show, following Foucault's example, the historical nature of sexual behaviors and types. In the wake of urban sociology and a certain anthropology, she proposes what she calls "sexual ethnogenesis," an approach to sexuality and sexual types that now has many followers. She describes, in particular, the grouping of American homosexuals in cities and their organization into quasi-ethnic communities as an effect of the population transfers spurred by industrialization.[193] More generally, she attributes the continuous production of new sexual types to what she calls the "modernization of sex." But if the formation of homosexual communities and the development of a "gay" culture stem, in general, from this "modernization of sex," the appearance of "Wendy Delorme," that is, of the bundled cultural phenomena that I gather under her name, attests to still another, more recent process.

If the formation of homosexual communities in cities is quite susceptible to a classic sociological treatment, the essentially "iconic" nature of the "Wendy" type requires a different approach. I use the term "iconic" to designate the type of identity building and display that is not rooted in ordinary social processes. Baudrillard characterizes it as "promotional" in "We Are All Transsexuals Now," and he connects it with what he names, resorting to English according to a logic whose necessity I have tried to account for, the "look."[194] Wendy's "look" refers exclusively to other "looks" that are found on large and small screens—for example, Marlene Dietrich's "look" in *The Blue Angel*. A "sexual type" of this sort is a media effect. Instead of—or rather, before—meeting it in the streets, we find it at the crossroads of images and discourses that circulate on the World Wide Web of instantaneous information. The Web speaks "English," as Wendy does. Let us say, rather, that Wendy speaks the English of the Web, from which she "descends," to a certain extent. If she moves into everyday behaviors and into the streets, her privileged stage remains that of the media. And because the instantaneous circulation of "information" short-circuits the traditional processes of diffusion and reception of a given cultural "trend" by ignoring frontiers and differences, it means that the *work of translation*—which implies that there is something in need of translation, thus some difference—can be supplanted by the *play of citation*, which stipulates that everything is imitable. "Wendy Delorme," in this sense, too, does not translate but rather "mimics" or "performs" gender theory as a theory of performance.

3

PARADOXES OF VISIBILITY IN / AND CONTEMPORARY IDENTITY POLITICS

"Feminism as I know it is resistance to invisibility and silencing," observes the American scholar Karlene Faith in a 1994 article titled "Resistance: Lessons from Foucault and Feminism."[1]

The statement is hardly original; in its apparent generality, it could be applied today to any form of resistance to oppression and discrimination, by any group that has been discriminated against or oppressed.

One can certainly agree that women have been made invisible in history, philosophy, and politics, as has already been forcefully argued by feminist theory. The Western division between public and private spheres has indeed been organized and conceptualized as a partition between the field of the visible and that of the invisible.[2] And until recently, the private or domestic sphere, to which women have long been relegated, remained the dark continent of political theory, history, philosophy, and even sociology. The philosophical, proto-ethnographic quasi-novel Montesquieu offered in his *Persian Letters* thus hinges entirely on the opposition between the domestic sphere as an obscure(d) space and the public sphere as the space of "broad daylight" and enlightenment, an opposition that the text makes manifest even while seeking to undo it. And Montesquieu's attempt to destabilize, if not to abolish, this partition between the visible and the invisible, by lifting the real and symbolic veils that maintain women in obscurity and by revealing the hidden face of so-called public actions, can be read as the accomplishment of a certain Enlightenment that makes un-veiling and emancipation coincide.[3]

But what interests me here is the now very common inscription of the motif of visibility and its corollary, invisibility, in the discourse of social and political protest, or in the analytic appropriation of such protest. I do not believe that the contemporary demand for visibility can be explained simply by the topological division of the spheres—domestic versus public—that I have just evoked, all the less so because the demand also emanates from social groups whose formation and history is not, like those of women, dependent on that partition, at least not entirely, and not in the same way, as I shall try to show.

But first, an observation: In the nineteenth century, in the West, op-pressed people "cried out" in order to make themselves heard. The influ-ential nineteenth-century Larousse dictionary described the "modern misery" of industrial workers who were prey to new forms of exploitation and poverty as "a *noisier* and more impatient misery, because of the use the worker makes of his rights, and of the sentiment he has acquired of his liberty." The new poor were indeed also heirs to the French Revolution and its "declaration" of the rights of man—an act of public speech that sparked an awakening of conscience. The communard newspaper founded by Jules Vallès was called *Le cri du peuple* ("The People's Cry"). Rimbaud, the great-est poet of the commune in many respects, defined the mission of poets in May 1871 this way: "The Poet will take the sobs of the Infamous,/The hate of the Convicts, the clamor of the damned."[4] In short, throughout that period, there was an emphasis on hearing the "voice" of the oppressed and making it heard.[5] Today, oppressed groups and diverse minorities seek above all to make themselves "visible," as if their liberation—or their struggle to achieve it—required catching the light; as if, to advance a cause, one had to get spotlights to shine on it.

Spotlights, yes, but from what vantage point? What does it mean today to be, or to feel, "invisible"? And what does one make visible—but perhaps also what does one make obscure?—when one succeeds in making oneself visible? Is making (oneself) seen or noticed the same thing as making (one-self) heard?

The shift of focus from the inaudible to the invisible—and thus from the desire to be heard to the demand for visibility—doubtless attests to a trans-formation in the forms, sites, and targets of oppression as well as in the conditions of political expression more generally. This seems glaringly obvious to me but also complicated, where the politics of gender(s) and sexualities are concerned.

Contemporary feminism sees itself, at least in part, as a form of "resistance to invisibility." I have just offered an example of that view. In the statement by Karlene Faith cited previously, though, the motif of invisibility figures alongside a more "nineteenth-century" motif, that of silence, the effect of a deafness or a prohibition on speaking (up) that would affect women more specifically.[6]

In a certain contemporary gay and lesbian politics, or in the emergence of a transgender claim, the problematics of visibility or of visibilization tend to occupy the foreground of discourse, for different but perhaps convergent reasons. In "Critically Queer," the concluding text in *Bodies That Matter*, Judith Butler thus stresses the deliberate theatricality of a certain "gay" cultural and political intervention in the Western public arena, a theatricality that culminates in spectacular gay pride parades or in the type of performances Butler had in mind in 1993: the provocative stagings of Act Up, a gay organization created to fight AIDS (or rather to fight the way the disease was being used politically). As its name indicates, Act Up combines—or combined, since the group is less active today—political action with theatrical action:

> To oppose the theatrical to the political within contemporary queer politics is, I would argue, an impossibility: the hyperbolic "performance" of death in the practice of "die-ins" and the theatrical "outness" by which queer activism has disrupted the closeting distinction between public and private space have proliferated sites of politicization . . . Mobilized by the injuries of homophobia, theatrical rage reiterates those injuries precisely through an "acting out," one that does not merely repeat or recite those injuries, but that also deploys a hyperbolic display of death and injury to overwhelm the epistemic resistance to AIDS and to the graphics of suffering, or a hyperbolic display of kissing to shatter the epistemic blindness to an increasingly graphic and public homosexuality.[7]

This strategy of hyperbolic exhibition could be interpreted as the response countering centuries of confinement in the famous "closet" in which Western homosexuals are said to have hidden themselves away, thereby staying out of sight and avoiding public sanction in the double sense of the term: condemnation, certainly, but also recognition. This is indeed what Butler's reading of this "queer" activism suggests. According to Butler, a certain theatrical action disrupts "the *closeting* distinction between public and private space."[8] But does this not amount to endorsing a sort of "repressive hypothesis" regarding the history of homosexuality, a hypothesis of which Foucault in his *History of Sexuality* has rightly taught us to be suspicious? Whether a certain contemporary gay exhibition is the hoped-for and anticipated effect of the exit from prolonged obscurity, thus of the end of the "repression" of homosexuality, or whether it stems from a new conception, or cancellation, of the distinction between private and public space, it belongs in any case to the discourse of "visibilization" that I am seeking to examine.

The question of visibility also arises in an acute way in the field of transgender politics and reflection, as Jamison Green stresses in *The Transgender Studies Reader*, an anthology of transgender studies and thought published by Routledge in 2006. Green, who is presented as one of the foremost American "FTM" (Female to Male) transsexual activists by the editors of the *Reader*, characterizes the problem of transsexuality as a problem of visibility in an article titled "Look! No, Don't! The Visibility Dilemma for Transsexual Men." According to him, the transsexual's dilemma, both social and political but also psychological, consists in the fact that he makes himself invisible as a transsexual precisely at the moment when he becomes one, that is, at the moment when he adopts visibly, if not fully, the "sexual" characteristics of the "gender" that he is claiming as his own; from this point on, he passes for a "man" like all the others.[9]

Starting with the title of his essay and continuing throughout his argument, Green presents this dilemma as that of transsexual *men*, as if it were not apt to arise for transsexual women (MTF). The question of visibility is thus embedded in a rhetoric and a politics of categorial specificity: in other words, an identity politics. And if Green identifies this dilemma (or this paradox) as the principal problem of the (male) transsexual, it is indeed because he conceptualizes gender (or gender identity) as a category that depends on a certain test of the visible. Gender trouble induces vision trouble and vice versa; the lack of visibility provokes a destabilization of gender. In so doing, it seems to me, Green positions himself firmly within a perspective that I shall provisionally call American.[10]

From the earliest elaborations of the notion of gender as role by John Money in the 1950s through the theorization of gender display by the sociologist Erving Goffman in the 1970s, and up to the Butlerian concept of gender as performance, gender has been and remains conceived as a quasi-theatrical social manifestation or production that, as such, mobilizes a central principle of visibility. Queer questioning of the gender partitioning and of the normative distribution of roles does not necessarily imply a way out of this paradigm. Even a certain "American" thinking about sexuality that invokes Foucault and challenges the primacy of the category of gender as a tool for analyzing the various forms of sexual oppression still subscribes, despite its denials, if not to a theatrical conception then at least to a theatrical practice of "sexuality." Now, as soon as there is theater, there are roles, and as soon as there are roles, gender tends to reconstitute itself visibly, even if in a queer fashion.[11]

If a certain politics of gender or of gender trouble in America is based on a "spectacular" conception of gender identity, in contrast an entire current of thought has undertaken to deconstruct the paradigm of visibility in an attempt to think of sexual differences differently (I use the plural "differences" to indicate that both differences of sex and differences of sexuality are in question). From Freud's warnings against the placid certainty with which we perceive a person as male or female when we enter into contact with that person for the first time, through Irigaray's critique of the "specular" organization of sexual economies and up to Derrida's injunction to "leap" (*sauter*: the term is his), as soon as this question comes up, from "seeing" to "reading,"[12] a number of thinkers find the very notion of visibility suspect, along with the role it plays, or may play, in a social problematics of gender identity, whether normative or not.

I seem to be presenting this debate as if it were a matter of cultural discord between Europe and America. It is true that this theoretical discord has common ground with certain cultural and historic differences between Europe and "America," but it does not simply coincide with them. After all, Derrida's thinking played an important role, as we know, in the intellectual genesis of American queer theory. Debord, Foucault, and Baudrillard, each in his own way, burnished the weapons of a "critique of spectacular reason." However, Martin Jay, an American specialist in French intellectual history, shows—albeit unwittingly—in *Downcast Eyes: The Denigration of*

Vision in Twentieth-Century French Thought, how the forms, places, and objects of analysis of these thinkers have contributed at the same time to the development and theoretical legitimization, even in France, of an epistemology of the visible, if not a politics of "visibility."[13] Still, it would be important to distinguish more clearly than Jay does, even within the confines of intellectual history, between the epistemology of the visible and the philosophy (or philosophies) of "vision." Philosophical and historical reflections on "seeing" do not necessarily follow the same logic or belong to the same realms as reflection on "making oneself seen" or "showing oneself," although for obvious reasons the two are often conflated. Finally, whole expanses of the discourse produced in France are in tune with the perspective I have characterized as "American," not because I subscribe to some culturalist myth, but because I am interested in tugging on some of the most salient threads in a complex genealogical fabric.[14] In this respect, the work that the anthropologist Catherine Deschamps has been devoting to the politics of the "bisexual minority" in France since the late 1990s is exemplary. It encompasses almost all the motifs that I am examining here: the emergence of a politics of sexualities conceived principally as an enterprise of mediatic visibilization; confusion between the notion of public space and the notion of visual field, the latter being constituted not by the organ of perception but by contemporary teletechnologies; conception of "identity" as a typifying, if not normative, system of display that plays on the "fixed image" (snapshot) and the "mobile image" (performance); finally, the articulation of a promotional "signaletics of the self" with a demand for power.[15]

My hypothesis is nonetheless the following: If we want to comprehend the emergence of a politics of visibility, at least as we understand that term today, then American political, cultural, and intellectual history offers us important keys.

In her 1991 article "The Evidence of Experience," the American feminist historian Joan Scott, educated in the school of "French thought," produces a critique of the ideological and methodological recourse to the notion of experience in order to establish in fact and by right what she calls "a history of difference," that is, a history of marginalized groups, and more generally of those groups left out by mainstream history or traditional historiography.[16] Appealing to one's "experience" or to the "experience" of the groups whose history one is seeking to write would be to subscribe naively to the truth value of lived experience, to confuse narrative—for there is no experience but narrated experience, as Walter Benjamin reminds us—and reality: in short, to succumb to an empirical illusion which is also, inseparably, a narcissistic illusion, for experience as Scott conceives it through the examples she gives of its use is always the experience of a subject, whether individual or collective. Thus experience is taken up in exemplary fashion by autobiographical discourse. For Scott, the question of experience is intimately connected with that of visibility, as is clear from the word "evidence" in the title of her essay. Evidence, in English, means literally, as in French, what is seen in vivid fashion (from *ex-videre*), but it is also a word used in the context of police work and in court: The evidence is the proof brought forward to demonstrate innocence or guilt; it is the basis, in a factuality or a reality that merges with the order of the visible (or that is recognized as "reality" only because it *appears* or may appear as such in the eyes of all), of a judgment that states both the law and the truth. By making itself visible or "evident," a given singular or collective experience would fallaciously acquire the status of irrefutable proof. Scott thus critiques the double value, veridical and juridical, of the demand for visibility. At the same time, she seeks to show that the "project of making experience visible" depends necessarily on a blind task. Because it espouses the viewpoint (and the blind spots) of a subject, it dissimulates or obliterates the historicity of the experience, in other words the discursive and material construction that made the experience possible: "The project of making experience visible precludes critical examination of the workings of the ideological system itself, its categories of representation (homo/hetero, man/woman, black/white)," Scott writes.[17] And she repeats the point a little further on:

> The project of making experience visible precludes analysis of the workings of this system and of its historicity; instead, it reproduces its terms. We come to appreciate the consequences of the closeting of homosexuals and we understand repression as an act of power or domination. . . . What we don't have is a way of placing those alternatives within the framework of (historically contingent) dominant patterns of sexuality and the ideology that supports them.[18]

But what especially interests me here is the example Joan Scott chose as the basis for her critique of recourse to "the evidence of experience": a passage from Samuel Delany's autobiographical essay, *The Motion of Light in Water*.[19] Delany is a gay black New Yorker who writes primarily from the perspective of sex rather than of race, as is clear from the subtitle of his book, *Sex and Science Fiction Writing in the East Village, 1957–1965*. In the passage Scott discusses, Delany describes his "discovery" in 1963 of a privileged site of homosexual erotic social life, the public St. Marks Baths in the East Village. He evokes his quasi-epiphanic vision of the bathhouse in the following terms:

> [The room was full of people, some standing, the rest] an undulating mass of naked, male bodies, spread wall to wall.
>
> My first response was a kind of heart-thudding astonishment, very close to fear.
>
> *I have written of a space of certain libidinal saturation before. That was not what frightened me. It was rather that the saturation was not only kinesthetic but visible*. . . .
>
> What *this* experience said was there was a population—not of individual homosexuals . . . not of hundreds, not of thousands but rather of millions of gay men, and that history had, actively and already, created for us whole galleries of institutions, good and bad, to accommodate our sex.[20]

Offering a reading of these passages in two stages, Scott shows the role played in Delany's discourse by the experience of vision and by vision as experience. Pointing out the way the author uses the metaphor of visibility,[21] she stresses the implicit articulation between vision (conceived as the transparency of experience), knowledge, and power. At the end of her essay, she calls into question the equation between visual perception and evidence (in the double sense of self-evidence and proof). She raises the question of the source and nature of the light that illuminates the scene, and she reads "the dim blue light, whose distorting, refracting qualities produce a wavering of the visible" as an allegory of the contingent, historically determined and necessarily distorted character of all "vision": In Scott's view, far from being the revelation of a preestablished truth and reality of gay identity, Delany's undulating vision and his retrospective grasp contribute to the production of gay identity at a specific moment.[22]

Oddly, Scott has very little to say about the historical context of the writing and publication of Delany's book, or about the period that it evokes.

The work "came out" in 1988; that is, just when the AIDS crisis was giving unprecedented visibility to the American male homosexual community, a macabre if not a negative visibility, but one with a spectacular impact that initiatives such as Act Up sought to turn to their advantage.[23]

Delany's memoirs are obviously overdetermined by this context. The writer evokes the period that preceded the cultural and political "coming out" of American gays, a "coming out" usually traced back to the so-called Stonewall riots, from the name of the gay bar in New York that was subjected to a brutal police raid in 1969, provoking protest riots in several major American cities. The scene Delany describes as a sort of epiphany in which the gay community was revealed to itself can be read as a stage in the process of visibilization that was preparing the emergence "into broad daylight" of the homosexual community as such, self-identified and henceforth publicly identifiable.

Yet the years 1957–1965, on which he focuses in his retrospective journal (1963 was the year of his "revelation"), coincide almost exactly with the era of the civil rights movement in the United States. Even if Delany does not say so, one can suppose that, if the question of visibility as a political issue and the rhetoric of visibility are so central for him, it is not only because he is gay but also because he is black.

The black American is, or was, an "invisible man," to borrow the title of Ralph Ellison's celebrated allegorical autobiographical novel, published in 1953. More precisely, as Ellison himself notes in a preface to the 1981 re-edition, the presumed or rather imposed "invisibility" of the black American male during the post-war years, even if he was "illuminated" by the torches of crowds prepared to lynch him or by the neon lights of urban commercial activity, is, in fact, the corollary of his phantasmatic "super-visibility": "[O]n the basis of his darkness he glowed, nevertheless, within the American consciences with such intensity that most whites feigned moral blindness toward his predicament."[24] It is because, to quote the novel's prologue, "the blackness of his invisibility" dazzles and "blinds" the white conscience (or rather the white unconscious) with its unbearable glare that whites choose not to see the "black" man—"blackness" is invisible—whom they nevertheless "see" everywhere.[25]

As I see it, the scene of revelation recounted by Delany cannot be understood without reference to Invisible Man. Delany's bathhouse is at once invisible to the uninitiated public and surrounded by the halo of an interior light that illuminates the author about the social and political meaning of his membership in the homosexual minority; does this bathhouse not recall the light-filled cave inhabited by Ellison's narrator-protagonist, whose "blackness" condemns him to invisibility in broad daylight? More generally, can one not say that the political and cultural status of the black American community, marked at once by its symbolic invisibility and its "imaginary" hypervisibility, along with the political history of that community (a political history that involves treating the problematic visibility of that minority), served as models for the aspirations of others, for example, the gay minority, and, today, the transgender minority?

In other words, the demand for visibility does not seem to me to stem solely from an implementation of the Western program of Enlightenment, as I indicated at the outset, nor does it stem solely from the constitution of contemporary societies as societies defined by technically engineered and generalized exhibition as well as panoptic modes of surveillance. These societies, moreover, can be understood as particular realizations of the Enlightenment project.

The insistent demand for political and cultural visibility, and more generally the massive recourse to the rhetoric of visibility in the field of minority struggles, are thus also the effect, as I see it, of the mark made by the American civil rights movement on the social movements that arose in its wake and that in many respects took it as a reference if not as a model: the women's liberation movement, for example, and the movements in support of sexual minorities. A specific historical juncture thus has to be taken into account if we are to understand the emergence of the motif of visibility in a certain "American" discourse.

However, the particular insistence of this motif also has its place, as I have suggested, in a vast theoretical current. The central questions brought together by this current are those of social identity and visibility, starting from a conception of social reality as a theatrical stage and social relations as role-playing. As an example of this way of thinking, which itself attests to a particular cultural outlook, I would like to evoke the work of Erving Goffman, a major figure in American sociology during the 1960s and 1970s. To be sure, the idea is not new. "All the world's a stage," Shakespeare reminded any naïve spectators who thought they could distinguish the theatrical stage (set up from scratch before their eyes) from social reality (whose construction remains invisible to its actors). Yes, "all the men and women"—since that is what this citation from *As You Like It* is about—"[are] merely players." But Goffman, like other sociologists of social interaction before him and after, has a tendency to reduce "play" to "display," as if the scene staged had no blind spot.

In the work for which he is best known, *The Presentation of Self in Everyday Life*, Goffman defined the individual both as a "character" in the theatrical sense and as a "performer" whose function is precisely to fabricate his own "character."[26] For Goffman, there is no pre-social identity; the "self" is produced when an individual is embedded in a social configuration conceived in theatrical terms, coupling intersubjective dynamics with a mobilization of preestablished social functions (in the theater these are called parts). But what interests me here are the terms in which Goffman extends his analysis of social identity to gender identity. In the mid-1960s, Goffman devoted two major essays to the question of gender: one, "The Arrangements between the Sexes," was published in the journal *Theory and Society*; the other first appeared in an anthropology journal and was republished in book form as *Gender Advertisements: Studies in the Anthropology of Visual Communication*.

In the first text, Goffman emphasizes the specificity of the social categories of sex in relation to the categories of class and race. According to him, if we can suspend the hierarchies of class and race within the family, thus in the private sphere (this supposes, as Goffman seems to, that families are homogeneous in terms of race and class), the particularity of sex roles is that they are initially learned within the family and continue to be played there. And how are they taught? Children are trained to distinguish between the sexes on the basis of social practices of "placement" and "labeling." Goffman called this set of practices an "identification system." His concept of identification has little in common with the psychoanalytic notion that goes by the same name. In his "system," what Goffman calls "appearance"—a way of presenting oneself that informs vision and inflects the way people who are looking at you behave toward you—plays a determining role. Appearance in this sense has nothing to do with bringing out the natural attributes of the sexes. It responds to codes that condition vision (as one talks about conditioning merchandise) and that allow others to identify the gender of a given person, and in so doing to situate that person in his or her proper place. Although Goffman notes that appearances can be deceptive in contemporary American society (he is presumably not thinking at this point about the allure of transgender individuals or "gay genders" but rather about the way one may hesitate upon seeing, from behind, someone of a certain height with short hair who is wearing jeans and sneakers), he suggests that "typing at a distance," the categorization enabled by the adherence of members of a society to one "system of identification" or another, is more effective for gender than for race. I cannot identify the "race" of a person I see at a distance and from behind. Conversely, Goffman says, "it is clear that the appearance established as appropriate to the two sexes allows for sex typing at a distance. Although recently this arrangement has developed some potential for error, still the system is remarkably effective at any angle and from almost any distance, saving only that viewing be close enough to allow perception of a figure."[27]

The veiling of women in certain societies or communities of yesteryear, and especially today, no doubt constitutes the most spectacular example of a coding of appearance that guarantees recognition of gender identity even from far away or from behind. And if black headscarves and cloaks have become widespread in contemporary Muslim societies and communities, superseding the traditional color symbolism associated with a given local culture or a particular tendency of Islam, is this not yet again because the color "black," if it is a color at all, signals visibility and invisibility at once, manifesting the hypervisibility of the "invisible" and consequently signifying, like the black American Ellison describes, the "blackness of invisibility"?

To return to Goffman, while he rarely uses the notion of "norm," his analyses of gender identification and differentiation unquestionably arise from a conception of gender as a "social norm" and, as such, a visible norm. This perspective brings out the fabricated character of categorial identities and helps make the fabrication process comprehensible; however, it does not have much to teach us about the mechanisms that produce gender hierarchies, or about the modes of gendered "subjectification," to use a contemporary idiom.

In *Gender Advertisements*, Goffman goes further in his reflection on mechanisms for constituting gender identities. He even goes so far as to propose a hypothesis that attempts to account for their hierarchical distribution: Gender identities, which develop first within the family structure, would be modeled on hierarchical parent-child relations, with women occupying a position in society analogous to the position of children within the family. Here Goffman's analysis turns on three terms: advertisement (and no longer arrangement), display, and style. To say that a gender advertises, or announces, itself, and consists in that "advertisement," draws the analysis of gender identity toward that of image effects, as when we study advertising to decode it or to make its coding more effective. These image effects are thus situated in the part of the public sphere that the notion of advertising, a form of "publicity" (in French, the word *publicité* explicitly links "advertisement" to the process of making public), evokes and defines. As his subtitle indicates, Goffman conceives of advertising as a particular form of visual communication. Gender conceived in terms of advertising thus brings together—by anticipation, as it were—the notions of gender identity, social visibility, and performance, advertising being a spectacular *act* (and art) of communication intended to produce certain effects and to provoke other acts (first and foremost that of consumption). Goffman is aware of the market connotation of the notion of "advertising." Thus he compares the mechanism for the production of genders to the process of manufacturing Ford cars.[28] Like advertising, the performance of gender would be in some respects a machine for arousing desires, such as the desire to consume.

But it is especially around the notions of display and style that Goffman articulates his analysis of gender manifestations and relations. The word "display" brings together once again the values of exhibition, scenography (thus also play), and advertising. "*Any* scene, it appears, can be defined as an occasion for the depiction of gender difference, and in any scene a resource can be found for effecting this display," Goffman writes.[29] Here the term "display" characterizes the theatrical staging of gender difference. All the world is indeed a stage for Goffman, as we can see from the lexicon he uses to define the space in which social relations are played out. But this difference is not simply shown or "depicted" by the display. It is literally produced *by* the display and *as* display. That is why Goffman affirms provocatively that there are no gender identities, but only what he calls a "*schedule for the portrayal of gender*": no gender identity precedes the scene in which this identity unfolds ("presents" itself) performatively. As in a play that is produced at regular intervals, and whose regularity is prescribed by multiple organizational considerations, gender identity is "put on"; it displays itself ritually on a certain stage and at a certain hour, in a space-time entirely governed by some particular social and cultural organization.[30]

Remaining in the register of gender as artifact, as social fiction in the strong sense of the term, thus in a certain way as work of art, Goffman tends to substitute the notion of gender "style" for that of gender "identity." "If . . . there are behavioral styles—codings—that distinguish the way men and women participate in social situations, then the question should be put concerning the origins and sources of these styles," he writes, translating styles as codings and vice versa.[31] But he clearly prefers the word style. Once again, the notion of style ("behavioral style," "gender style") allows Goffman to develop a model of gender identity that is less expressive than performative: According to him, *expressions* "of subordination and domination" *constitute* the hierarchy rather than manifesting a preexisting hierarchy. They are *at once*, Goffman writes, "the shadow," as in "shadow theater," and the "substance" of the hierarchy. In conclusion, he writes, "And here gender styles qualify."[32] Such a "style," as Goffman conceives it, is thus a shadow appearing *as* substance. It seems clear that the notion of style, which Goffman is not using in its etymological sense as a singular inscription but rather in its modern and almost opposite sense as a characteristic common to a set of objects, includes, for him, a higher coefficient of visibility than the notion of "code."[33] Style draws us into the vicinity of what is called fashion, with its function of aesthetic emphasis and mystifying seduction. Even if masculine and feminine "behavioral styles" are not necessarily "stylish," as Goffman notes humorously, they participate in what he calls, slipping in a metaphor from the arts, a "choreography."[34] Far from "expressing" a femininity constituted in advance, that is, before its "representation," the style of feminine behavior would have a social and political function: Its adoption would produce femininity by subtly obliging women to embody the feminine norm and thereby enabling women's occupation of the place that is assigned to them.[35]

Gender Advertisements dates, as we have seen, from the mid-1970s. This was the period of the first translations of "French thought," and the period during which the first women's studies programs were established in American universities. There are scarcely any traces of these developments in Goffman's text, even if his interest in the question attests to his awareness that something is in the air.[36] And yet his work constitutes an interesting and in some respects crucial stage in the shaping of American "gender theory."

The idea that gender identity is elaborated within the structure of the family converges with a certain psychoanalytical axiomatics. In the same way, the notion of style may overlap to a certain extent with the psychoanalytic notion of masquerade. From Rivière to Lacan, as we know, this notion made it possible to situate both the experience and the performance of sexual identity in the field of desire, at the point where this field gives rise to a ritualized scene, thus to what Goffman calls "social interaction." In this view, women (but also men, according to Lacan) would constitute themselves as objects of desire for the other through and in "masquerades." By now, and above all, readers of Judith Butler have no doubt recognized a prefiguring of the Butlerian conception of gender in Goffman's text. With the exception of one article from 1988, Butler almost never cites Goffman.[37] Yet her arguments and her language come peculiarly close to his formulations. At several points in *Gender Trouble*, she defines gender as the "repeated stylization of bodies."[38] In so doing, she links the notion of style or stylization, a term she often uses herself to designate the way in which subjects embody social norms, with that of performativity (a notion tied to that of repetition) as it applies to social relations. It is partly because she conceives of gender as a *spectacular* manifestation that she attaches so much importance to drag scenes, to theatrics, and to the theory of cross-dressing.[39] If gender is a matter of style, thus of appearance, and not a matter of essence or inner stance, if a gender style has meaning and existence only when it is exhibited on the social stage, thus when it is understood as display and demonstration, then it is the destabilization of what Goffman calls "visual communication"—a blurring or troubling of visual norms and thus a "politics of visibility"—that a certain politics of gender subversion might, or ought to, embrace, whether the agenda at stake is feminist or queer.

While Goffman and Butler turn toward the spotlights to explain or challenge the formation of gender identities, for Derrida the question of sexual differences (I shall return in a moment to the theoretical displacements induced by this change of idiom) belongs on the contrary to the *penumbra*. To the double question raised by Christie McDonald in *Choreographies*—

What are our chances of "thinking 'difference' [différance] not so much before sexual difference," as you say, "as taking off 'from'" it? What would you say is our chance and "who" are we sexually?

Derrida replies, indirectly:

> At the approach of this shadowy area [*pénombre*] it has always seemed to me that the voice itself had to be divided in order to say that which is given to thought or speech.[40]

The word *pénombre*, "penumbra," whose composite signifier (*pen/umbra*) connotes both the masculine and the feminine, thus, if not bisexuality, at least more than one sex and more than one sexuality, is indeed here "shade" or "darkness" rather than "shadow." And each time Derrida ventures into the vicinity of these questions, he emphasizes that they are located, for him, on the side of what Ellison calls "the blackness of invisibility." The ant (*la fourmi*) or rather the word "ant" (*le fourmi*)—at once the insect and the word that designates it in French while subverting its gender, since no French dictionary has ever listed an ant as masculine—the "ant," then, in the meditation that bears this name in the plural, allegorizes the *unfigurable* of sexual difference.[41] "Of an ant (*d'une fourmi*)," Derrida writes,

> **it is very difficult to see**, if not to know, the sexual difference . . . , and not only **because it is imperceptibly black**, but because as soon as the word *fourmi* is masculinized in a dream, for example Hélène's dream, **we see it at once removed from vision, doomed to the obscurity** [*noir*] **of blindness but promised in this way to reading**. *Une fourmi* can be seen perhaps but already to challenge you to identify the sex of this little black living creature. As for *un fourmi*, it is already the adventure of reading and interpretation, it swarms [*fourmille*] with thousands of meanings, a thousand and one [*une*] images, a thousand and one [*un*] sexes.[42]

In the same way, the *silkworms* (*vers à soie*) cultivated in his childhood proliferate in a thousand and one sexes and thousands upon thousands of meanings; the memory of these worms comes back to assail Derrida, he says, just before he closes his eyes, in the penumbra of half-sleep, and also just before he finishes writing the strange text that bears once again the name of an imperceptible insect: *Un ver à soie: points piqués sur l'autre voile* [A Silkworm: Pinpricks on the Other Veil]. In this text, Derrida meditates on the limitations of the logic of unveiling, at once an apocalypse of meaning, and an epiphany of the world, in the light of perception and knowledge. What the child that he was sought to uncover by observing the worms was something like the secret and the truth of sexual difference.

But the latter eluded perception. To be sure, silkworms are whitish and not black, but their whiteness is blinding—Derrida qualifies their sericigenic secretion moreover as "white [sleepless] *night*"—and their small size makes it "impossible to discern a sex."[43] There is no use looking, one sees nothing, and the motif of blindness punctuates this fantastic evocation.

The blackness or darkness of the (word) ant, the nocturnal whiteness of the silkworm, their undecidable—because at once multiple and minuscule— features make these creatures literally *imperceptible*, thus invisible, irreducible to the logic of visibility. And it is because the (word) ant is condemned to the "obscurity of blindness," Derrida writes, that it is "promised . . . to reading." The "darkness of invisibility" is thus the condition of this leap from "seeing" to "reading," of the shift from a logic of representation to the adventure of deciphering that Derrida anticipates.[44]

The operation of reading, as Derrida conceives it, makes it possible to leave the terrain of veridictional and jurisdictional discourse to which the logic of visibility refers and confines us, according to him (and also, as we have seen, according to Joan Scott):

> (. . . thenceforth, sexual difference remains to be interpreted, deciphered, decrypted, read and not seen. Legible, therefore invisible, an object of testimony and not proof—and in the same way problematic, mobile, uncertain, it goes by, it passes from one to the other, by one and the other [*par l'un et l'autre*], from one [*l'une*] to the other like *une fourmi*, *un fourmi* of a dream), the word insect, therefore, as it is heard without being seen, as on the telephone, teems with meanings and gives us to read all that can be deciphered on the programme of this colloquium.[45]

To say that "sexual difference" can be only *readable*, not *visible*, is an invitation to move beyond appearances, thus at once beyond the (false) certainty offered by the display of a certain number of physical features, but also beyond the play with identity that Goffman terms "display," a form of play that produces "visual communication" and takes place through that communication. For Goffman, as we have seen, gender identity is not a matter of anatomical conformation, nor even of unconscious identification in the psychoanalytic sense; it is a system of identification with models— Butler calls them "regulatory ideals"—that passes essentially through visual recognition and that is linked to the dynamics of social interaction. (We are not very far removed here from the notion of "role model," whose importance in American sociology and mass psychopedagogy is well known.) If Derrida and Goffman agree on disqualifying anatomical "self-evidence," "display" nevertheless produces identity effects that are foreign to the Derridean concept of "sexual difference(s)." Thus Derrida warns against the comic illusion produced by the adoption of gender roles in another passage of *Fourmis*. Evoking his appearance alongside Hélène Cixous on the stage of the conference at which he was reading this paper, he invited the listeners/spectators not to be fooled by the stage set-up and by the apparent distribution of roles:

> If Hélène and I were here to *figure* and, God forbid, if we appeared then as a mated figure of sexual difference *itself,* if we played the staged role of sexual difference here from the platform, from the pulpit or rostrum [*chaire*], sexual difference *ex cathedra,* if we were here to *interpret,* each in our own way and separately, our score [*partition*], in English our *part,* our part of separation—sexual difference in a reading for two hours, one actor, myself, playing the man, the other, her, playing the woman—one should only fall for this game, and believe in it, as at the theater or as "in life," on two conditions: *on the one hand*, it must be said that we are *interpreting* sexual difference in the sense that we are reading it, which is to say without seeing it, only so as to bear witness to it beyond the anatomical fact, beyond the proof of the civil status, beyond every system of so-called objective criteria of sexual identification—thus by passing from *seeing* to *reading*; *on the other hand,* we must remember the absolute leap that, in passing from *seeing* to *reading,* presupposes such an experience, such an endurance of blindness, such a test of witnessing, where it involves the abocular moment, . . . such an act of faith, therefore, that she and I could well have, we could still and we could always take the wrong place in play/by playing, pretend to play at mistaking our place without meaning to, interpret the role of the other and at every instant cross the line of the assigned partition.[46]

Thus "sexual difference" for Derrida does not refer to separate and stable identities, whether "performed," "produced," or "constructed." Now, the production of separate and stable identities is a condition sine qua non for establishing and maintaining hierarchies. Like differance with an "a," about which we cannot say whether it departs from or is part of "sexual difference," unless it is the other way around, "sexual difference" "passes," to use Derrida's formula, "it goes by, it passes from one to the other, by one and the other, from one to the other like *une fourmi, un fourmi* of a dream." And, in passing, it makes identities wobble, if not waltz.

But then why insist on the phrase "sexual difference," which may induce belief in some stable division between beings according to their sex, and which seems to refer, among other things, to the use that a certain Freudo-Lacanian psychoanalysis makes of this expression? I have addressed this question elsewhere;[47] here, let me simply recall the first part of my answer, namely, that to retain the phrase "sexual difference" is to engage in dialogue with psychoanalysis and to assume its legacy, even if in a critical manner. Derrida inherits the notion of sexual difference bequeathed by modern epistemology and dialogues with modernity as an "age of sexuality" (in particular, with "Freud's legacy") by playing with that expression. But it would nevertheless be a mistake to confuse the Derridean *reading* of sexual difference with the psychoanalytic interpretation.

In "Homo-ness and the Fear of Femininity," an article devoted to Leo Bersani, the queer essayist Patrick Paul Garlinger sums up the difference between the two theoretical paradigms that still dominate thinking about gender and sexual differences in the Anglophone intellectual world:

> Femininity as gender refers to a set of *cultural images and attributes* associated with the category "woman" as a sexed being. Under compulsory heterosexuality it is assumed that female bodies will be feminine and that male bodies will be masculine. In a sexual difference paradigm, the "masculine" is posited as the site of subjectivity and *the "feminine" as a site of lack, of unrepresentability.* While *gender theory would take visible characteristics or attributes as femininity itself,* sexual difference emphasizes *the incommensurability of any living being to represent femininity:* femininity in a sexual difference paradigm is not an attribute of gender.[48]

I shall leave aside the question of the way in which the theoretical paradigm of gender and the paradigm of sexual difference are articulated with each other or not. As I have tried to show in "The Theater of Gender," American *gender theory* is less inclined to oppose these "paradigms" than to superimpose them, as Judith Butler does, for example. But what interests me here is the axis of their distinction according to Garlinger. This distinction hinges essentially, in his view, on the opposition between visibility and invisibility. In the paradigm of gender, the analysis of femininity depends on its visibility: *"[I]mages* and cultural attributes," coincidence or lack of coincidence between a sexed body and the gender of its staging, *visible characteristics* all converge to support this perspective; in the paradigm of sexual difference as psychoanalysis (and especially Lacanian psychoanalysis) understands it, femininity is on the side of the *unrepresentable*, an unrepresentability that Garlinger stresses on several occasions. He is right, I think, to relate the paradigm of "sexual difference" as it is mobilized in Anglo-Saxon discourse on these questions to a Freudo-Lacanian approach. The latter is much more widespread than the Derridean perspective, which is more difficult to generalize.

It is true that, for Freud, and even if Freud relies on an "ocular moment" to evoke the "discovery of sexual difference" (a "discovery" that cannot be reduced, however, to the experience by the boy of a simple visual perception of the girl's lack, since that "perception" is organized in advance by the fear of castration), neither femininity nor masculinity is defined or recognized by visible attributes but rather by the adoption of unconscious positions that, as such, are "invisible." In Lacanian language, sexual difference, the effect of an identification of the subject with the "ideal type of her/his sex" which results from the "castration knot," is neither a reality nor simply an imaginary construct: It is "symbolic," that is, it does not belong—or belong only—to the order of representation and fantasy; it exists through what it *signifies*. But the psychoanalytic problematics still remains, to a certain point, a problematics of identity, or at least of identification (feminine or masculine), and in this sense it ends up rejoining gender theory, as I noted previously with regard to the relation between the theater (or the theatricality) of gender and masquerade. In this sense, the psychoanalytic interpretation of sexual difference differs from its *reading* by Derrida.

To say, as Derrida does, that sexual difference is and can only be readable, that is, *read*, is also to suggest paradoxically that it remains indecipherable, thus inaccessible to hermeneutics, including psychoanalytic hermeneutics. It *remains* "to be interpreted, deciphered, decrypted, read and not seen," Derrida writes in a passage cited earlier ("Ants," p. 21). In other words, in Derridean language, there is always a remainder, something that escapes reading, or rather that escapes, that "remains" *still* to be deciphered through and thanks to reading. For the process of reading, as

Derrida conceives it, is an infinite movement, impossible to stop even if it can always be interrupted, contrary to interpretation, which is finite, or at least aims at an end.[49] In short, sexual difference according to Derrida is a species of—or belongs to the species of—"text." Let us recall the first paragraph of "Plato's Pharmacy": "A text is not a text unless *it hides* from the first comer, *from the first glance*, the law of its composition and the rule of its game. A text remains moreover, forever *imperceptible*. Its laws and its rules are, however, harbored in the inaccessibility of a secret; it is simply that *they can never be booked, in the present, into anything that could rigorously be called a perception*."[50]

This, of course, does not mean that sexual difference consists only in words. The world, bodies, social relations—everything is "text" for Derrida, *that is to say, remaining to be read. And not to be seen.*

I began with the question of political protest as a demand for visibility, and I return to this question to conclude.

It is easy to see how an identity politics can take form and be formulated—one could supply any number of concrete examples—and how it passes or must pass through a demand for visibility. There is no "social identity" that holds together without recognition, and what is called recognition—the intersubjective mechanism that allows one unquestionably to call out to—or to believe one is calling out to—a given subject as a member of a socially and culturally identifiable category—presupposes or induces visibility.[51] Symmetrically, and as Leo Bersani shows in his book *Homos*, "visibility"—for example, the sudden public display of the gay community in the mid-1980s owing to the AIDS crisis—produces effects of identity definition, however ambiguous these may be.

(Let me open a parenthesis to point out that I do not want to join the debate here over the necessary but difficult articulation between, on the one hand, an identity politics that is generally articulated on the basis of a situation of discrimination or the perception of a deficit of "recognition," and, on the other hand, a politics of equality. The struggles based on race or gender membership (historically more recent than class struggles) have contributed to promoting identity politics. Indeed, in this case, categories of identity are perceived as non-dialectical: existing or presumed to exist "in themselves," even if they are contingent and historically overdetermined, they require a politics of inclusion in the social body and the cultural community.[52] In the case of class struggles, the dialectical confrontation of social categories aims at their mutual transformation, or even their abolition.)

But is there a possible politics of "sexual differences" in the sense in which Derrida conceives them, that is, the sense in which they escape precisely not only from the logic of binary opposition (whether involving the man/woman opposition or the homo/hetero opposition) but also from the logic of recognition, since they are unstable, destabilizing, fundamentally "imperceptible," and heterogeneous to the order of proof, *which does not mean that there are none*?

The question, I will be told, is in many respects irrelevant and the answer should be "no." First, "difference" or "differences" in Derrida's sense cannot be confused with what is called "diversity" today in France and has had that label for more than twenty years in the United States. Diversity maintains the principle of identity. If the principle of "diversity" were to win out, we would pass from a political regime or a social and cultural model based on a uniform or hegemonic identity to a model of multiple identities. This is not what is at stake in Derrida, since every claim of identity is ruined or undermined in advance by the movement of differance that works and disturbs it from within. But above all, Derridean thought about sexual differences is not a thought about power and power relations. In this respect, it does not belong to the domain of politics, if this domain necessarily implies the question of power, whether power is understood here as strategic relations of force, the practice of domination, the exercise of control, the deployment of surveillance, or even simply the ability to act in view of modifying a given situation.

And it is perhaps precisely because "sexual differences" as Derrida thinks and dreams them (i.e., not in terms of hierarchical distribution and identity formations) are "invisible," or escape from the enterprise of visibilization, that they do not really grant a place or a hold to "power," in the various meanings of that term. For Linda Alcoff, an American promoter of a certain identity politics of race and gender, visibility and power are intimately linked. Alcoff is, of course, not the only one who has theorized the relations between visibility, identity, and power, but I mention her because she takes on the task precisely of conceptualizing their consubstantiality in a recent book, *Visible Identities: Race, Gender and the Self* (2005). In her introduction, "Identity and Visibility," she defines her project in these terms:

"In one sense, my aim is to make identities more visible, to bring them [out] from their hiding places where they can elicit shame and obscure power."[53] Not only does Alcoff connect the affirmation of identity and the demand for visibility but she conceives of exiting from a certain "obscurity" as a condition for the emergence of power, or of a power. If, when they are "hidden," identities are not identifiable and are thus not identities—properly speaking—and if, especially, what obscurity makes invisible is "power" ("[in] their hiding places . . . [identities] can elicit shame and obscure power"), it is indeed because power, like identity, depends on its display: There is no power without a *demonstration* of power.[54] And only the demonstration of power can transform shame into its opposite, pride, an at once social and moral notion that, in its contemporary sense, combines affirmation and self-legitimization with exhibition, and which is enjoying today a political success that is as widespread as it is unprecedented (I am thinking about the various forms of "gay pride" and their avatars, of which the most recent, in France, is "academic pride").

A similar logic informs Deschamps's study of the specific political difficulty encountered by the bisexual "community" that is coming into being in France. If, according to Deschamps, bisexuals have not succeeded in "coming out" politically on the French stage, unlike other sexual minorities, it is because "a collective without visuals is cut off from part of its power." And bisexuals, like the transsexuals Jamison Green discusses, "are less easily grasped in fixed snapshots than others."[55] In other words, if a "stable image" (i.e., a photo) that shows two women or two men embracing suffices to signal and by the same token signify homosexual identity, "nothing permits bisexuality to be shown in a single visual image."[56] Thus bisexuals find themselves at a disadvantage in a Western culture in which "images are the principal vector of communication" and in which "the time imparted to each task has to be the shortest possible." If we add that bisexuals "lack performative experience" and "don't know how to play on derision and the inversion of stigmata"—stigmata referring literally to the visibility of the wound—it is understandable that the maintenance of "identitary bisexuals" in a "dominated" position is connected with "their inability to stage themselves through images."[57]

Is it not, in a way, this solidarity between identity, visibility, and power, generally formulated in view of obtaining one's rightful place in the sun within "democratic societies," that Bersani rejects, celebrating the necessarily *obscure* modes of jouissance in which identity is undone and the will to power is dissolved?[58]

It is a long way, in many respects, from Bersani to Derrida. But might we not say that Bersani's attempt to interrogate not only the contemporary politics of identity and sexuality but also the very meaning of the political, starting from an erotic experience that stems, for him, from the dark continent of the unconscious and of jouissance, in a sense rejoins the praise of the penumbra in which, for Derrida, the questions having to do with sex and sexuality dwell irreducibly? To be sure, erotics and politics are in a certain way incommensurable. And Bersani's "antisocial" erotics differs from the one that is sketched out between Derrida's lines. But while there may be no possible politics, in the most common sense of the term, of "sexual differences" and of their dance, embodied yet unfigurable, Derridean thought in this domain is not heterogeneous to the political, either. The interrogation of the political, and first of all a certain articulation between power and visibility that is central to its definition and to its history, starting from a "place" that is unthought or unthinkable by politics, has already, or still has, a political import.[59] Doesn't Foucault himself, when he suggests valorizing the claims of "bodies and pleasures" against the "grips of power" in *The History of Sexuality*, set forth a challenge—an ever-so-political challenge—to the political itself, conceived as the place and the mode of these "grips of power"? And does he not do this from the starting point of both an erotics and an ethics—lived or dreamed—of the pleasures of the body, an erotics and an ethics that escape the laws of gender and their disciplinary manifestations, to be sure, but perhaps also escape their spectacular transgressions, where these latter leave intact, or even contribute to the consolidation of, the relation between display, identity, and power effects?[60]

4

THE ENDS OF AN IDIOM, OR SEXUAL
DIFFERENCE IN TRANSLATION

WHAT ARE THEY TALKING ABOUT?

In a 1994 interview titled "Sexual Traffic,"[1] Judith Butler questioned Gayle
Rubin about the political and theoretical reasoning that had led her to drop
the paradigm of gender in favor of a theory and politics of sex. Rubin re-
sponded as follows:

> I was trying to deal with issues of sexual difference and sexual variety.
> And when I use "sexual difference" I realize from reading your paper
> "Against Proper Objects" that you are using it in a very different way
> than I am. I am using the term to refer to different sexual practices. You
> seem to be using it to refer to gender.[2]

Rubin is alluding here to an essay by Butler published in the same special issue of *differences* as "Sexual Traffic" that calls into question the philosophical and methodological premises of gay and lesbian studies, in this
instance their exclusion of "gender" as an object of sexuality studies.

The dialogue that follows might have come straight out of a play by
Ionesco, Tardieu, or even Beckett: Two characters ask themselves and each
other what they are talking about when they talk or believe they are talking
(to each other) about sexual difference, or, in Lacanian parlance, what it—
sexual difference—is talking about:

> JB: You mean, I am using "sexual difference" in the way that you were
> using gender in "Traffic in Women"?

GR: Well, I'm not sure. Tell me how you are using "sexual difference," because I am not clear on it.

Butler then tries out a definition of sexual difference that she prudently refuses to represent as her own, as the quotation marks indicate. And she immediately associates the paradigm, or what she calls the conceptual framework, of sexual difference with a certain use of psychoanalysis:

JB: . . . most of the people who work in a "sexual difference" framework actually believe . . . there is something persistent about sexual difference understood in terms of masculine and feminine. At the same time, they tend to engage psychoanalysis or some theory of the symbolic. . . .

A little later in the discussion, Rubin returns to the terminological issue:

GR: I found [the gay male political] literature fascinating and thought it was not only helpful in thinking about gay male sexuality, but also that it had implications for the politics of lesbian sexual practice as well. *And then there was just the whole issue of sexual difference. I am using that terminology of sexual difference here to refer to what has otherwise been called perversion, sexual deviance, sexual variance, or sexual diversity. By the late 1970s, almost every sexual variation was described somewhere in feminist literature in negative terms with a feminist rationalization. Transsexuality, male homosexuality, promiscuity, public sex, transvestism, fetishism, and, sadomasochism were all vilified . . . .*[3]

Rubin thus uses the phrase "sexual difference"—which she puts in the plural in "Thinking Sex"[4]—to designate, as she says, "what has been called perversion, sexual deviance, sexual variance, or sexual diversity." For now, I shall set aside the question of why she seems to prefer "sexual difference" to "sexual variation" or "sexual diversity" here. What is striking, if we can agree that the notion of sexual difference stems from the field of psychoanalysis or refers back to it (a point that Butler makes immediately in response to Rubin's question), is that Rubin is clearly giving it a "perverse" twist. The notion of perversion was developed in the field of psychopathology and more specifically within psychoanalysis at the end of the nineteenth century. In psychoanalytic terms, everything that amounts to denial of sexual difference is akin to perversion, sexual difference being understood as recognition by sexualized subjects of the irreducible male/female duality, and—the inexorable corollary—acceptance of the symbolic effect of castration; the "perversions" Rubin enumerates (transsexualism, homosexuality, fetishism) are cases in point. (Let us note in passing that "fetishism" seems to be the "fetish" perversion of a certain "queer" discourse on sexuality, from Foucault—who reserves a particular fate for it in his *History of Sexuality*— to Rubin, who proposes an anti-psychoanalytic "materialist" reading of fetishism in "Sexual Traffic." Is this because the fetishist perversion, according to its Freudian interpretation, consists precisely in denying sexual difference and its consequences? Is it not also because fetishism helps to reveal a certain complicity between contemporary sexual "arrangements" and market capitalism? On this topic, see my analysis in "Roxana's Legacy," in the following chapter.)

Then how does one move from the psychoanalytic notion of "sexual difference," linked as it is to the "knot" of castration that serves to bind each subject to his or her gender destiny, "masculine" or "feminine," to its "queer" use to designate the variety of the sexual practices or inclinations called deviant, that is, the "perversions" in which psychoanalysis, at least in its most normative and most widespread version, recognizes precisely a "denial of sexual difference"? I shall leave that question in abeyance for now. What I would like to emphasize for the moment is the obvious instability of the use of the phrase "sexual difference," an instability that cannot be attributed simply to ignorance, to lack of precision, or to the fact that its "original" contexts have been forgotten. Rubin's first essay, "The Traffic in Women," suffices to attest to her knowledge of the psychoanalytic field, especially in its "Franco-German extension" (Freud and Lacan).

Geneviève Fraisse, a French philosopher known for her nuanced positions in the field of French feminist thought and also for her reservations about American gender and queer theory,[5] refuses for her part to use the expression "sexual difference." She prefers the formula "difference between the sexes," arguing that the first expression already has a determined content.[6] I do not know what Fraisse means by the word "content," a term of which she is fond, and I am not sure that the distinctions it presupposes can be rigorously maintained. From the standpoint of either a pragmatics or a philosophy of language, how can one differentiate between a form without content and a form with content, between a floating signifier and a signifier aligned with a meaning, between the presumed "semantic void" of the "difference between the sexes" and the loaded meaning of "sexual difference," between the neutrality of one expression and the tendentious charge of the other?[7] Nevertheless, I imagine that Fraisse has in mind reflections on "sexual difference" by thinkers such as Luce Irigaray, whom she mentions, Antoinette Fouque, whom she does not mention, Hélène Cixous, whom she mentions, or Derrida or Lacan, whom she scarcely mentions but who use the expression.[8] But one can hardly reduce the phrase "sexual difference," as used by Derrida, Lacan, Irigaray, Cixous, or Fouque, to *one* and *only one* content. While it is true that the phrase has a particular intellectual history in France, this history is by no means homogeneous. It is by definition susceptible to the historicist treatment that Fraisse claims to be privileging in her approach to the questions surrounding the "difference between the sexes."

In any case, seen or read from the United States, the assertion that "sexual difference" has *one* content (precise and immutable) risks being illegible. All the more so in that it would be quite difficult to find an idiomatic translation that could bring out the distinction between *la différence des sexes* (difference between the sexes) and *la différence sexuelle* (sexual difference) and that would not play on the disjunction between "sex" and "gender," which Fraisse also challenges. To designate the "difference between the sexes"[9] in English today in Fraisse's sense(s), "gender difference" would arguably be the first expression to come to mind, as Fraisse herself hints.[10] And since American feminists and postfeminists are being translated in France in increasing numbers, the flow of discourse coming from the Anglophone world cannot help but provoke re-readings of the French corpus and consequent misalignments or realignments of the French theoretical scene in this realm.

These are not the hairsplitting arguments of a semiotician. At issue is rather what we call cultural history today and how we go about "doing" it. One usually studies cultures as if they were securely bounded and unified entities. Cultural history is generally the history of a single culture. The relation between cultures is thus seen as a variable relation between stable entities, whose territorial boundedness both figures and provides the ground for its internal coherence. Yet territorial unity and internal coherence are undermined by the way a number of contemporary cultural phenomena and discourses travel across space and especially virtual space, bypassing borders, material and immaterial. The display and circulation of "information" on the Web has thus contributed to inflecting the meaning of the word "culture." Notions of "culture" and "cultural space" or "areas" are traditionally tied to a notion of "location" as a bounded and "oriented" space. Virtual space does something more and something other than simply putting different geographical, linguistic and political spaces in permanent communication with one another: it *dislocates* and *disorients* location(s). It unhinges culture and "the cultural" from their traditional anchors. It therefore modifies the task of translation.

SEXUAL DIFFERENCE IS NOT ONE

I would now like to examine several different uses of the idiom "sexual difference." I am calling it an idiom and not a concept in order to stress the textual and contextual particularities of its use rather than the universal scope and abstract quality of the concept. The appeal to (and of) "sexual difference" is not only determined by history and by cultural particularities, as we have just seen, but also by the singular relationship between those who use the expression and the language they speak and with which they play.

In Greek, *idios* connotes both particularity and strangeness. An idiom is a highly particular and therefore untranslatable element of a language, or rather of the way a language is used. In any given language, idioms connect linguistic features with cultural features in a singular way, thus linking a text to a specific context. Every idiomatic formula has a context and a history, or rather contexts and histories. In this sense, none of the terms we use can be said to be pure concepts, universally translatable and abstractly universalizable.

To support these contentions, I shall evoke very briefly five idiomatic contexts in which the phrase "sexual difference" is used, five corpuses to which I attach singular names: 1) Sigmund Freud, 2) Hélène Cixous, 3) Jacques Derrida, 4) Gayle Rubin, and 5) Judith Butler.

1. I begin with Freud because it is he—in other words, it is psychoanalysis—that gave a new theoretical meaning to the notion of sexual difference, establishing it as a quasi-concept[11] and ensuring for the lexicon of sexuality a renewal, extension, and diffusion without precedent in the history of Western thought. Let me specify that I am gathering under Freud's name an entire European continent of thought and preoccupations to which Freud gave the most sophisticated formulations; thus I am also implicitly referring to Breuer, Kraft-Ebbing, Havelock Ellis, and many others.

As Foucault reminds us in the first volume of his *History of Sexuality*, the discourse on and of sexuality, and consequently the lexicon of sexuality that simultaneously translates and produces this discourse, are dated. This allows Foucault to advance the hypothesis of an "age of sexuality" that has clear historical and geocultural contours. "Sexuality"—as an idiom, an epistemological category, and an object—and thus the "sexual difference" that stems from this lexicon and from the range of questions it purports to address are modern Western inventions.

The adjective "sexual" (*sexualis*) certainly existed in Latin, but it referred exclusively to the female sex. Similarly, the word *sexe* was used in French to designate women (English did the same in expressions such as "the sex," "people of sex," or "the fair sex") until the eighteenth century. It was precisely in the eighteenth century that the adjective "sexual" took on its modern meaning, henceforth designating features of either sex or sexuality in general. From this point on, something like "sexual difference" became thinkable as such. Similarly, "sexuality" was a neologism that appeared in Romance languages in the first half of the nineteenth century, during the period when the epistemology and the politics of sexuality were being established.

Freud uses the Latinate neologism *Sexualität* to name and describe his new field of inquiry. But when he uses the modern expression *Sexuelle Differenz* (or its plural form *Sexuelle Differenzen*), the term does not necessarily have the meaning attributed to the comparable expressions in contemporary French and English. As gay activist and theorist Simon Watney points out in "The Banality of Gender," an article published two years after "Thinking Sex" in a special issue of *The Oxford Literary Review* titled *Sexual Difference*, there are indeed two "lines of thought" in Freud's work on this question. Under the label *Sexuelle Differenzen*, Freud attempts to conceptualize not so much the male/female or masculine/feminine distinction as the variety of sexual behaviors, or even sexual orientations, anticipating the way some queer theorists use this term.[12] To designate what is called sexual difference in English (French *différence sexuelle*), he uses the conventional German term *Geschlechtigkeit*—from a pre-theoretical lexicon, one might say; he speaks about *Unterschied der Geschlechter*, or, more often and even more simply, of *Geschlecht*. In the German notion of *Geschlecht*—Geneviève Fraisse and Jean Laplanche rightly stress this point—"sex" and "gender," as distinguished today in English and the Romance languages, are precisely indistinguishable, or at least very hard to dissociate.[13] Like the Latin *genus*, from which the word "gender" derives, *Geschlecht* can designate race, family, or gender; however, unlike the Latin word, which belongs to the lexical family of genetics and generation, nothing in the etymological origin of *Geschlecht* suggests the "genetic" or natural character of the social categories it "expresses." Finally, contrary to what the French and Anglo-American gloss on Freudian thought might imply, *Unterschied der Geschlechter* appears in Freud's discourse as an infra-theoretical locution that can refer to ordinary—pre-psychoanalytic, as it were—conceptions of the difference between the sexes. In contrast, Freud's frequent recourse to the (Latinate) lexicon of "sexuality" (in certain texts, the substantive *Sexualität* and the adjectives *sexual* and *sexuel* can be found as many as ten times on a single page) underscores the innovative character of his reflection on the various sexual organizations and orientations. Indeed, in the indexes to German editions of Freud's texts, *sexuel*, *sexual*, and numerous lexical kin appear with high frequency, signaling the particular theoretical status of the lexicon of sexuality. The word *Geschlecht*, no doubt deemed infra-conceptual, is not included.

In any case, when we read Freud we must take into account the pragmatic and semantic distinction that he establishes between the lexicon of "sexuality" properly speaking and the Germanic vocabulary of *Geschlechtigkeit*. I shall offer just one example of this play, or gap, between the German language and the Romance (or Greco-Latin) languages as purveyors of the idiom of sexuality. In his 1931 lecture on "femininity," when he invites his public to consider the coexistence of "masculine" and "feminine" traits as a manifestation of bisexuality, Freud writes this: "Sie [die Wissenschaft] sieht in diesem Vorkommen das Anzeichen *einer Zwiegeschlechtigkeit, Bisexualität*, als ob das Individuum nicht Mann oder Weib ware."[14] "Bigendericity" (*Zwiegeschlechtigkeit*) is interpreted in psychoanalytic terms as "bisexuality" and can be characterized only in this way.[15]

As his readers know well, Freud conceives of *Geschlecht* or *Unterschied der Geschlechter* (rendered in English as sexual difference, in French as *différence sexuelle*) not as the set of anatomical differences between male and female but as the manifestation of different unconscious positions that drive human subjects to privilege one path or another in their social and erotic lives. As Lacan himself repeatedly stressed, the psychoanalytic concept of "sexual difference" does not make reference to any sort of "biological essentialism."

It might be helpful, however, to look into what we project, and reject, when we refer to "biology." The term tends to be condemned out of hand too often and too quickly in gender studies today, at least in their most widespread summary version. Are we sure that we know what set of phenomena this word designates in the scientific field that bears its name? Is biology as a discipline truly "essentialist" in its approach and its goals? Above all, can the terms "essence," "nature," "body," "life," and "sex" that are associated with "biology" or called upon to answer for it really substitute for one another in an unproblematic synonymy? Not according to Foucault, at least. "Sex," for Foucault, is a speculative, indeed the most speculative, effect of sexuality. In contrast, the "body," that is, the living body, retains its physicality while it is being "disciplined." And Foucault certainly does not conceive of the relation between *bios* and *polis*, or between politics and "the body," as one of opposition and mutual exclusion. As for the distinction between *bios* and *zoé* on which Giorgio Agamben bases his version of "biopolitics," it is hardly problematized by Foucault, and one could show that it is as instable in his case as it is in Aristotle. Whether we take a "Foucaldian" approach to "sex" and "sexuality," "biology"—the discourse or study of *bios*—need not be anathematized. It deserves a less simplistic approach than mere exclusion from the speculative horizon of gender and sexuality theory.[16]

To return to the question of *Geschlecht* in Freudian theory, the difference between woman and man, or rather between the "feminine" and the "masculine," is not given; one is not born a woman—or rather *Weibliche*, feminine; it is a matter of becoming. Freud says this and seeks to demonstrate it well ahead of Simone de Beauvoir. Here again, it would be necessary to account for Freud's differentiated use of *Weib* and *Weibliche* on the one hand and *Frau* on the other.[17] The adoption of a sexual identity and orientation is the result of a complex process that implies identifications, transferences, cultural and social categorizations, and so on.

2. Hélène Cixous has inherited the Freudian notion of "sexual difference" through its French translation, and she plays purposefully with this legacy. Let us consider just one example of such play. "Sexual difference"—not the thing itself but the formulaic phrase—features in the title of a "reading" presented in 1990 at the first major international multidisciplinary

conference organized by the Center for Women's Studies at the University of Paris VIII. The conference was titled "*Lectures* de la différence sexuelle" (*Readings* of Sexual Difference): The aim was precisely to present "readings" rather than demonstrations or proofs (e.g., of the existence or nonexistence of sexual difference). The title was thus an invitation to read "sexual difference" both as a fact of language and as an effect of discourse. Cixous's contribution was part of a duet, with the other part voiced by Jacques Derrida. Each one played at playing his or her part or score (the "woman" part and the "man" part) while complicating and questioning the distribution of parts to the point of rendering the score untenable or unsingable without multiple voices. Cixous titled her part "Tales of Sexual Difference," emphasizing in literary terms what would be called discourse in para-Foucaldian terms. "Tales" here does not mean "lies" (as in "Are you telling me a tall tale?" or "What are these tales you've been telling?"), for literature does not moralize (even when it seems or seeks to do so), and in this sense it is not concerned with the opposition between lies and truth. Cixous's title nonetheless points toward fiction and its powers. And indeed, in these "tales," sexual difference is transformed by a stroke of the poetic wand into "DS," an acronym for *différence sexuelle* and a homophone of *déesse*, the French word for goddess, thus bringing into play the pagan goddesses that have been marginalized by monotheistic religions. Some will pounce on this point and say: we told you that she worshipped sexual difference as if it were a divinity! But that's because they haven't read the text. What is "divinized" and thus embodied, what is changed into an unexpected trope, is not the thing called "sexual difference" but the formula itself. And DS is precisely not sexual difference. It is a fact, a phenomenon—*un fait* (or as H. C. would say, with another homophone, *une fée*, a fairy) of language. Here is what Cixous says:

> [DS] is not a region, nor a thing, nor a precise space between two; it is movement itself, reflection, the reflexive Se,[18] the negative goddess without negativity, the ungraspable that touches me, that, coming from what is closest to me, gives me in a flash the impossible me-other, makes the you-that-I-am appear, in the contact with the other.[19]

This DS, which in passing destabilizes all signs and assignments, this not-so-well-behaved (*pas sage*) goddess of the passage of one toward the other and of one in the other, has no more to do with anatomical destiny than with a regulated distribution of roles. Rather, it has a great deal to do with certain psychic mechanisms studied by psychoanalysis, such as the formation of the ego, the self's various ways of relating to the other, love, or, conversely, when there is no (tres)passing, hostility.

3. Derrida, a powerful deconstructor of what he calls "sexduality," the dual logic underlying the traditional idea—but also to a great extent the psychoanalytic notion—of sexual difference and of sexuality in general (starting with the opposition between heterosexuality and homosexuality), nonetheless remains attached to the idiom of sexual difference. Why and how does he preserve this idiom while continuing to denounce and break down the phallogocentric hierarchy that slips into every difference treated as an irreducible opposition? The fact is that idioms, and this idiom in particular, interest Derrida on several counts; moreover, deconstruction does not work by censuring, reducing, or erasing the structures it purports to dissect.

To retain the idiom "sexual difference" is to accept a certain historical legacy and to reflect on this legacy, even if in a critical manner.[20] Derrida inherits the notion of sexual difference from modern epistemology, and by playing with the idiom he engages in a dialogue with modernity (an "age of sexuality") and especially with "Freud's legacy." He approaches the phrase as a poet or poetician, too, playing as Cixous does with the feminine gender of the French term, and with the word "difference," which, as he reminds us in "Choreographies," connotes both mobility and instability. Difference (a noun derived from a verb), the differentiating act of difference, is not a state and certainly not a state of opposition; it is a dance. The Latin verb *di-fero* literally means to carry away, to move, deport, or displace (oneself) in multiple directions. It comes close to what Derrida calls dissemination: Difference, in this sense, in no way resembles the categorical immobility of a distribution of traits. The philosopher calls on philology to bring out the cutting edge of the epithet "sexual." The word "sex" and its derivatives come from the Latin *secare, sectum*, meaning to cut, to divide into sections. Language thus invites us to think sex, sexuation, and the sexual, as phenomena and experiences of cutting, partitioning, even wounding. Sexual identity would then refer to a specific incision, an imaginary and symbolic cut in and of the very fabric of each human being.

We know the role that reflection on cutting—always both an interrogation and a deconstruction—plays throughout Derrida's work, for both philosophical and autobiographical reasons, via the circumcision motif, for example (and thus for historical reasons as well, since autobiography is a writing of history at the individual level). With "sex" and its lexical derivatives, we find ourselves in the vicinity of thought about cutting and infinite divisibility but also at the heart of an inseparably psychical and cultural experience of the cut as a wound, of division as resistance to totalization, of the "not all/whole her" and the "not all/whole him," "not all-mighty" that we all are as sexed beings, subjected to sectioning and therefore bound to intersect.

Derrida prefers to talk about sexual differences in the plural. He holds onto the idiom of sexual difference while dividing it infinitely and hence pluralizing it in the hope of escaping from binary constructs as well as from conceptual frames. A concept is always spelled out in the generic singular. Indeed, when sexual difference in the singular is taken seriously, that is, as a concept, it cannot help but produce effects of sexduality.

For Derrida, finally, holding onto this idiom is also a way of preserving the possibility of thinking about the relation between the cut, or the experience of the cut, and the experience of love. Without sex, without the thought of sex, there would be no love dance. Without cutting, that is, without the cut of sex, there would be no self-interruption, no self-limitation. We would risk losing the differences (understood as plural, because the line of demarcation between them is neither "one" nor clear) between auto-eroticism and allo-eroticism. Without interruption or alteration of the love for oneself, there would be no possible love for another.

4. Let us now leap back to the other continent where these questions are in play and return to Gayle Rubin. In "The Traffic in Women," Rubin seeks to show the importance of psychoanalysis and structural anthropology in the development of a feminist epistemology and politics. Indeed, these are the only two "human sciences" or discourses where what she calls the "sex-gender system" (i.e., "the set of arrangements by which a society transforms biological sexuality into products of human activity, and in which these transformed sexual needs are satisfied" [p. 159]), plays a central role.

Rubin offers one of the earliest feminist definitions of "gender," for example, when she declares that "[g]ender is a socially imposed division of the sexes" (p. 179), but she also provides the most convincing defense and illustration of the usefulness of psychoanalysis for feminist theory:

In Marx's map of the social world, human beings are workers, peasants, or capitalists; that they are also men and women is not seen as very significant. By contrast, in the maps of social reality drawn by Freud and Lévi-Strauss, there is a deep recognition of the place of sexuality in society, and of the profound differences between the social experience of men and women. (p. 160)

In France, gender theory proper has often ignored psychoanalysis. And yet it is impossible to understand Judith Butler's work and that of her contemporaries in gender studies and/or queer studies if we fail to take into account their debt to psychoanalysis and to some sectors of anthropology. At the same time, it is true that psychoanalysis remains a major bone of contention within these fields. While Rubin followed through with her commitment to anthropological reflection and ethnographic work, she gave up on psychoanalysis in the name of a new, radical distrust of any interpretive gesture with respect to sexuality: "Sexual acts are burdened with an excess of significance," she claimed in "Thinking Sex" (p. 11). At virtually the same time, Simon Watney was arguing for a Foucaldian reading of Freud, or (perhaps more accurately) a Freudian reading of Foucault, and he also proposed abandoning the theory of gender in favor of a theory of sexuality or sexualities. But, unlike Rubin, he appealed to a Freudian notion of desire and the instability of identity in order to do so.[21]

"Thinking Sex" is for queer theory what "The Traffic in Women" was for the establishment of gender studies, a foundational text.[22] That these two texts were written by the same author is particularly interesting.

In "The Traffic in Women," we begin to see the seeds of the thesis that Rubin developed subsequently in "Thinking Sex," namely, that the deconstruction of gender as a social and political category involving the binary regulation of sexual life *and* social life has to result in the eventual abandonment of that category, both in theory and in practice.

Cultural evolution provides us with the opportunity to seize control of the means of sexuality, reproduction, and socialization, and to make conscious decisions to liberate human sexual life from the archaic relationships which deform it. Ultimately, a thorough-going feminist revolution would liberate more than women. It would liberate forms of sexual expression, and it would liberate human personality from the straightjacket [*sic*] of gender.[23]

Rubin thus calls for liberation from gender in a radical contestation of the way social identities are produced. Whether it is possible to drop gender altogether in favor of thinking (about) sex and sexuality more thoroughly and more freely is an object of debate and even dispute within queer theory. The field is split between those who hold Rubin's position and those who endorse Butler's, with each side finding support in Foucault on different grounds. As Rubin herself reminds us, the word "sex" in English refers ambiguously to the sexual identity or characteristics of human beings *and* to sexual practice (as in the act of "having sex"). In contrast, in French it is possible to "have a sex" but not to "have sex"; one can only make love. Yet for political reasons that are at the heart of her essay, Rubin seeks to make a sharp distinction between these two uses of the term.

In "Thinking Sex" (a richly idiomatic and amphibological formula that we must not be too quick to translate into French as "*penser le sexe*": It could just as legitimately be translated as "*penser sexe*" or even "*sexe pensant*"), the idiom of sexual difference still occupies center stage. But it is pluralized, as in Derrida's work, and it is not used to signify generic differences between masculine and feminine, since Rubin refutes this dichotomous polarization, nor is it used to designate the differences in sexual orientation that are thought to be a by-product of a heterosexist conceptual matrix that sees difference or binary opposition everywhere (between men and women, but also between heterosexuality and homosexuality). Instead, "sexual difference" is used to refer to all sorts of sexual practices and identifications, which are understood to be historically contingent. For Rubin, dropping gender does not mean returning to a naturalist notion of sexuality. She seeks rather to delve further into Foucault's analysis of sexuality and pursue the full consequences of his principled indifference to the question of gender(s).

Rubin denounces the social pressures and the political repression that are applied against anyone who breaks away from the dominant model of sexual behavior in any given society:

The notion of a single ideal sexuality characterizes most systems of thought about sex. . . . *Progressives who would be ashamed to display cultural chauvinism in other areas routinely exhibit it toward sexual differences.* We have learned to cherish different cultures as unique expressions of human inventiveness rather than as the inferior or disgusting habits of savages. We need a similarly anthropological understanding of different sexual cultures.[24]

I have already stressed Rubin's apparent lexical preference for the phrase "sexual difference(s)," for which she also proposes a series of imperfect equivalents that only express the full meaning of the preferred phrase when she lists them all together, as she does in "Sexual Traffic": sexual deviance, sexual variety, sexual diversity. It is as though the word "difference(s)" allowed her to maintain a balance between a clearly pejorative term such as "deviance," which has meaning only in relation to a norm that Rubin is intent on contesting here—for her there are no normal or abnormal sexualities—and another term, "diversity," whose euphemizing and neutralizing value is by now well known in both the French and American contexts. Difference separates and upsets people; diversity reassures people and brings them together. The former threatens the principle of identity; the latter does not.[25] Rubin's goal is thus to decriminalize so-called "deviant" behaviors instead of "normalizing" them on the basis of the liberal ideology of "individual choice."

What, then, is the status of these sexual differences and these different sexual cultures? What social and psychic forms can their practice or experience take? Is it possible to leave all "generic" categorization and qualification behind? I shall leave these questions unanswered for now, and simply add that, for Rubin, the sexual question is not a pre-political question but is at the very root of politics. Even so, her position can only be fully understood in the context of the cultural history of politics and the political in the United States. In particular, one has to take into account the centrality of the focus in "American" politics on everything that has to do with what has been called biopolitics, in Foucault's wake. Rubin is advocating not a new politics of the genders or sexes (whether we count two of these or, following Plato, three) but a politics of sex and sexualities that cannot be reduced, according to her, either to Marxism as a theory of workers' liberation or to feminism as a theory of women's emancipation.

5. Have we then reached "the end of sexual difference"? My question is actually a quotation. I borrow it from the title of an article by Judith Butler first published in *Feminist Consequences* in 2001 and reprinted in *Undoing Gender*. Butler's title is indeed formulated as a question, and she herself intends it "as a citation of a skeptical question."[26] She answers in the nega-

tive. The question of sexual difference (both as an idiomatic expression and as a notion) will have to remain troubled and troubling (which is why the title is indeed an open question) if we are to avoid impoverishing the field of feminist reflection. Here are Butler's final words in the first version of her essay:

> That the sexual freedom of the female subject challenged the humanism that underwrites universality suggests that we might consider the social forms, such as the patriarchal heterosexual family, that still underwrite our "formal" conceptions of universality. The human, it seems, must become strange to itself, even monstrous, to reachieve the human on another plane. This human will not be "one,"[27] indeed will have no ultimate form, but it will be one that is constantly negotiating sexual difference in a way that has no natural or necessary consequences for the social organization of sexuality. By insisting that this will be a persistent and an open question, I mean to suggest that we make no decision on what sexual difference is but leave that question open, troubling, unresolved, propitious.[28]

"The End of Sexual Difference?" is above all a meditation on the idiom of "gender," thus on gender *as* an idiom, not in the philosophico-philological mode of Derrida or in the poetic fashion of Hélène Cixous, but rather in a pragmatic and political mode that makes room for a questioning of language and discourse as the author reflects on the semantic variations of the term and on the various political aims or effects of its use within different contexts. Butler writes, "More important than coming up with a strict and applicable definition of the term [gender], is the ability to track the travels of the term through public culture."[29] Her essay does not advocate a soft intellectual pluralism; rather, Butler argues for the necessary complexity of a theoretical field that only becomes richer as it indexes multiple idioms and sometimes contradictory formulations.

Some of Butler's subsequent work on gender, collected in *Undoing Gender* (2004), also attempts to address a new set of concerns that have come to the forefront of American discourse on such questions. This new set of concerns is again making trouble in the already troubled area of gender as a social category and as a conceptual tool: I am, of course, referring to the development of the double social phenomenon of transsexuality and transgenderism, a development spurred by the theoretical attention it has received. The discourse and the practice of "crossing" assume a symbolic, social, physical, and phantasmatic alignment of gender with sex in its transsexual version, while in its transgender version it plays instead on the discrepancy between sexed bodies and declared gender identities. In both cases, these cultural phenomena invite us to continue to situate our analyses at the crossroads of cultural history, social theory, and psychoanalysis, and above all to keep open the irksome question of sexual difference(s).[30]

WHEN LANGUAGE TAKES US FOR A RIDE: A FEW REMARKS, TO END BUT NOT TO CONCLUDE

1. In "Sexual Traffic," Gayle Rubin reminds us that in the early 1970s, a time when "women's movements" were starting to make their presence felt throughout the Western world, Marxism in its various forms was the dominant paradigm among "progressive intellectuals."[31] These women's movements were both real political movements, capable of mobilizing public opinion in favor of contraception and abortion, for example, and reflexive moves that resulted in the gradual development of *feminist* theory in the 1980s and the early 1990s. What is called second-wave feminism thus grew out of a complicated relation to Marxism.[32] In her first essay, "The Traffic in Women," Gayle Rubin pointed out the shortcomings of Marxism and spelled out the epistemological and methodological conditions for an autonomous feminist thought. However, her essay was also conceived both as commentary on and homage to Friedrich Engels' *The Origin of the Family, Private Property and the State*. In "Thinking Sex," Rubin affirms her debt to Marxism when she analyzes the ambiguous but substantive relations between certain forms of modern sexuality and the market economy.[33] Marxism supplied and continues to supply feminism with productive ways of thinking about the connection between theory and politics, and more specifically between a theory of domination and a politics of emancipation. But while Marx has his share of interpreters and has elicited a wide range of readings, Marxism in all its forms nevertheless has only one source and is grounded in a fairly stable conceptual apparatus. There is general agreement on the meaning of terms such as "capital," "labor," "surplus value," "exchange value," and so on, or at least on their definition and meanings in Marx's work. The same cannot be said of "feminist theory." The key terms in its vocabulary are regularly disputed and consequently undergo a continuing

process of "resignification," to use a term coined by Butler to describe the semantic shifts and redeployments that are so characteristic of contemporary thinking about gender and sexual differences. No single author or authority stands out in feminist or postfeminist thought today: neither Marx nor Freud, neither Irigaray nor Beauvoir. For feminist theory, this is at once a misfortune and an opportunity, but perhaps especially the latter, since the heterogeneity of its sources and the constitutive instability of its "foundations" bring to light, by contrast, what any attempts at conceptual stability owe to the double ("patriarchal"?) principle of textual unity and authority.

2. Toward the end of the augmented version of "The End of Sexual Difference?" that appeared in *Undoing Gender*, Judith Butler reflects on "the Anglo-European division" and initiates a dialogue with "European" feminist philosopher Rosi Braidotti. At one point, Butler asserts that "theory emerges from location."[34] This remark on the "location" of theory may well have been inspired by Homi Bhabba's work on the "location" of culture. In any case, it is a way of reminding the reader that no theorization is possible without a *point of view*, and that there is no point of view that does not imply a place or a site from which the "viewing" activity, or the *theorein*, can take place. In the wake of this remark, Butler points out that "location" itself, as a unified or at least identifiable site of collective enunciation, is actually in a state of crisis in Europe:

> Theory emerges from location, and location itself is under crisis in Europe, since the boundaries of Europe are precisely what is being contested in quarrels over who belongs to the European Union and who does not, on rules regarding immigration (especially in Belgium, France, the Netherlands), the cultural effects of Islamic communities, of Arab and North African populations.[35]

But this crisis of location, which is a crisis of the belief in the unity of location (a unity which in Europe is declared and asserted through the figure of the Union and without which no location can "take" or stay in place), does not affect Europe alone. The literal dislocation of viewpoints affects the whole of contemporary theory and especially feminist theory, as Butler herself suggests. Immediately after her remarks on Europe, she hastens to add: "I am an American, but I am trained in European philosophy."[36] She then goes on to offer a quasi-"confessional" statement about her relation to European languages in general and German in particular. What is the connection between her meditation on the crossing of languages and her questioning of the meanings and uses of the terms "gender" and "sexual difference"? In both cases, the issue is one of dislocation, of the severing of the link between language and its—or *any*—place of utterance. What language am I speaking, and from what location(s), when I use the word *sex(e)* today in French? Sociolinguists have shown that this term has taken on meanings in French that it lacked fifteen or twenty years ago, to such an extent that when we speak (about) *sexe* in French we are actually speaking English. One historical dictionary of the French language confirms this relation between "speaking sex" and speaking (in) English when it notes that many derivatives of the words *sexe* and *sexualité* in contemporary French come from English: This is the case of the series of words with the prefix *trans-*, such as *transsexualisme*, first attested in French in 1956, and *transsexualité* (1960) or *transsexuel* (1965), and, today, *transgenre*, a term that had not yet made it into the dictionary in 2000.[37]

The English language, which no longer refers back to a unified place or culture, is today both the paradoxical location and the vehicle of this generalized dislocation. It has thus become advisable, perhaps even necessary, to ask ourselves what happens to the "content" of "différence sexuelle"/"sexual difference" when the French term crosses the Atlantic or the English term heads back from San Francisco or New York.

The semantic instability of such a locution is, of course, an effect of the particular character of our "knowledge" in the area of sexual difference(s). All "knowledge" of the subject matter, all rationalizations, all epistemological or political propositions concerning sexual differences are necessarily "affected"—Geneviève Fraisse uses this term in her introduction to *L'exercice du savoir et la différence des sexes*—or at least overdetermined and therefore undercut by both the intimate experiences and the unconscious positions of those who speak on the subject. Above all, such "exercise of knowledge" is affected by the at-once *undecidable* and *insurmountable* limit that separates knowledge of oneself from knowledge of the other, however uncertain the former may be. Where "sexual difference" is concerned, the knowing subject is condemned to the misrecognition or lack of knowledge that characterizes his or her apprehension of the other as well as of him- or herself. Knowledge of the other can therefore only be a system of presumptions; Lacan would call them, jokingly, convictions.[38] This is why, in Western feminist politics and theory alike, it is so difficult—indeed, impossible—to reach agreement on questions of "sexual identities," in which we all have personal and unconscious stakes, while it is so easy to agree on the necessary struggle for equality.

"As for sexual difference, we will always wonder . . ."[39] (*La différence sexuelle, nous nous demanderons toujours* . . .), Derrida writes at the end of his "reading of sexual difference" titled "Ants." And to stress the grammatical undecidability of the "*nous nous demanderons*" (literally either "we will ask ourselves" or "we will ask one another"), a pronominal quandary that inserts the *inter*locution into the *allo*cution and the question *to* and *of* the other into solitary reflection, Derrida adds: "But that's it, sexual difference, if sexual difference has something to do (*quelque chose à voir*) in this situation: se demander. And to ask oneself, (from) the other (*se demander, à l'autre*), if there is such a thing, if it is an accessory determination, . . . a secondary supplement or an essential antenna across all separations . . . ."[40]

If the question of sexual difference, or rather the multiple questions gathered together under its name, remain, as both "troubling" and "troubled" questions, the idiom (or the segment of an idiom) "sexual difference," which speakers of the Western languages in which it is rooted continue to use, no longer functions today as the key element of an "oriented" discursive arrangement. Disoriented and disorienting, it opens up in discourse— whether it is a matter of ordinary speech, scholarly speech, or militant speech—what Laurent Dubreuil calls, with respect to a certain colonial phraseology, "a contradictory *and* yet meaningful space."[41] At once available and ungraspable, it does not bequeath to us a doctrine or an ideology but an injunction to keep open, and continue to interpret actively, the meaning or rather the meaning(s) of its legacy.[42]

5

ROXANA'S LEGACY: FEMINISM AND CAPITALISM IN THE WEST

CRISIS IN FEMINISM, FEMINISM IN CRISIS

Feminist theory was constituted almost immediately as a field of crisis and in crisis. For the crisis in feminist theory coincided almost exactly with its rise to prominence. In their introduction to *Conflicts in Feminism*, a volume published in 1990 that recapitulates ten years of theoretical and political quarrels in American academic feminism, Marianne Hirsch and Evelyn Fox Keller recall that "a decade ago there was no professional or indexical category called 'feminist theory'; rather, there were (a few) people who were 'doing theory,' and doing it as feminists."[1]

What had happened, then, between 1980 and 1990? Hirsch and Fox Keller point to the explosion of "feminist" research during that period. But why did the term "feminist theory" take hold just at that moment, and why did "theory" supplant "criticism"—the key term in the research landscape of the humanities and social sciences since the 1970s—in the labeling of this field? The first answer, of course, is that what has been called "French theory" in the American academy reached its peak during this period. But although "feminist theory" borrows a number of its concepts, axioms, and foundational texts from "French theory," it is not simply a disciple of the latter and a member of the same intellectual family. In a short book on "literary theory," Jonathan Culler, who has been an advocate and one of the best exponents of French structuralism and post-structuralism in the United States, observes that, while the body of work known as *theory* falls within a line of "critical thought" going back to the Enlightenment, *theory* is nevertheless distinguished from "critical thought" by its unprecedented practice of interdisciplinarity[2] and by its metadiscursive character: *Theory*, whose discursive particularity and historical singularity are highlighted by the absolute construction of the syntagma by which it is designated, takes as its privileged object of inquiry the very tools and categories with which we think.[3] In other words, *theory* is self-reflexive: Not only does it question its own presuppositions but it also elaborates and reinforces itself in the very gesture of calling itself into question. If "feminist epistemology" is inter- or trans-disciplinary, since any knowledge or statement about sexual differences and hierarchies necessarily requires collaboration among philosophical, anthropological, sociological, historical, meta-psychological, semiotic, and other approaches, *feminist theory* was conceived, recognized, and designated as such from the moment when it devoted the better part of its efforts to interrogating its own procedures and aims. Most of the essays in *Conflicts in Feminism*, written in the 1980s, have an explicitly metacritical scope. From Katie King's "Producing Sex, Theory and Culture: Gay/Straight Remappings in Contemporary Feminism" through Peggy Kamuf's challenge to feminist criticism ("Replacing Feminist Criticism") and the evocation of the internal contradictions or limits of a certain feminist critique of the biological, zoological, and medical sciences by Helen Longino and Evelynn Hammonds ("Conflicts and Tensions in the Feminist Study of Gender and Science") to the final essay in the volume, "Criticizing Feminist Criticism," written jointly by Jane Gallop, Marianne Hirsch, and Nancy K. Miller, most of the contributions engage in a form of "immanent critique" of their own space and mode of deployment.

"Immanent critique": As we know, this is how Judith Butler qualifies her own intervention in the field of feminist theory in *Gender Trouble*, published a few months after *Conflicts in Feminism*. But while Butler's angle of attack is different, her work consistently constitutes the most telling point of an at-once self-reflexive and self-critical gesture that serves more to found feminist theory as such than to undermine it. One might say that, to the extent that gender theory is rooted in this internal or "immanent" critique of the subject or the object of feminism, a critique that is the source both of its strength and of its specificity, "gender theory" is simply the name of feminist theory in its crisis state.

So just as what is now called "second-wave" Western feminist theory was being consolidated, first as "feminist theory" and then as "gender theory," its object and reason for being—the object "woman," or "women"—was splintering apart under the pressure of a virulent "immanent" challenge to the internal unity and the exclusivity of this object, and in response to a corollary challenge to the epistemological and political pertinence of the framework that had previously circumscribed feminist action and thought. From this point on, under its "crisis" label of gender theory, feminist theory took a melancholic turn: It became the site and target of an endless mournful reflection on the impossibility of its own enterprise. The practitioners of gender theory, female and male alike, are thus indeed, in this sense, (post) feminists.

Two essays by Wendy Brown, a political theorist and a committed (post) feminist, are exemplary in this respect. The first, "The Impossibility of Women's Studies," initially published in 1997 in the journal *differences*, observes that the field of women's studies is running out of steam.[4] As its title indicates, the article questions the possibility and the relevance of maintaining such programs of study in American universities, even as "gender studies," that is, in the name of a "critical, self-reflexive" conception of gender rather than a "normative or nominal" one.[5] Brown's other key essay, "Feminism Unbound: Revolution, Mourning, Politics" was originally published as "Women's Studies Unbound: Revolution, Mourning, Politics": The change in title seems designed to highlight the theoretical and political project of women's studies (i.e., feminism), rather than its institutional structure.[6] Here, Brown analyzes the "critical state"[7] of feminist theory in the light of the larger crisis in modern political thought, which she sees above all as a crisis in the revolutionary hope that has oriented "progressive" thought in the West and has helped shape political force fields since the revolutions in the eighteenth century.[8]

Nancy Fraser, another thinker who focuses on political and feminist theory, makes a similar observation in a 2009 essay, "Feminism, Capitalism, and the Cunning of History."[9] Her perspective, however, is different from Brown's. Refusing to adopt the "melancholic" posture of a certain (post)feminism, and determined to reposition the feminist struggle if not within a "revolutionary" logic then at least within a project of global social transformation, she denounces the ambiguous convergence of what I shall call the "new spirit of feminism," in a parody of the formula used by Luc Boltanski and Eve Chiapello, with the "new spirit of capitalism."[10] The displacement of feminist struggles from the "social" to the "cultural" terrain, the new political formations and demands of "identity politics," and, finally, if not the absence then at least the secondarization of a "critique of political economy" at the heart of these trends—these are all signs, according to Fraser, of a profound change in the political paradigm.[11] She describes this change as the shift from a "politics of redistribution," inspired by an ideal of social justice for all, to a "politics of recognition," moved by an ideal of cultural legitimation of oppressed and/or stigmatized minorities. The problem, according to Fraser, is that this demand for cultural recognition comes to terms too easily with the contemporary economic order, in this case the forms and effects of globalized capitalism.

If we are to believe Brown and Fraser, in its newest and most "visible" political manifestations as well as in its new theoretical orientations (gender theory and its queer avatar), contemporary Western (post)feminism is no longer seeking either to "change life" by working toward the "revolution of the symbolic" nor to "transform the world" by proposing a radical critique of the socioeconomic order. It has given up because it has ceased to believe in the possibility of bringing a different world into being. It has thus ceased to be "utopian."[12] It is precisely this "absence of utopia," or better yet this strange "pragmatism," that characterizes the politics of the "subversion of sexual norms" that Geneviève Fraisse—a skeptical observer of the "American" (post)feminist political and theoretical field—deplores.[13]

In *Beyond Accommodation: Ethical Feminism, Deconstruction and the Law*, first published in 1991, Drucilla Cornell, who declares herself both a Marxist and a feminist, proposed a deconstructive defense of the "utopian" penchant of a certain 1970s "French feminism," viewed as a necessary heuristic condition for theoretical and political progress: Without the dream of "a different world" or "a different woman," where would the desire or the power to work toward transforming the present come from?[14] In contrast, the opening sections of *Gender Trouble* not only question the identity, unity, and universality of the "subject of feminism" (i.e., the subject "woman") but also challenge the "controlling fictions" of utopian feminism, whether this latter invokes a "before" or an "after" of the androcentric order.[15] But while Butler skillfully convokes Marx to legitimize her political and theoretical critique of the tendency to fall back on the fictions of a past or a future presumed to be immune from the power relations that characterize the historical present,[16] she is following in Foucault's footsteps when she defines the new task of (post)feminism: The task is no longer to *change worlds* in order to change *the* world, but to *resist* the dominant sociocultural order from within, since there is no possible way out of the "field of power."

MARX, RETURN OF THE SPECTER

The abandonment of a macro-politics of "revolution" in favor of (plural) micro-politics of "resistance" advocated by Butler is thus carried out in Foucault's name. Are Fraser and Fraisse—among others—right (or at least partly right) to see in this Foucaldian—or presumed to be Foucaldian—"turn" of feminist theory, a turn that coincides with the moment when this theory is becoming "postfeminist" by turning against itself, the subtle form taken by a certain "accommodation" between (post)feminism and the global capitalist order?

No one better illustrates both the strength and the ambiguities of this "turn," perhaps, than Gayle Rubin. In "Sexual Traffic," her interview with Judith Butler, Rubin recalls the historical and theoretical debt of "second-wave" feminism toward Marxism and the revolutionary movements of the late 1960s.[17] Isn't Rubin's first major essay, "The Traffic in Women: Notes on the Political Economy of Sex" (1975), a perfect illustration of the "indebtedness" of the emerging feminist theory to Marxism, an indebtedness that Nancy Fraser also proclaims and emphasizes?[18] On the one hand, Rubin attempts to disengage the new feminist epistemology from the Marxist perspective by emphasizing the theoretical and political limits of Marx's thinking on the subject. On the other hand, she maintains her innovative analysis of the "sex/gender system" in the orbit of Marx and Marxism. Indeed, "The Traffic in Women" was conceived in the first place in homage to the work of Marx's fellow thinker Friedrich Engels. Rubin brings feminism into the embrace of Marxism, especially at the end of her essay, when she suggests using the new epistemological advances of feminism to support a critique of economics and a political project of the Marxist type.[19] Rubin's choice of title attests to the decisive imprint of Marxism on her thought: Rubin—like Irigaray, moreover, during the same period—prefers the notion of "market," and even "traffic," to the Levi-Straussian notion of the "exchange of women," thus drawing structural exchange toward market exchange and systemic analysis toward a historicized and modernized analysis of that exchange.[20] Finally, her subtitle, "Notes on the Political

Economy of Sex," indicates clearly that Rubin intends after all to focus or remain focused on political economics rather than on kinship systems. In "Sexual Traffic," a dialogue with Judith Butler first published in an issue of the journal *differences* devoted to the "encounter" between feminisms and queer theory, Rubin reaffirms Marx's importance and contemporary relevance. She even goes so far as to use the term "tragedy" to characterize a certain tendency to forget Marx's teachings and Marxism: "I find the current neglect of Marx a tragedy, and I hope to see a revival of interest in his work. Marx was a brilliant social thinker, and the failure to engage important and vital issues of Marxist thought has weakened social and political analysis."[21]

However, in "Thinking Sex: Notes for a Radical Theory of the Politics of Sexuality" (1993), Rubin clearly situates her attempt to theorize the disjunction between questions of gender and questions of sexuality (or rather of "sex") in Foucault's wake, especially following Foucault's analysis of the modern disjunction between "kinship system" and "sexual arrangement."[22] The anthropologist asserts in this essay that "Michel Foucault's *History of Sexuality* has been the most influential and emblematic of the new scholarship on sex."[23] In "Sexual Traffic," she relates her encounter with Foucault at length—a meeting with the man first of all, then with his text, and she describes her reaction to the first volume of *The History of Sexuality*, in terms that recall the erotic-euphoric evocation of the fetishist universe in which she had immersed herself not long before (we shall come back to this point).[24]

Thanks be to Foucault, then, and yet the specter of Marx nevertheless comes back to haunt "Thinking Sex." But this is no longer the Marx found in "The Traffic in Women." The name Marx no longer serves as an intellectual guarantee for the dream of a "humanity liberated" thanks to the deployment of a new political economy of sex, a dream that comes up more than once as such in Rubin's first essay.[25] Quite to the contrary, Rubin summons Marx to the rescue at the very moment when—deploring the social stigmatization in the United States of the various sex industries or enterprises, such as pornographic publications and firms, or "sex work"—she is advocating the social and cultural legitimation of the sex market in all its forms, in the name of a certain axiological neutrality of capitalism. "Marx himself," she writes, "considered the capitalist market a revolutionary, if limited, force. He argues that capitalism was progressive in its dissolution of pre-capitalist superstition, prejudice, and the bonds of traditional modes of life."[26]

And she cites a passage from the *Grundrisse* concerning the historical triumph of "capital" and the advent of "bourgeois society" where Marx expresses himself in these terms: "Hence the great civilizing influence of capital, its production of a stage of society compared with which all earlier stages appear to be merely local progress and idolatory of nature."[27]

Is Marx making an objective observation here about social progress under the "civilizing influence of capital" or is he mimicking the discourse of the self-satisfied bourgeoisie? Perhaps he is doing both at once. In any event, we cannot be certain that this pronouncement lauding the superiority of bourgeois society is not tinged with irony—as such statements often are with Marx. It is not certain, either, that he must be read the way Rubin reads him. To be sure, capitalist bourgeoisie ceases to be subjected to "Nature," which "becomes for the first time simply an object for mankind," Marx writes immediately after the passage cited by Rubin.[28] But the same Marx, in the same manuscript, also warns against what he calls "the deification of free competition by the middle-class prophets,"[29] and against the illusion that competition is the absolute form of individual freedom.[30] In short, Marx remains more circumspect than Rubin is willing to acknowledge as regards the "progressive" or even "revolutionary" character of the "capitalist market." And if he indeed insists on several occasions in the *Grundrisse* that "[b]ourgeois society is the most highly developed and most highly differentiated historical organization of production" (p. 390), he does not simply confuse "development of the productive forces" with moral or social "progress."

THE "VICES" OF SEX OR THE VIRTUES OF THE MARKET

How are we to understand Gayle Rubin's appeal to the "virtues" of the marketplace to defend the "vices" of sex? What are the forms, reasons, and effects of the complacency manifested by a certain (post)feminism toward the same capitalist social and economic order that "second-wave" feminism put on trial for a time, following the example of other modern "revolutionary" movements?

I have already stressed the central place that "fetishism"—its theoretical invocation and its ideological celebration—occupies in a certain "queer" discourse. Foucault designates "fetishism" as the "model perversion" of late-nineteenth-century psychopathologies, which recognized it, he says, as "the way in which the instinct became fastened to an object in accordance with an individual's historical adherence and biological inadequacy."[31] Freud, for his part, saw "fetishism" as a way of denying "sexual difference" in both its psychological and its biological dimensions. Fetishism brings to light the always-possible divergence between "psychic" evolution and the "biological function"—between "history" and "nature," as it were—in an individual's sexual behavior, a divergence or "deviation" that precedes or exceeds any question of "sexual orientation"; this may be why fetishism has become, symmetrically, the "fetish-perversion" of queer theorists. But Rubin shows us yet another analytical path. As she sees it, fetishism, and the sado-masochism that she derives from it, in a sense, are incomprehensible unless one takes into account the modes of production and circulation of the objects and accessories necessary to the erotic setup of fetishist and sado-masochistic scenes. I have already mentioned the passage in "Sexual Traffic" in which she clearly takes pleasure in evoking the erotic apparatus in question:

> I do not see how one can talk about fetishism, or sado-masochism, without thinking about the production of rubber, the techniques and gear used for controlling and riding horses, the high polished gleam of military footwear, the history of silk stockings, the cold authoritative qualities of medical equipment, or the allure of motorcycles and the elusive liberties of leaving the city for the open road. For that matter, how can we think of fetishism without the impact of cities, of certain streets and parks, of red-light districts and "cheap amusements," or the seductions of department store counters, piled high with desirable and glamorous goods ... ?[32]

What is this description of the conditions of emergence and development of fetishist and sado-masochist "perversions" if not an evocation, as "voluptuous" as it is "materialist," of the erotic resources of industrial and market capitalism, from the manufacture of rubber (inseparable, in the West, from colonial expansion), to the eye-catching spectacle of merchandise stacked up in department stores, not to mention the Harley Davidsons zooming down the highways that are part of twentieth-century "American" mythology? The landscape depicted in this evocation, between big cities with their red-light districts and their amusement parks (or "parks of attraction," to translate back from the French) and roads crowded with gleaming motorized vehicles, is a landscape of "made in America" industrial modernity. If "fetishism" is the modern perversion par excellence, is this not precisely because it aligns sexual "deviance" and sexual pleasure with the production of artifacts and the circulation of merchandise—in other words, because it attests to, and depends on, the material and cultural triumph of capitalism? Is it not a way of affirming solidarity between a certain regime (or "arrangement") of sexuality and the economic regime of merchandise? Is it by chance, finally, that Gayle Rubin resorts to the same lexical field of sparkle, shininess, and wealth to speak about motorcycles, silk stockings, *and* Foucault: "gleam," "glamour," and "piled up" merchandise on the one hand, "brilliance," "descriptive richness," "dazzling insights," and "proliferation" (of perversions) on the other?[33]

This historical affinity between the structural and cultural effects of "capitalism" and a certain (post)feminist position is acknowledged by some thinkers, ignored or denied by others. Nowhere is the complexity of its discursive forms and its stakes as manifest, perhaps, as in the treatment of another "topos" that has taken on particular relief since the mid-1990s: I am referring to "prostitution," a (cultural) notion and a (social) question that a certain (post)feminism has taken up energetically, both to test concretely its capacity to "subvert the norms" and to bring to light its quarrel with "second-wave" feminism (the feminism espoused, for example, by Fraser and also by Carole Pateman, about whom I shall have more to say later on) through the prism of a highly divisive political and theoretical object.

THE "WRONG" TYPE OF (POST)FEMINISM

The word "prostitution" (from *prostitutio*, which means "debauchery" or "profanation" in the Latin of Christianity) has not always designated "the fact of delivering up one's body for remuneration." Etymologically, to "prostitute" oneself means to expose or exhibit oneself in public (*pro + statuere*: literally, to place or hold forward, in front), as if the exposure of one's body, its literal "obscenity," were the source or the paradigmatic form of a sexual outrage. As a historical dictionary of the French language reminds us, the modern sense of the term took hold in the Romance languages in the seventeenth century, consigning its other meanings to oblivion.[34]

But an objection may be raised: While prostitution indeed designates a market form of sexual proposition today, this does not necessarily imply subscription to a capitalist ideology, or even positioning within a capitalist logic. After all, market exchanges are far older than the system of production, accumulation, and circulation of material goods that Marx called capitalist. What would authorize us, then, to see a certain feminist or postfeminist defense of "prostitution" as a form—avowed or disavowed, tranquil or uneasy, subjective or objective—of subscription to the capitalist economic and cultural order?

It is when she argues that the sex industry and market, prostitution in particular, should be fully integrated, culturally and legally, into the "capitalist market" that Rubin summons Marx to her rescue in "Thinking Sex": A Marx whose seeming apology for capitalism is all the more striking in that it is, a priori, unexpected. But after all, as Rubin writes, "keeping sex from realizing the positive effects of the market economy hardly makes it socialist."[35]

The question of "prostitution" plays a determining role once again in Rubin's account to Butler of her own change in theoretical orientation and political affinity: her abandonment of the terrain of feminism, defined as a practical and theoretical struggle against gender oppression or discrimination, in favor of a "politics of sexuality," which for her entails identification with the gay and lesbian movements above all. The narrative of her encounter with a prostitute named Carol Ernst occupies the very center of "Sexual Traffic." Fairly long (two full pages), it is explicitly constituted by Rubin as a moment of revelation and political conversion. This is the only place in the dialogue where Rubin abandons the dual register of theoretical analysis and intellectual history in favor of a "confessional" register. The narrative reports Ernst's "exploits" and the political lessons to be learned. The story is moving—Ernst was killed in a tragic automobile accident— and it helps make a heroine of its central character. In traditional rhetoric, this insertion in discourse of a simultaneously edifying and pathetic narrative would be called an *exemplum*. An instrument of persuasion, this passage, too, has a metadiscursive dimension, since it tries to persuade by telling the story of how the author was "persuaded" by the heroine of her narrative.

What lesson is Carol Ernst offering here, both in words and by example? It is a lesson in two dimensions. The first, presented explicitly, concerns the politically harmful effects of a certain rhetorical stigmatization of prostitution. Rhetorical recourse to "prostitution" (the word and what it is presumed to designate) generally takes two forms, both condemned by Ernst: either the term and its more or less crude equivalents are used as insults, or else "prostitution" serves to evoke in a paradigmatic way the misfortune of the female condition, seen as degrading. In both cases, the rhetorical operation is one of condemnation through verbal stigmatization of prostitution. "Destigmatization" then comes about through a change in labeling that itself corresponds to a change in perspective on, and in the analysis of, the prostitutional activity. Ernst does not conceive of herself as a "prostitute" but as a sex worker. (I shall come back to the multiple theoretical and political implications of this new label.) The second dimension of the lesson Rubin draws from her encounter with Ernst, even if it is not explicitly thematized in their exchange, concerns the need to break away from the identification with women or among women that is the basis for the traditional feminist enterprise. The mention of Ernst's brutal death may arouse in readers, especially female readers, a burst of sympathy that encompasses both the victim and the one who mourns her. This circulation of melancholic affects makes identification with the "prostitute" and her lesbian friend possible. In this sense, it constitutes an effective counterweight to the ambivalence that often characterizes women's reactions to "prostitutes," in the very name of solidarity among women. In so doing, it contributes to the disidentification of "women" as such with other "women" like themselves.

In the wake of this narrative, Rubin speaks out at length against what she calls, with reference to Adrienne Rich, the "lesbian continuum," that is, against the idea that lesbianism would be simply the most successful manifestation of solidarity among women. "She was right. I finally realized that the rhetorical effectiveness came from the stigma and decided that my rhetorical gain could not justify reinforcing attitudes which rationalized the persecution of sex workers," Rubin concludes, speaking of Ernst. And she continues: "I was also getting more and more alarmed at the way the logic of the woman-identified-woman picture of lesbianism had been working itself out. By defining lesbianism entirely as something about supportive relations between women rather than as something with sexual content, the woman-identified-woman approach essentially evacuated it . . . of any sexual content."[36]

Against Rich and against a certain "feminist" reading of the motif of female friendship in nineteenth-century Europe, Rubin takes care to distinguish lesbian sexuality from any form of "gender solidarity."[37] In fact, Carol Ernst is not simply a "sex worker." She is a "lesbian." Rubin remarks playfully, moreover, that in Ann Arbor, "sex workers," at least the ones she knew, who worked as Carol did in "massage parlors," are for the most part lesbians.

It is no accident that the critical "queering" of feminism, which I have also characterized, following the example of many female colleagues in *theory*, as a (more or less) postfeminist turning point, is accompanied by the "heroizing" of the prostitute figure. This "heroizing" becomes apparent in the centrality of a certain defense and illustration of prostitutes and prostitution among queer theorists, especially among those who, like Gayle Rubin and Gail Pheterson in the United States (but also in Europe, in Pheterson's case), or like Elsa Dorlin or even Virginia Despentes in France, identify themselves as lesbians. The "prostitute" cannot be the "subject of feminism," or at least not its "proper" subject. For, as these queer thinkers and activists make every effort to show, a "prostitute" is not a "woman," and even less so if she is a lesbian.

The idea that the prostitute disobeys the rules of gender is actually not a new one. To be sure, during the "apogee of capitalism," to borrow the formula Walter Benjamin used in his study of Baudelaire and the first "modernity," "gender" was not yet an "analytical tool" or a classified "concept." But wielders of language such as Zola and Proust knew perfectly well that in playing on the word "gender," which in French refers inevitably to the grammatical masculine/feminism dimorphism, they were bringing in the entire system of cultural and ideological oppositions that this term made it possible to index. Thus it is no accident that the question of *genre* arises in their texts as soon as it is a matter of pinning down a character who is a "prostitute" or of evoking the society of "prostitutes" and other *demimondaines*. The infinitely equivocal remark that closes the account of Swann's love for a *cocotte* is well known: "To think that I wasted years of my life, that I wanted to die, that I felt my deepest love, for *a woman who did not appeal to me, who was not my type* [French *genre*]!"[38]

As for Zola, he reports the vague thoughts of the guests who throng to a supper given by Nana, the eponymous heroine of one of his novels, in the following terms: "In order to be fun, supper parties had to be dirty.

Otherwise, if you put on a show of high principles and good form [*bon genre*], you might just as well be in good society, where you wouldn't be any more bored."[39]

If the prostitute, or rather the fantasy of a prostitute, triggers "gender trouble," it is because she transgresses the constitutive oppositions between masculine and feminine in the age of bourgeois "sexuality." Neither a spouse nor a good mother but a woman of the streets, she crosses the boundaries of the "holy family" and the domestic sphere to which women are assigned. She goes out into the streets, at night no less, just like a man. She also circulates, potentially, between social spheres. In fairy tales, scullery maids can become princesses by marrying princes. In the chronicles of modern life, among children of the masses, only "prostitutes" can attain the economic and social sphere of "duchesses" even as they escape marriage, the fools' market of the day. Thus Nana, a girl from the streets of Paris, lives for a while like a countess.

Spatial mobility, social mobility, power of economic exchange, legal independence, separation between sexual activity and "sentiment": We understand why "the whore" could have been viewed as "a man like any other," to paraphrase the provocative title of an essay by Elsa Dorlin. In this essay, Dorlin focuses on the masculinizing construction of the prostitute's body by medical discourse from the seventeenth to the nineteenth centuries.[40] This construction is obviously the translation, in the medical sphere, of the gender trouble induced by the social situation and behavior of prostitutes, at least as they are represented in bourgeois novels and proto-ethnographic literature, from Alexandre Parent-Duchâtelet to Proust.

Finally, as queer theorists have understood very well, trouble of or in gender necessarily reveals or produces trouble in sexuality, if not in sexual orientation. In his study of nineteenth-century "women for hire," Alain Corbin notes that Parent-Duchâtelet, a great observer of the phenomenon of prostitution and an advocate of its regulation, is obsessed with what he calls prostitutes' *tribadisme* or lesbianism, making this the defining feature of their sexuality.[41] Without necessarily seeing it as a determining feature, Zola and Proust, too, connect the transgression of gender norms with sexual "deviance." Nana discovers love between women with Satin, a girl who first refuses to submit to police control but finally gives in. Odette maintains a Sapphic relation with Madame Verdurin. With Proust, the language of "species" and "gender" serves, as we know, to point to troubled sexualities.

What does Swann, or rather Swann's formula, insinuate when he notes that Odette "is not his type" (*genre*)? That she *is* of a gender different from his? Or that she does not *have* the gender he desires, in an idiomatic substitution of "being" for "having"? What "is" Swann's "type" or "gender," then? And to what type or gender does Odette belong? Ambiguity wins out in the end. If there has been an error regarding gender, it is impossible to decide whether the error involves the person, the nature of the relationship, or both at once.

We can thus understand why "the (female) prostitute"—and I insist here on the feminine because we are concerned now not with real prostitutes but, to echo Simone de Beauvoir, with their "myth"—is not and cannot be the "proper" object of feminism. We can also understand by the same token how the (female) prostitute could have become the (proper) subject of "crisis feminism," the crisis having to do, as we have seen, with the subject of feminism (woman). That being locked up at Saint-Lazare should produce the same effect on "girls" as seclusion in a convent did for nuns, according to Diderot; that prostitutes became *tribades* because they were "disgusted with men" or, conversely, that a woman's lack of taste for men should have eased her entry into prostitution; that the opprobrium and social stigmatization directed at both groups should have encouraged the association between "lesbians" and "prostitutes"—the explanations hardly matter; each one is plausible and all are inadequate to account for the counter-idealization through "projective lesbianization" of the prostitute. What I want to stress here is that it is precisely to the extent that the "prostituted person" was not—or was no longer—a "woman" that she was able to become a theoretical and political icon of a feminism of the "wrong" type focused on the "wrong" gender: the queer (post)feminism that no longer identifies itself with women as such.

SEX WORKERS OF ALL COUNTRIES . . .

But let us look at the new designation of "prostitutes" as "sex workers," a designation that is now accepted by consensus in the West in the media-dominated space that shapes opinion and influences social policies, thanks to the alliances and collaborative efforts of sex workers, militants for sexual minorities, and queer feminists or (post)feminists. In English, of course, the notion of "sex worker" avoids the systematic association of a (feminine) gender with the word "prostitute." In French, the use of the collective term "sex workers" is what neutralizes the question of gender, since masculine plural forms can be read as gender-neutral. Thus a "point of view" published in *Le Monde* on January 5, 2012, and signed by a (male) member of the Syndicat du travail sexuel (Sex Workers' Union), Thierry Schaffauser, was titled "La majorité des travailleurs du sexe ne sont pas victimes de la traite des êtres humains" (the majority of sex workers are not victims of human trafficking).

Now, the French word *travailleur(s)*, especially in the masculine plural, refers, like its English homologue "worker(s)," to a historically dated conception and organization of labor: Again, according to Alain Rey's historical dictionary of the French language, the word took hold in the nineteenth century in Europe to designate the socioeconomic category of salaried industrial workers. During this period, the noun *travail*—"work" or "labor" in English—used in an absolute construction (in expressions such as "*le travail* [labor in general]" or "*le monde du travail* [the world of labor]") came to be used as an abstract synecdoche for the world of industrial workers. Thus toward the end of his life, Zola wrote a sort of novelistic apologue in a neo-Fourierist vein titled simply *Travail*; it depicts the creation of a working-class community and the social reorganization of work during the era of industrial capitalism.[42]

So we find ourselves once again referred back to Marx: While he was not the only one who theorized "labor" on the basis of a study of the social and economic relations between "salaried workers" and "capitalists," he nevertheless proposed the most thoroughgoing and influential analysis of the organization of labor in the industrial capitalist regime.

Yet if "prostitution" is—or seeks to be—considered henceforth as "work" in the West, for Marx, conversely, it is "work" that is a form of "prostitution": "Prostitution is only a *particular* expression of the *universal* prostitution of the *worker*, and since prostitution is a relationship which includes not only the prostituted but also the prostitutor—whose infamy is even greater—the capitalist is also included in this category," he wrote in 1844.[43] This text is devoted in part to the "relation of man to woman" as a relation of appropriation. In it, Marx criticizes the inadequacy of pre-Marxist French socialists such as Proudhon, Fourier, and Saint-Simon in their analyses of "private property." The "wholly crude and unthinking" character of the modes of "communism"[44] advocated by one or another of those thinkers is revealed in particular, according to Marx, in their conception of the sharing of women. "Just as women are to go from marriage into general prostitution, so the whole world of wealth—i.e., the objective essence of man—is to make the transition from the relation of exclusive marriage with the private owner to the relation of universal prostitution with the community."[45] Holding women in common, far from abolishing private property and ending women's alienation, would only extend the regime of private property, which would shift from being exclusive to collective. This is where Marx adds, in a note, the remark I cited earlier. But what does Marx mean, exactly, when he compares the situation of workers with that of prostitutes (male or female)—persons defined not by their gender but by their activity and their relation to the "prostitutor," as signaled by the neutrality of the German term Marx used[46]—to the point of making prostitution—sex work—a special case of the general condition of industrial workers? And what establishes for him, then, the equivalence he suggests in this passage between "the capitalist" and "the prostitutor"?

Let us note right away that Marx avoids distinguishing (or chooses not to distinguish) between the "proxynete," or pimp, and the "client." "The prostitutor" ("whose abjection is even greater" than that of the prostituted person, according to Marx) is an equivocal formula that can designate one or the other of these functions, or even both, since both enter into the definition of the prostitutional "relation." In this way, it would indeed be the "class" of men or rather "men" as a class (i.e., as "prostitutors," whatever specific role—pimp or client—men might play toward the prostituted person) that Marx would compare with the bourgeois class, since "the capitalist" functions in Marxist rhetoric as a representative of the interests of the bourgeois class, thus of Capital as a whole.

To understand the meaning and import of the analogy thus proclaimed between wage labor and prostitution, we need to recall Marx's main theses concerning the nature and status of the work in question. To be sure, Marx's thought evolved in this area, between the manuscripts he wrote in 1844, his early writings on "wages" in 1847, the 1849 lectures later collected in a volume titled *Wage-labor and Capital*, and the first volumes of *Capital*, which he drafted in 1859. But if Marx explicitly distinguishes "labor power" from "labor" itself only starting with the 1859 texts, we can still identify three major lines of argument in his analysis of wage labor that varied little over the years. The first concerns the equivalence between labor (or labor power), wages, and merchandise; the second, the fact that the wage laborer is a "free" worker; and the third, the fact that, if the wage laborer "owns" his "labor power" in his quality of "free worker," he does not and cannot own or "possess" the product of his labor.[47]

In what way do these theses clarify the Marxian analogy between wage labor and prostitution?

Let us start with the first thesis: It is because the work of the industrial wage-earner is exchanged for money, because, as Marx writes in *Wage-labor and Capital*, the capitalist buys the workers' labor power with money, and, reciprocally, the workers sell their labor power to the capitalist for money, that "labor-power . . . is a commodity, no more, no less so than is . . . sugar. The first is measured by the clock, the other by the scales."[48] Everything that is obtained by money or exchanged for money becomes a commodity, since "possession" of money has as its effect and as its only goal the acquisition of merchandise. With a given sum of money, Marx explains, the worker will be able to purchase a given quantity of food or drink. With a given sum of money, the capitalist will be able to pay for so many hours—"clock" at hand—of a worker's labor (or labor power). Thus if labor power is the "commodity" sold by the wage laborer to the capitalist, the wage itself is equivalent to a commodity, since it corresponds to the sum of merchandise that the laborer will be able to acquire by this means. There still remains the task of calculating the "exchange value" of the "labor commodity," a calculation that is inextricably economic and political.

This relation of money to commodities, or merchandise, is described by Marx in *Capital* as a quasi-sexual relation: Money "desires" merchandise and merchandise "attracts" money. Thanks to his famous rhetorical sleight-of-hand that consists in causing not "the merchant," nor even his agent, money, but merchandise itself to "speak," in a dazzling prosopopeia, it is to merchandise that Marx grants the status and the anthromorphizing privilege of "subject of desire." It is thus merchandise that figures in his discourse as the instigator of a market transaction that closely resembles, in fact, a scene of prostitution: "A born leveler and cynic," Marx writes, "[a commodity] is always ready to exchange not only soul, but body, with each and every other commodity, be it more repulsive than Maritornes herself."[49] Venal, merchandise is ready to "sell its body" to any buyer at all. The modalizer Marx uses here ("not only . . . but also . . .") suggests that selling one's body is a more serious sin than selling one's soul.[50] Perhaps because if

I sell my soul, as Faust did, I at least prove that I have one—or because life can always go on without "a supplement of soul" (*Seele*) but not without an animated body. In the following chapter, Marx again depicts "merchandise" as the merchant of its own charms, characterizing prices as "those wooing glances cast at money by commodities."[51]

It is thus as if every market relation were for Marx a prostitutional relation for which the initiative would be attributed not to the "prostitutor" but to the prostitute herself. Let us note in passing that, in this "deal," as in the one that takes place, even without their knowledge, between the wage laborer and the capitalist (since there is prostitution as soon as there is an exchange of commodities), neither Marx nor his "merchandise" distinguishes between "rental" and "sale" of the "body" of this latter. While Marx forcefully distinguishes "free labor," including that of the industrial wage laborer, from slavery, it matters little to him that the worker rents his labor power, and that through him the merchandise lends its "body," *for a definite time period*: As soon as the transaction involves money, the deal belongs fundamentally to the order of buying or selling, by virtue of the fact that money, which "is all other commodities divested of their shape, the product of their universal alienation," transforms what transits through it into merchandise.[52] Now, merchandise is made to circulate. Owing to its constitutive "alienability," it cannot belong to a single owner. "Rental," in exchange for a "salary" or retribution, of the body of a laborer or a prostitute—or of the labor power of the one and the service rendered by the other, if we consider their respective bodies as work "tools"—is thus nothing but a short-term sale.

The second major thread of Marx's analysis of wage labor concerns the statutory freedom of the worker. This freedom is asserted by Marx at various points in *Capital*. In a passage devoted to labor power (Book I, chapter 6, section 2), he thus writes:

> [L]abour-power can appear on the market as a commodity only, and in so far as, its possessor, the individual whose labour-power it is, offers it for sale or sells it as a commodity. In order that its possessor may sell it as a commodity, he must have it at his disposal, he must be the free proprietor of his own labour-capacity, hence of his person. He and the owner of money meet in the market, and enter into relations with each other on a footing of equality as owners of commodities, with the sole

difference that one is a buyer, the other a seller; both are therefore equal in the eyes of the law.[53]

The legal equality between the two parties involved in this exchange (the industrial worker and the capitalist) is guaranteed—and is guaranteed only—by the fact that each disposes freely of his own "merchandise": money in one case, labor power in the other. In *Wage-labor and Capital*, Marx reminds us that "[l]abor-power was not always a *commodity* (merchandise). . . . The *slave* did not sell his labor-power to the slave-owner, any more than the ox sells his laboring force to the farmer."[54] Freedom is thus the condition for the insertion of labor and labor relations into the regime of market exchange, the condition for the transformation of work into "merchandise." Reciprocally, the exchange of his labor power for wages frees the worker from the old forms of personal dependence on his employer. In his 1847 lectures on "wages," Marx was already insisting on what he called the "positive side" of the wage system, prefiguring the analyses that Georg Simmel would devote some fifty years later to the relation between a cash economy—by virtue of which money becomes the general equivalent of merchandise—and individual freedom. Thus we read the following in Marx's preliminary notes: "[A]s the workers realized through the general saleability that everything was separable, dissoluble from itself, they first became free of their subjection to a given relationship. The advantage both over payment in kind and over the way of life prescribed purely by the (feudal) estate is that the worker can do what he likes with his money."[55]

In *Capital*, Marx goes as far as to stress the profit that the capitalist himself can draw from the worker's freedom: "For the transformation of money into capital," he writes, "the owner of money must find the free worker available on the commodity-market . . . ."[56] Thus accumulation and surplus value would also depend on a free worker putting his labor power on the market. But if Marx insists on the worker's freedom and on the intrinsic relation between freedom and the market regime, he places just as much emphasis on the equivocal nature of this freedom as the "freedom to sell oneself." Just after noting that "[f]or the transformation of money into capital, . . . the owner of money must find the free worker available on the commodity-market," he goes on to specify that "this worker must be free in the double sense that as a free individual he can dispose of his labour-power as his own commodity, and that, on the other hand, he has no other commodity for sale, i.e. he is rid of them, he is free of all the objects needed for the realization [*Verwirklichung*] of his labour-power."[57]

Thus the deprivation of the wage laborer, who is "free" of everything, makes him dependent on the employer, who will allow him to realize his labor power. The "freedom" to sell his labor power then becomes a necessity. And if the "free worker" belongs to no one in particular, unlike the slave—if, as Marx writes in *Wage-labor and Capital*, "[h]e does not belong to this or that capitalist [emphasis added]," he nevertheless belongs "to the *capitalist class* . . . ."[58] Similarly, if, as soon as a prostitute "sells herself of her own accord, and on the retail market," to paraphrase what Marx says here about the worker, she is affirming her freedom in this gesture, she nevertheless thereby "belongs" not to *a* man, but to men, to the class of men. This is at least what is implied by the analogy between "wage labor" and "prostitution," and by the idea expressed by Marx in his 1844 manuscript that the capitalist is a "prostitutor."

This structural "belonging" of the free worker or the "prostitute" to the "class" that employs their labor power or their "services" does not encroach on their legal freedom. To this "belonging" that is based neither on an ownership contract nor on the always-singular violence of a gesture of appropriation, Marx gave the Hegelian label "alienation." The alienation of a worker is fully understandable only if we take into account the third aspect of Marx's definition of wage labor, in the case in point the fact that, while the worker may be the owner of his own labor power, he does not own either his means of production or the product of his labor.

In his lectures on wage labor and capital, Marx explains to his listeners at length that "the product of [the worker's] activity . . . is not the aim of his activity. What he produces for himself is not the silk that he weaves, not the gold that he draws up the mining shaft . . . . What he produces for himself is the *wages*."[59] Now, for Marx, the fact that the worker's "life activity" is only a means, his only means, of subsistence, or that "[l]ife for him begins where this activity ceases," attests to the worker's fundamental alienation: Since the work he "produces" or helps produce does not accrue to him, he is himself reduced, like a machine, to the rank of means of production of commodities or wealth alienable by the capitalist who employs him. He does not live in order to produce; he "produces" in order to subsist. And since he spends twelve hours a day "weaving, spinning, boring, turning," simply in order to earn enough "to sit down at a table, to take his seat in the tavern, and to lie down in a bed," this activity which is neither the goal nor the work of his life "is rather a sacrifice of his life."[60] In reality, the worker's alienation, or rather the alienation of his labor power, is two-fold: His labor power is alienated because it is put at the service of others in such a way that his production becomes the property of others, and it is alienated by virtue of the fact that it is exchanged for a monetary payment, thus becoming a commodity, that is, by definition an "absolutely alienable" good.[61] Thus Marx advocates the collective appropriation by workers of their means of production and the end of the wage system, entailing an exit from the market relation between employer and employee. The "dis-alienation" of workers' labor power is the condition sine qua non of their emancipation.

Simmel, as we shall see, offers an entirely different reading of the separa-tion between "labor" and "life" that results from the transformation of labor power into a commodity, as soon as this commodity can be exchanged for money.

But let us turn to the (post)feminist defense of prostitutes as "sex work-ers." For Gayle Rubin, Carol Ernst's struggle to win recognition for pros-titutional work was not simply a matter of "destigmatizing" that activity, along with all "deviant" or minority sexual practices. Ernst was also a champion of workers' rights. She led a unionization movement against massage parlor owners, and she fought to organize a sex workers' union. In the era of the triumph of financial capitalism and the inexorable de-industrialization of the West, while there are still people who work, there are fewer and fewer "workers" in Marx's sense. The productive industries are being gradually replaced by "service" industries, and "workers" are giv-ing way to "employees." The label "worker" thus resounds all the more as an appeal, if not to Marx, at least to what the name "Marx" continues to stand for. To gain recognition today as a sex "worker," male or female, is to claim one's place in the historical—and also cultural and social—lineage of in-dustrial wage laborers. The demands of sex workers and their supporters, in fact, evoke, in their language and their aims, the great era of the work-ers' struggles encouraged and theorized by Marx: calls for solidarity and support for labor unions; demands for decent working conditions, equitable wages and benefits, legal work contracts, health insurance, pension rights; and so on. After all, sex workers are sometimes actual "wage-earners": for example, when they are employed in massage parlors or bars. But above all, like the workers Marx described, when this work is their principal occupation rather than an occasional activity, they have no other means of subsistence, no tools for earning money but their bodies.

. . . GET RICH!

Nevertheless, through the reference to Marx and to the struggles of industrial laborers, an entirely new conception of work and the worker's status, an entirely new relation to the market economy, are brought to light, if not in the statements or political actions of sex workers themselves, at least in those of their supporters.

As we have seen, Marx stresses a paradox: The wage laborer's freedom is the condition of his alienation in the capitalist regime. Similarly, while the philosopher acknowledges that bourgeois society has put an end to the old servitudes and to the ties of personal allegiance that characterized the feudal order, his description of the reign of commodities, which have "seized power" thanks to the monetarization of the economy, is eminently critical. Here again, he sees new modes of alienation of life and liberty taking shape as a particular market relation is generalized.

What is striking, on the contrary, in a certain defense of sex workers, is the stress placed on their freedom, an apparently impregnable liberty which, in its forms and in its expression, may have something to do, paradoxically, with subscribing to the economic and symbolic regime of merchandise.

Thus in *The Prostitution Prism*, a collection of essays published in 1996 that has become the standard reference on the question of defending prostitutes and prostitution in the sphere of contemporary feminist and (post) feminist thought, Gail Pheterson places the emphasis, in turn, on prostitutes' "freedom," "autonomy," and "independence," attributes that are at once demanded and postulated. "Women must have the freedom to choose whether or not to work as prostitutes," Pheterson declares, citing the recommendations of the Dutch Ministry of Social Affairs and Employment, which activists like herself helped formulate.[62] A little further on in her introduction, she notes that "fallen women" "are punished for exactly the *sexual autonomy*, geographic mobility, *economic initiative* and physical risk-taking that bestow respect upon noble men."[63] Basing her arguments on certain sociological investigations, she notes that prostitutes who were questioned about what led them to adopt that line of work cited their desire to earn money and remain independent.[64] In "The Whore Stigma: Crimes of Unchastity," republished as chapter 4 of *The Prostitution Prism*, Pheterson justifies the comparison between the social position of a (female) prostitute and that of a lesbian in the following terms: "The prostitute, the professional, and the lesbian woman are models of female autonomy in sexuality, work, and identity. They are each independent of marriage for sex and money, and they are defined by their own lives rather than by the lives of men."[65]

In "*Red light district* et porno durable!," Marie-Hélène Bourcier, who writes chiefly about the pornographic film industry but who rightly stresses the kinship between the problematics of "pornography" and that of "prostitution," since both belong to the "sex industry" today, similarly asks us to believe a "porn" actress when the latter declares "that she feels *empowered* in the feminist sense of the term when she works, that she controls her acts, that she defines them performatively . . . ."[66]

In so doing, both writers are in agreement with the line of defense of prostitutes and prostitution adopted by the French Syndicat du travail sexuel (Sex Workers' Union). Thus in the op-ed piece in *Le Monde* cited earlier, Thierry Schaffauser, spokesperson for the union, strives to demonstrate that "the majority of sex workers are not victims of human trafficking"; in other words, these women and men carry out their activities on their own behalf, in complete freedom.

According to the Office central pour la répression de la traite des êtres humains (Central Office for the Suppression of Human Trafficking), cited in the *Le Monde* essay, 80 percent of the prostitutes practicing in France are of foreign origin. It must be noted that this agency essentially bases its statistics on street prostitution, thus on the most exposed and most impoverished branch of the profession. But does the prostitution practiced by immigrant women always mean that these women are victims of trafficking? Not necessarily, if we are to believe Pheng Cheah, an astute theorist of capitalist globalization who teaches in the United States. In "Female Subjects of Globalization," Pheng Cheah reflects on the status of the new female migrant workers in the context of globalized capitalism. He is particularly interested in women and girls from developing countries who offer their domestic or sexual services to clients from wealthy countries. Yet while he describes these women on the one hand in Marxian or Lévi-Straussian terms as "commodities in a circuit of transnational exchange that profits many parties," on the other hand he, too, insists on the ability of these women to assess their own situation and calculate their own interests: "These women are not hapless victims who are blind to their true interests and needs. They see themselves as full earning members of the household and are considered so by others because their remittances help to bolster the family's agrarian economy."[67]

And, he adds, speaking now of women who hire themselves out as domestic servants abroad: "[t]heir oppression/subjectification occurs not by silencing them, but by incorporating their very needs and interests in the fabric of global capitalism. Whatever the role of ideology in making the wills of these women migrants, they also go with the firm desire to improve their lives because this is how their needs and interests have been shaped by governmental technologies."[68]

Shifting thus here from Marx to Foucault, Pheng Cheah sees the expression of "desire" on the part of these women (as a desire for a better life) and their aptitude for acting in their own interest less as proofs of their autonomy in decision-making than as effects of their successful "incorporation" of "governmental technologies." It is by appropriating the requirements of bio-power subjectively and "embodying" them that female migrant workers become voluntary servants of Capital. Pheng Cheah nevertheless insists that these women are not "victims," and above all that their choices and their modes of existence do not depend on men or on their relations to men. If in his more "Marxist" vein he does consider migrant workers as "human capital" and as "commodities" in a circuit of transnational exchange, he does not relate this form of "exchange of women" to the position of these women within a "patriarchal" social organization. Moreover, he takes pains to minimize the argument according to which female migrant workers, by agreeing to exile themselves under such conditions, would be behaving as good mothers, sisters, or spouses.[69] And if he does not go as far as to say, like Gail Pheterson, that prostitutes are "defined by their own lives" (a statement that is at best equivocal, if not maladroit), he refuses to analyze female prostitution or domesticity in their contemporary forms as signs of servitude or dependency with regard to men. For him, as for Pheterson, these women are not "defined by the lives of men."

"Freedom," "choice," "control," "autonomy," "interest," "independence" (in particular with regard to men): Despite the reference to Marx and despite the mobilization of a neo-Marxist rhetoric in defense of sex workers' rights and in the social battles waged in their name, the conception of work and the position of the sex worker that is outlined in the discourses of Rubin, Pheterson, and Bourcier breaks—the appearance of continuity notwithstanding—with Marxist analyses of the alienation constitutive of the "free" worker. Marx called for the abolition of the wage system because that system transforms labor power into merchandise and empties work of meaning by separating it from the rest of "life" whenever the producer is deprived of the material or symbolic enjoyment of the product of her or his work. A prostitute, male or female, may well be an employee of a bar, a salon, or an agency, when she or he is not working independently. The defenders of "free" prostitutional activity, salaried or independent, for their part, see this rather as a way of escaping another form of "alienation" of the subject, the form that results from bonds of personal dependency.

It is precisely the transformation of the sexual service provided into a commodity that is considered here both as the condition and the sign of the "disalienation" of its purveyor. By conceiving of the market relation as a vector of emancipation, Rubin, Pheterson, and Bourcier, to cite just those three, distance themselves from Marx and fall into step, knowingly or not, with another late-nineteenth-century German philosopher, Georg Simmel.

MONEY, (F)ACTOR OF EMANCIPATION

In *The Philosophy of Money*, a masterwork dedicated to the examination of the modes, meaning, and deep sociological and psychological effects of the monetarization of the economy, Simmel devotes part of his reflection to the study of the relation between monetary transactions and what he calls "individual freedom."[70] The formula, banal today, is not anodyne. Simmel, in fact, seeks to show that the generalization of monetary exchange has helped shape the "individual" as such, and to make individuals the principal support—at once agents and stakes—of social, legal, economic, and political relations in the West. In terms that in a way prefigure Marcel Mauss's work on the modalities of social exchange and the notion of "person," Simmel shows that the notion of the individual, and with it, individualism, have developed in the West thanks to the generalization of money in exchanges, thus literally ruining the system of personal relations, solidarities, and dependencies that prevailed before the triumph of money. How and why? Because money is a breaker of bonds. Unlike the system of gift and counter-gift in archaic societies described by Mauss, the monetary system does not produce a social bond between reciprocally obligated "persons" who recognize one another through presents functioning by synecdoche as gifts "of themselves." On the contrary, it produces de-linking: I am not linked to other persons in any lasting or personal way through money. The one I pay, or who pays me, a sum of money is indifferent to me on that basis. If I have a debt, it is wiped out, and my creditor along with it, as soon as I have paid up.

Simmel thus tries to show, on the one hand, that money allows for an infinite number of "economic dependencies"—as distinguished from "personal dependencies"—since I can owe money simultaneously to a large number of individual or collective social, legal, or governmental agencies, and I can likewise receive money from multiple sources; but he also argues, on the other hand, that money "is conducive to the removal of the personal element from human relationships through its indifferent and objective nature."[71] In this sense, "individual relationships" are not "personal relationships" understood in Mauss's terms: "The modern individual" is not the same as the statutory "person" whose emergence and place in ancient societies Mauss described.

Simmel has certainly read Marx. Taking up Marx's analyses of wage labor, he nevertheless proposes a totally different reading of the effects of the work/life separation for industrial wage-earners, indeed for all salaried employees. Like Marx, he notes that once the modern labor contract had transformed work into a "commodity" measurable in units of time (so much money for so many hours; here is Marx's clock again), the worker "no longer feels subordinate as a person, but rather contributes only an exactly prescribed amount of work—prescribed on the basis of its monetary equivalent—which leaves the person as such all the more free, the more objective, impersonal and technical work and its regulations become."[72]

But, unlike Marx, he deems the separation of work from personal life conducive to individual freedom. The separation introduced between the worker, his tools, and the product of his work through the organization of the wage system may lead to the alienation of the worker as such; in exchange, however, it enables the autonomization of the individual "person":

> The separation of the worker from his means of production . . . would in a completely different sense appear as a salvation. This would be true if such a separation were to mean the personal differentiation of the worker as a person from the purely objective conditions in which the techniques of production placed him. . . . Money, by driving a wedge between the person and the object, not only goes on to destroy the beneficial and supporting connections, but also paves the way for the independence of both from each other so that each of them may find its full satisfactory development undisturbed by the other.[73]

Money has the effect of atomizing a society by disengaging individuals from the old forms of allegiance and community. A factor contributing to the objectification of monetized products and exchanges, as well as to separation and individualization, it also leads, according to Simmel, to the "atomization" of individuals themselves, through the "differentiation" (or splintering) and "objectification" of their internal components.[74] These latter can, here again, give rise to contradictory evaluations: Thus the worker's "labor power," which depends on his physical condition, is detached from his person as soon as it becomes a commodity, and the same thing holds true for the prostitute's body.

It is precisely in his analysis of "the typical relation between money and prostitution" that Simmel pushes his reading of this "process of differentiation" through money the furthest—to the point where the signification of the process becomes irreducibly equivocal.

Just as, for Marx, "prostitution" functions as the paradigm for workers' dependency on capitalists in a monetarized market regime, so for Simmel the "prostitutional relation" is the model, if not the essence, of the monetary relation. "In so far as one pays with money, one is completely finished with any object *just as fundamentally as when one has paid for satisfaction from a prostitute*," he writes.[75] Money cancels out the "personal" value of the object it touches, as it cancels out the "persons" of the prostitute and her client. Paradoxically, it allows persons to be "finished with" the objects to which it gives access, objects without "power," that is, without "personality" or "aura" once they have been bought and sold, unlike the objects given as gifts in Mauss's schema.

Like the (post)feminists I am talking about here, Simmel envisages the "prostitutional relation" only as a hasty transaction, a bargain that is over as quickly as it is made:

> Only a monetary transaction corresponds to the character of a completely fleeting inconsequential relationship as is the case with prostitution. The relationship is more completely dissolved and more radically terminated by payment of money than by the gift of a specific object, which always, through its content, its choice, and its use, retains an element of the person who has given it.[76]

In this passage, Simmel again stresses, in pre-Maussian terms, the difference between a monetary payment and the gift of a specific object, which, symbolically representing the donor's person, potentially creates gratitude toward that person along with a durable bond. In so doing, he also indicates the difference between those who used to be called "kept women" and prostitutes who, like "lesbians" and "working women," are, according to Pheterson, the real models of female autonomy. The "kept woman" maintains a lasting personal bond with her "keeper" owing to the "gifts" he offers her, since she does not know how (or is unable) to maintain control of her own financial resources. Neither a wage-earner nor independent, she is structurally in the same position as the traditional married woman, minus the legitimacy. Balzac's Esther, in *Splendeur et misère des courtisanes*, is a kept woman; what is more, she is sold as a lure by her diabolical *souteneur*, to the benefit of her lover. Nana devours men's fortunes, but she depends on them. Wildly extravagant, she demolishes and decapitalizes everything she touches, herself included, incapable as she is of appropriating the money she "earns" for herself.[77] These women have nothing in common, then, with unionists struggling for fair business practices and measurable profits.

But let us come back to the "atomization" of the individual himself (or herself) and its consequences, as analyzed by Simmel. The sociologist notes yet again that the prostitutional relation is indeed the prototype for all monetary relations, since it privileges "means" at the expense of "ends," or rather it takes the "means" as the "end" or goal of human activity, as the expression "having the means" suggests, in a way. According to this logic of means, an individual's body is no longer the synecdochal representative of the person but becomes one "means" among others to acquire "the means."

Constituted as a detached or detachable "object" by and in the market relationship, the body is then treated not as a scrap of being but as something one has, a possession of the individual that can be sold or debited, one that the individual can enjoy and put into play at will. It is in this respect that the notions of "individual" and "property" are intimately linked. We shall come back to this point.

In the wake of Marx and Mauss, a significant number of anthropologists, inheritors like their predecessors of one strand of Enlightenment thought, have deemed it possible and necessary to distinguish between things that are absolutely inalienable—*sacra*—on pain of desecration, and things that are alienable, that can be claimed for oneself or relinquished without limits, such as money, a commodity (or a "meta-commodity," as it were) that is characterized as "absolutely alienable" in Marxian terms. Might Simmel and his improbable heiresses have it right, rather than Marx and Mauss? Hasn't the old humanist distinction between alienable and inalienable objects become obsolete under the reign of the person (male or female) whom Carole Pateman calls "the individual owner"?

Logically, Simmel ought to defend prostitution, since according to him it constitutes the model and the most extreme form both of the interindividual relation "unbound" by money and of objectivization of the thing exchanged. But here the moralist gets the better of the sociologist, and Simmel in his turn appeals to Kant in order to denounce the reduction of the "ends of man" to his "means" and to stigmatize prostitution.[78] The fact remains that, at the end of his reflections on prostitution, Simmel's analysis touches on an aporia that owes nothing to morality. He notes that the process of infinite differentiation of individuals that the monetary economy has made possible has a corollary as troubling as it is seemingly paradoxical: To the extent that money, a factor of independence, has become at once the standard and the equivalent of the most varied commodity-objects, the individualization of social relations in the monetary regime has as its corollary the interchangeability of bodies and the axiological indifference of things and persons.[79]

FREEDOM, SOVEREIGNTY, PROPERTY

A prostitute (male or female), as we have seen, may be a wage laborer. But the ideal sociological, economic, and legal model that has taken shape in arguments supporting prostitution is rather that of the independent worker or self-employed entrepreneur, that is, an individual who contracts directly with her or his clients to supply a service. Thus we read in the opinion pages of *Le Monde* a declaration signed by Francis Caballero, a lawyer, and Sauveur Bourkris, the president of an association for the recognition of the social rights of prostitutes: "The prostitution contract is not a sales contract, nor even a rental or loan contract. It does not bear on a thing. It is a contract for supplying a sexual service in exchange for remuneration."[80]

For Marx, as we have seen, but also in a certain way for Simmel, whenever a contract implies a monetary transaction, there is "objectivizing" and thus also "objectification" or "thingification" of the commodity exchanged, whether this latter is a "service" or a worker's "labor power." This is why, in a Marxist perspective, the distinction between "rental" and "sale" is not relevant. In this sense, too, the argument made by Caballero and Boukris on behalf of sex workers challenges the validity of the Marxian conception of wage labor. Both sides subscribe nevertheless to the same definition of "contract" and the contractual relation. The legal notion of "contract," which formalizes "the agreement between two or several wills,"[81] presupposes the freedom and formal equality of the contracting parties. No "will" can, in fact, be expressed and implemented without freedom on the part of the subject of volition. When the contract is a market contract, that is, whenever its purpose is to exchange "commodities" of any nature through a monetary transaction, it presupposes that the contracting parties also recognize one another reciprocally as private owners. This is not my own claim; Marx himself says as much in *Capital*: "In order that these objects may enter into relation to one another as commodities, their guardians must . . . recognize each other as owners of private property. This juridical relation, whose form is a contract, whether as part of a developed legal system or not, is a relation between two wills which mirrors the economic relation."[82]

Regarding the interindividual relationship that such a "legal relation" outlines, he adds, in terms that prefigure Simmel's analyses: "Here the persons exist for one another merely as representatives and hence owners, of commodities."[83]

In her critique of the "sexual contract," the feminist political theorist Carole Pateman, in turn, formulates the intrinsic connections between the notions of "contract" and "individual ownership," thus situating herself in a direct line of descent from Marx. However, unlike Marx, she sees the contract agreed on by two "individuals" as the pivot not simply of labor relations in a free-market capitalist regime but of "the modern social whole of patriarchal civil society."[84] What allows her to support such a thesis? Once again, it is the analysis of the prostitutional relation that constitutes the crux of her argument. Pateman seeks to show that the "sexual contract" that formalizes the relations between the sexes and consecrates the inequality of their statuses and their respective situations does not concern solely the private or domestic sphere to which marriage and family relationships are too often relegated. Prostitution, which is a non-domestic contractual relation, constitutes in her eyes "the most dramatic example of the public aspect of patriarchal right."[85] She also seeks to show that, under the cover of free-market liberalism, "contractualism" reinforces and abusively extends the rights of "individual owners" of the male sex. It constitutes on this basis the most pernicious philosophical ally of capitalism *and* of patriarchy. "[S]ale of labor power, in contrast to sale of labor or the person, is what makes a man a free worker," Pateman notes in chapter 5 of her book.[86] In contrast, according to her, the wife who "contracts" a marriage is not free (and is thus not an "individual owner") since she receives no salary in exchange for her domestic work.[87] Excluded from what Marx calls the "economic relation of wills," she herself becomes property: By contract, the man thus has "legitimate access to sexual property in the person."[88] As for the prostitute, if she does enter into an authentically "contractual" relation in Marx's sense, she does not escape the process that objectifies the goods exchanged—even if these "goods" are "services"—of which Simmel speaks, an objectification that Pateman describes and critiques in these terms: "The contractualist argument is unassailable all that time it is accepted that abilities can 'acquire' an external relation to an individual, and can be treated as if they were property. To treat abilities in this manner is also implicitly to accept that the 'exchange' between employer and worker is like any other exchange of material property."[89]

In comparing marriage to a legitimate and lasting prostitution contract, since this contract aims, as she sees it, to ensure the man's permanent sexual access to the "person" of his wife, Pateman locates herself as a direct inheritor of the critiques addressed to marriage by the proto-feminist thinkers in the West who, from the late seventeenth century on, emphasized the perverse effects of women's economic dependency.[90] Moreover, by engaging in a radical critique of the "commodification" of the self—since, unlike

Simmel, she challenges the idea that one can really separate one's body, and even one's labor power, from one's person by constituting them as divisible or detachable "material properties"—she situates herself within a humanist tradition that is vigorously contested today by a (post)feminism that is also, in many respects, a posthumanism.

Pateman's critique targets not only the "sexual contract" but the very notion of "contract" and the "contractualist ideal" as a whole. For the "contract," inasmuch as it expresses or is presumed to express the "agreement of wills" as a free agreement, is the basis and legal form for market exchange. It makes such exchange possible and legitimate by masking the dissymmetry of the actual positions of the persons involved under the formal equality of the contracting parties. And since everything can be sold or rented, as soon as "individual owners" enter into a bargain, their contract—any contract—legally and factually establishes prostitution, which turns out once again to serve as a paradigm for the contractualist ideal.[91]

The title of Pateman's book, *The Sexual Contract*, clearly refers to Rousseau's *Social Contract*. The "social contract," a sort of founding pact made between the governed and the governors, is, as we know, a philosophical fiction that allows us to consider political bodies and forms of government not as reflections of some natural or divine order but as expressions of the general will shared by the partners making the pact. It is to the political manifestation of this general will that Rousseau, in an inaugural move, gave the name "sovereign."[92] In so doing, the philosopher, like Grotius and Locke before him, anchored the political order in the natural freedom and formal equality of the "contracting" individuals. For her part, Pateman seeks to show that the "social contract" contains a hidden contract of a different type, which, if it is just as conventional and thus potentially as modifiable as the first one, consecrates the nonegalitarian organization of the relations between men and women. It is as though the "social contract" were tacitly founded on a "sexual contract," as though the freedom and equality of one party, which the "social contract" reveals in the contractual act itself, were supported by the dependency of the other party.

In *The Price of Truth*, a work that deals with the antagonism between gift relations and market relations in the West from "the Greeks" to our day in a neo-Maussian perspective, Marcel Hénaff contrasts the "social bond" as an expression of the "gift relation" (between persons) with the "contractual bond" (between individuals).[93] In the wake of Simmel and

Marx, he identifies the latter fully with "market relations," hence this warning: "When equitable exchanges of goods are involved, gift-exchange relationships must give way to commercial relationships. There is a precise converse to this requirement: *Commercial relationships* are not capable of forming bonds between humans and cannot aim to do so. Let me go further: *The contractual bond* is not and must not be the social bond."[94] Hénaff, in fact, sees the imposition of the "contractual relationship" as a "model for all public and private relations" as one of the most serious questions facing modern societies.[95]

While Hénaff and Pateman are equally critical toward what they see as a contractualist drift in modern societies, Hénaff nevertheless warns against the confusion, possible in his view but mistaken, between the form and theory of the market contract, which he says is his exclusive concern, and the form and theory of the political contract, summarized previously. In a note accompanying the lines I have just cited, he thus states: "It goes without saying that these claims do not apply to the theories of the contract as founding pact found in authors such as Grotius and Rousseau. The latter involve a model of representation of civil society as originating from a convention assumed to have constituted a break with an earlier state of nature. This would involve a different and considerable debate."[96]

And yet confusing "social" (or political) contracts with market contracts is exactly what Pateman does. She sees in the development of contractual relations at the heart of the capitalist marketplace, as they regulate the labor market, for example, both an application and an extension of the contractualist theories of the late-seventeenth- and eighteenth-century philosophers. Is Pateman wrong to bring together what Hénaff thinks he can and must separate? I am not sure. Both the market contract and the "social contract," both the legal pact and the political pact, stress implicitly or explicitly the contractants' free exercise of their wills. And it is indeed because the prostitute is acting freely—one would say today that she is "performing" her freedom"—and because she is demanding contractual equality between "providers" and "clients" while fully "assuming" the market character of her transaction, that this "individual owner" of a new type (*genre*) appears to some observers as an icon of the free woman in the capitalist regime. Hénaff himself recalls the way a certain Enlightenment philosophy—hardly "Rousseauist," to be sure, in this respect—powerfully articulated the idea that "there is an essential association between commerce and institutions respectful of public liberties."[97] And one could easily show that contractualist political theories are contemporary, on the one hand, with the large-scale development of international commerce, and, on the other hand, with the beginnings of the dematerialization of "cash" (with the invention of bills and drafts), developments that hastened the capitalist revolution of modes of production and circulation of merchandise in Europe.

By pointing out the circular solidarity between the notion of "contract" and that of "individual owner," Pateman invites us to meditate on the link between "freedom" (since every contractual act is supposed to put into play, as such, a free will), sovereignty (as the manifestation of that will), and property. However, her demonstration lacks a "deconstructive" analysis of what connects a certain concept of "freedom" and the concepts of "sovereignty" and "property," both genealogically and intrinsically. To be sure, a whole feminist movement has developed in the West owing to and in favor of that triple call for freedom, sovereignty, and property, from the declarations of Olympe de Gouges and Mary Wollestonecraft to the slogans brandished in Europe and the United States during the 1970s proclaiming that "our bodies belong to us."[98] Marx himself recognized the usefulness and even the inevitability of the "proprietorist" argument in the formulation of a project of emancipation, even as he was fighting against capitalist forms of appropriation.[99] Pateman sums up this aporia as follows: "The idea that individuals own property in their persons has been central to the struggle against class and patriarchal domination. Marx could not have written *Capital* and formulated the concept of labor power without it; but nor could he have called for the abolition of wage labor and capitalism . . . if he had not also rejected this view of individuals and the corollary that freedom is contract and ownership."[100]

The fact remains that a project of emancipation based on this trinity—freedom, sovereignty, property—always runs the risk of being "overtaken," philosophically and politically, by its market "double": free-market liberal individualism as embodied in the contemporary figure of "sex work," conceived as the autonomous exercise of a commercial activity and as the affirmation of the freedom to "contract" without limits, since it does not recognize normative distinctions between licit and illicit commerce.

Let us add, in a final echo of Marx's theses, that by accepting the risk, or the opportunity, of market "objectification" of her or his work instrument—in the case in point, her or his "sexual body"—the sex worker helps extract this body from the domain and the domination—real or conceptual, but always mystifying—of "nature." By making the body a tool (for herself or himself) and a toy (for the client), the sex worker participates, in a way, in the realization of the inextricably philosophical and economic program of capitalist society that Marx described in the *Grundrisse*. Here are the passages from that work that immediately precede and follow the excerpt cited by Gayle Rubin as mentioned previously:

> Thus . . . production which is founded on capital . . . creates a system of general exploitation of natural human attributes, a system of general profitability, whose vehicles seem to be just as much science as all the physical and intellectual characteristics. . . . Hence the great civilizing influence of capital . . . Nature becomes for the first time simply an object for mankind, purely a matter of utility; it ceases to be recognized as a power in its own right; and the theoretical knowledge of its independent laws appears only as a stratagem designed to subdue it to human requirements, whether as the object of consumption or as the means of production.[101]

ROXANA'S LEGACY

The fetishist exaltation of erotic gadgetry, the defense of prostitution and the sex industry, the "subversive" use of the resources of the market economy, the rhetoric of "interests" and "rational choice" or of "costs" and "benefits"[102]: Do these constitute an ideological "perversion" of Western feminism and a deviation from its "natural" trajectory? Or do they help uncover, on the contrary, if not one of the roots of feminism, at least one of its original potentialities?

Carole Pateman situates her critique of the "sexual contract" in a line of Anglophone feminist thinkers running from Mary Astell, the author of a seventeenth-century pamphlet titled "Some Reflections upon Marriage" (1700), through Mary Wollstonecraft's *A Vindication of the Rights of Women* (1792) to the countless texts published on the topic in the 1960s, '70s, and '80s. Along the way, she singles out a particular early eighteenth-century "feminist" who is quite well known in the English-speaking world but hardly at all in France: Roxana, the eponymous character of Daniel Defoe's last novel, which was published in 1724.[103] Roxana is, if not its "author," at least the spokesperson for a proto-feminist critique of Western marriage whose force and power of conviction are unequalled. The novel is essentially a sort of picaresque narrative told in the first person feminine. The reflective pause imposed on the narrative by this critique is thus all the more remarkable; it is something like the modern, feminist pendant of Achilles' shield, the most celebrated *ekphrasis* in Western literature. Pateman cites Roxana's discourse on several occasions, even bringing in Mary Wollstonecraft's declarations on women's servitude in marriage as a kind of reprise of Defoe's writings.[104] *Roxana*—both the novel and its heroine— are thus recognized as pioneers of the theses that Pateman defends in her work. No matter that the novel's author is a man, inaugurating (along with Montesquieu and the Abbé Prévost in France) a series of first-person feminine narratives that will punctuate eighteenth-century European literature and help give it its proto-feminist accents.[105] It is precisely because, to paraphrase Rimbaud's famous formula, a fiction writer's "I" is always an other, whatever the naïve author or reader may say or believe, that a certain literature has always crossed the line between—and thus blurred the opposition of—genders.

But Roxana's anti-contractualism where marriage is concerned does not make her an adversary of all "contractual relations." The novel, which was initially published anonymously (like Montesquieu's *Persian Letters*), was first called *The Fortunate Mistress*, a title playing on the literal and figurative senses of the adjective "fortunate." It tells the story of a person who takes up the career of prostitution—"whoring" or "whoredom" are the narrator's preferred terms for describing her activity—after having been abandoned with small children in abject poverty by a husband she describes as an incompetent idiot. Unable to meet her children's needs, she abandons them in turn. Thanks to a series of liaisons, always chosen with care, she makes a fortune and becomes an exemplary manager of her property. Aware that she would lose all legal and financial autonomy by marrying, she rejects the marriage proposal of a wealthy merchant who had become one of her lovers. Some twenty years later, at the peak of her wealth and protected from reversals of this type of fortune, she meets her merchant again. Seemingly converted to her "equitable" version of sexual relations, he proposes marriage once more, on the basis of an absolute separation of property. He also promises to put real property in her name, and the title that goes with it. Eager for titles of all sorts (titles of nobility as well as titles to land), she gives in to the lure of this ultimate good fortune. In the end, though, ordinary morality appears to reassert itself: Persecuted by a daughter from her first marriage who is fruitlessly seeking her mother's recognition, the "unworthy mother" goes through a difficult patch that obliges her to remain confined, like a "real woman," within the domestic space of her good Quaker friend. But the affair is settled in the end by the elimination of the cumbersome offspring. The novel concludes with an evocation of the misfortunes that necessarily befall a sinner of this sort. However, neither the narrator nor the author takes enough interest in this moral to develop its circumstances. The vaguely edifying story of Roxana's ultimate reversal of fortune is covered in a single paragraph.

Couldn't Gayle Rubin or Gail Pheterson claim affinity with Roxana today—even more so, on several counts, than Carole Pateman? Isn't Roxana in effect a sophisticated Western prototype of the "autonomous" woman celebrated by Pheterson?

While her first act of "whoring" is clearly designated in the narrative as an attempt to escape the poverty in which her conjugal misadventure had plunged her, Roxana goes on prostituting herself when she no longer needs to, because of her overt taste for money and "the game."[106]

Pheterson notes in one of her essays that a particular lexical item that designates both the "play" of actors and the "game" of money—essentially, "game playing"—is a popular term used in the Netherlands to characterize prostitutional activity.[107] The "theatrical" episode in which Roxana disguises herself as a "Turkish" dancer has a metanarrative value, since it is on this occasion that the narrator receives the nickname "Roxana"—which will become the name of the novel itself—from her excited spectators. In this sense, the episode constitutes at once an allegory and a sort of obligatory stage in the process in which the heroine turns into a prostitute. It is in becoming a prostitute that she becomes "Roxana," a pseudo-Oriental dancer. This becoming-Roxana will be interpreted later on by the narrative itself as becoming "transgender." Toward the end of the story, when Roxana's "disavowed" daughter is maneuvering to get herself recognized by her mother, and when the latter is playing at being someone who has never "played the game," a loaded dialogue takes place between the two women about the "Turkish" incident. Roxana characterizes the game of the person she is pretending not to be as follows: "Why, *says I to her*, this was no *Persian* Dress; only, *I suppose*, your Lady was some *French* Comedian, that is to say, a Stage *Amazon*, that put on a counterfeit Dress to please the Company, such as they us'd in the Play of *Tamerlane*, at *Paris*, or some such."[108]

In England, as we know, women did not have the right to act on stage until the late seventeenth century. If men were destined to play women's roles, as we saw in "Theater of Gender," earlier, becoming an actress thus necessarily meant acting like a man. This is just what Roxana herself suggests when she characterizes the "French Comedian" she claims not to have been as a "Stage Amazon": The figure of the Amazon already referred, in the repertory of the period, to the transgender figure of a woman in arms and at war against men. Let us note in passing the amusing coincidence between this borrowed masculinity of the woman "in drag" and "Frenchness," French women having obtained the right to perform on stage earlier than English women did. Let us add to this the relations that Roxana maintained with her servant Amy, her agent for fiscal and other exchanges, her emissary, her double, her right arm, and her frequent companion in bed.[109] Roxana and Amy often shared the same bed and sometimes the same man, and Roxana could easily be classified today, if not as a "lesbian," at least as a "queer" before her time.

On another level, as I suggested earlier, Roxana embodies to the highest degree the spirit of commerce, that "first spirit of capitalism" celebrated by a certain number of Enlightenment thinkers.

In his study of "women for hire" in the nineteenth century, Alain Corbin notes the sociological and iconic link between prostitutes and tradeswomen. He thus recalls "the women who owned small mobile stalls, especially the many flower-sellers, who were often lesbians and haunted the streets of the center of Paris and the Champs-Elysées."[110] Similarly, he associates the provocative visibility of street prostitution during the Second Empire with the new forms of merchandise display, owing to the establishment and rapid development of display windows in shops. Paris, he notes, "had become 'the city of food on offer.'"[111] In so doing, Corbin is engaging in a form of urban sociology or anthropology, whose role in the emergence of "queer" or "sexuality" studies is well known. From Sébastien Mercier's proto-ethnographic writings on the "streets of Paris" and Restif de la Bretonne's musings on "Paris nights" through Parent-Duchâtelet's treatise and

Balzac's novels to Corbin's own work and Jill Harsin's,[112] the study of "prostitutional territories" has supplied a model for the contemporary cartography of homosexual communities in urban settings. Gayle Rubin was the first to recall, in "Thinking Sex," the debt sexuality studies owes to "urban studies," a field that in her eyes offered a key angle of approach to the problem of the "ethnogenesis" of modern sexualities.

But the urban commerce evoked by Corbin is commerce on a very small scale. As for Roxana, she is "a Woman of Business, and of great business too, I assure you."[113] Thanks to her "business," she acquires astounding knowledge in the area of speculative investments and financial strategy, knowledge she seeks to share with her Quaker friend on condition that she, Roxana, will also make a profit from leading her friend on the path to fortune.[114] We learn on the very first page that the heroine's father, who emigrated from France to England to escape anti-Protestant persecution, was an excellent businessman, very clever in his dealings. A worthy daughter of her father, Roxana herself becomes a "She-Merchant,"[115] a merchant "in drag," as it were. On this basis, she travels about as a man, or as an "autonomous woman," among the principal marketplaces of the day: London, Paris, and Rotterdam. She takes boats as readily as "businessmen" take planes today—a way of precipitating, following, incorporating, and embodying the movement of capital.

To be sure, this commercial proto-capitalism, however enterprising it may be, does not yet have the form or the scope of the industrial capitalism analyzed by Marx. It is not characterized by an overturning of the relations of production; more importantly, it does not draw its principal resource from labor (or, to put it more precisely, from the exchange value of labor power): Roxana continues to make her capital grow, even when she has stopped "working." But in her celebration of the generation of ever-higher interest owing to the intelligent investment of a fortune that was initially material (jewels and household objects) but that becomes more and more dematerialized, doesn't Roxana prefigure, in a way, the post-industrial capitalism that is characterized precisely by financial speculation rather than the production of goods?

Recent literary criticism, which has taken an interest in *Roxana*'s "feminism" and in its eloquent denunciation of the "sexual contract," has wondered endlessly about the "real" meaning of Roxana's anti-marriage declaration. Just before reproducing her general critique of marriage in the name of women's natural right to independence—a critique formulated in terms that announce *A Vindication of the Rights of Women* and that give an elevated, philosophical "turn" to her rejection of the merchant's marriage proposal—Roxana actually gives readers a different explanation of this refusal:

> I was obliged to give a new Turn [to the refusal to marry] and talk upon a kind of elevated Strain, which really was not in my Thoughts at first, at all; for I own, as above, the divesting myself of my Estate, and putting my Money out of my Hand, was the Sum of the Matter, that made me refuse to marry; but, I say, I gave it a new Turn upon this occasion . . . [116]

Thus the critique of marriage and the defense of women's rights are presented by the narrator as a clever "turn" played on the merchant, a way of paying him off in play money, in short, an elegant pretext for turning him away. The desire to keep the upper hand in the management of her money was, according to her, the real reason, the hidden motive, for her rejection of the merchant's proposal. Faced with the apparent duplicity of this double discourse, most contemporary critics have chosen either to take the narrator's discourse at face value or to credit the discourse attributed to the heroine. In other words, they have chosen to treat the feminism of *Roxana*/Roxana either as a pretext making it possible to veil the heroine's greed or, on the contrary, as the avowed truth of her position, whatever the narrator may say after the fact. They have made one choice or the other depending on which they judged to have the highest moral or political "return." Which is more serious or more disturbing: showing oneself to be a "feminist" out of "interest" or declaring oneself "interested" so as to attenuate the import of one's "feminism"?

Perhaps the problem is badly put. Rather than considering Roxana's feminism and her business sense as divergent if not contradictory positions, rather than believing that one is a lie if we believe in the truth of the other, shouldn't we think differently about the articulation of these two "positions": that of the feminist before (or rather in) her time and that of the "She-Merchant"? If "feminism" has successfully sought to make women's economic independence possible, conversely, hasn't the triumph of a certain "market ideology" contributed to the blooming of feminism in the

West? And what if *Roxana* were recounting for us, prefiguring Simmel's analyses of the relation between monetary exchange and emancipation, the history—not the reality, but the myth and the truth—if not of the birth, at least of one of the births, of Western feminism? In the contemporary debates and the current forms of (post)feminism, we might still have some reckoning to do with this (hi)story.

NOTES

1. PARABASIS (BEFORE THE ACT)

1. Janet Halley and Andrew Parker, eds., "After Sex? Writing After Queer Theory," special issue, *South Atlantic Quarterly* 106 (Summer 2007). The title of the special issue obviously plays on the confusion between two meanings of the word "sex" in English, with a reference both to the decrease in excitement that follows sexual intercourse and to the wholly "theoretical" question of what can be thought and formulated when one has taken—or abandoned—"sex" as an object or a category of thought.

2. Joan Scott, "Gender: Still a Useful Category of Analysis?," *Diogenes* 57, no. 1 (2010): 7–14.

3. This does not mean, of course, that such research was not already being done in France. As early as 1973, Hélène Cixous created a research center and a doctoral program in women's studies. Feminist researchers at the Centre National de la Recherche Scientifique, such as Christine Delphy and Geneviève Fraisse, also began to publish in this field in the late 1970s. But only in the last few years has the existence of such a research field been both acknowledged and supported by French institutions of higher education and research.

4. I am thinking in particular of "Genre et sexualités" (Gender and Sexualities), the new collection at the Éditions La Découverte headed by Eric Fassin and Elsa Dorlin.

5. The final sentence of the introductory volume in Foucault's *History of Sexuality* is well known: "The irony of this deployment is in having us believe that our 'liberation' is in the balance" (159). The statement in effect governs Foucault's whole argument. The "deployment" in question is what the author calls the "organization" of sexuality, designating thereby "the entire technical machinery" deployed in "the production of 'sexuality'" (114) in the modern West. This "technical machinery" combines techniques of speech (from Christian confession to psychoanalysis),

techniques of government (with the implementation of what Foucault calls bio-politics), and sociopolitical uses of new forms of knowledge (from demography to a certain practice of medicine for body and soul); far from having as its goal and its effect the repression of human sexuality, it has on the contrary, according to Foucault, helped "produce" this sexuality, placing us "under the sign of sex, but in the form of a Logic [and a politics] of sex" (78–80). At the time when Foucault was writing his *Introduction*, "sexual liberation" was still the credo and the horizon of the new struggles of women and sexual minorities that arose in the wake of the protest movements of the 1960s. What Foucault seeks to show, contesting the illusion of his contemporaries, is that the centrality of the sexual question in the modern and contemporary West is less the effect of a drive toward freedom or a will to liberation (even though he himself believed he had experienced this drive or will in San Francisco) than of a complex technology of power. If he speaks in his turn of "sex" and "sexuality," it is thus in many respects in order to dismantle the myth of their epistemological preeminence in the human and social sciences, as well as to bring to light the mechanisms of their political utilization and the forms of their cultural "hegemony." But even as he denounces the omnipotence of "sex," which he himself qualifies as a "monarchy" (159) and which he sets out to "decapitate" on this basis, hasn't he himself helped consolidate its "reign"? The fact is that, with queer theory, whose advocates claim on one basis or another to be followers of the Foucault of *History of Sexuality*, questions of sex and sexuality have made a remarkable comeback; the resulting philosophical reflection and scientific inquiry are perhaps comparable in intensity and effects only to the work done on the subject by Freud and his contemporaries.

6. Alice Jardine, *Gynesis: Configurations of Woman and Modernity* (Ithaca, N.Y.: Cornell University Press, 1985).

7. Eve Kosofsky Sedgwick did her undergraduate work at Cornell and later returned as a visiting scholar. Jane Gallop and Peggy Kamuf, two important players in the spread of "French thought" in the American university context and recognized in their own right as feminist critics, both earned their doctorates at Cornell. During their studies, their professors included Hélène Cixous and Jacques Derrida, both of whom did several stints at Cornell, lengthy ones in Derrida's case. Julia Kristeva and Sarah Kofman also lectured there. Biddy Martin, a lesbian feminist critic little known in France but widely recognized in North America taught there in the 1980s and '90s before becoming university provost. Judith Butler visited several times after the publication of *Gender Trouble*. Leo Bersani, Wendy Brown, Gayatri Spivak, Chandra Mohanty, and many others were also frequent presences.

8. Simone de Beauvoir published *Le deuxième sexe* (*The Second Sex*), a work that bears numerous traces of her American experience, in 1949, a year after the publication of *L'Amérique au jour le jour* (*America Day by Day*), a kind of diary devoted to her stay in the United States.

From this standpoint, too, the bibliography of the introductory course in women's studies given at Cornell in 1970 is revealing. This course, called "The Evolution of Female Personality: History and Prospects," proposed to study the evolution of the status and image of women, family roles, and the influence of the environment and social status of women on the construction of the "female personality." The bibliography that accompanied the course description was rather slim; not until the 1980s could one speak of a real "library of feminist studies." But *The Second Sex* was among the three books that were required reading, in its first English translation by H. M. Parshley (New York: Bantam, 1968; first published by Knopf in 1962). In the 1980s the most prominent representatives of "French feminism" on women's studies reading lists were Hélène Cixous, Luce Irigaray, and Julia Kristeva, and also occasionally, Sarah Kofman or Michèle Montrelay (on this subject, see Elaine Marks and Isabelle de Courtivron, *New French Feminisms* [Amherst: University of Massachusetts Press, 1980]). Today, these authors have almost disappeared from the feminist, gender, and sexuality studies curriculum (Cornell adopted the new program name in 2000); students are now reading "American" (including African American) feminist and postfeminist authors. But this (or these) new feminism(s) nevertheless remain nourished by readings from Francophone thinkers: the aforementioned "French feminists," still, but also and especially Franz Fanon, Michel Foucault, Monique Wittig, Jacques Derrida, and even Jacques Lacan and Claude Lévi-Strauss.

9. This is the topic Eric Fassin has taken up; see, for example, *Le sexe politique: genre et sexualité au miroir transatlantique* (Paris: EHESS, 2009).

10. On this subject, see "Traversées de frontières: postcolonialité et études de genre en Amérique," an interview I published in *Faut-il être post-colonial?* ed. Laurent Dubreuil, special issue, *Labyrinthe* 24 (2006): 10–37, and my remarks in "Les lieux et les moments," introduction to *Genre et postcolonialismes: dialogues transcontinentaux*, ed. Anne Emmanuelle Berger and Eleni Varikas (Paris: Éditions des Archives contemporaines, 2011), 3–10.

11. In its May 26, 2010, issue, noting the introduction of an obligatory course in gender studies at Sciences Po (an elite institute for study and research in political science), the newspaper *Libération* published an article under the title "Les *gender studies* débarquent en France" (Gender Studies Have Landed in France). The media flurry around this academic initiative tended to present the introduction of such a field of inquiry and teaching as a novelty in France, ignoring a historical reality that was certainly complex and neglected (or marginalized) in the "hexagon" but well recognized elsewhere. In the context of Franco-American intellectual relations, the metaphor of "landing," however banal it may have been, inevitably revived the memory of another "American landing," one destined to save France (and Europe) from the Nazi threat. This presumed new "landing" thus helped accredit the idea that the field of "gender studies" was arriving just in

time to "save" a field of study that might not have lived or survived without such intervention.

12. Judith Butler, *Gender Trouble: Feminism and the Subversion of Identity*, 2nd ed. (New York: Routledge, 1999); regarding the question of the act, see p. 185; for the characterization of heterosexuality, see p. 166.

13. I borrow this expression from Judith Butler, who uses it to describe the eventful voyages of the notion of "gender" throughout the world in "The End of Sexual Difference?" (see *Undoing Gender* [New York: Routledge, 2004], 184).

14. Obviously, this difference in meaning despite the apparent homonymy is not limited to the relation between words of different languages. As we have just seen, it is also an intra-linguistic phenomenon or property: Thus the expression *différence sexuelle* can vary greatly in use and meaning within the French language alone.

15. A proto-feminist Cartesian philosopher who has been neglected in French manuals of history and philosophy, Poullain de la Barre would probably have remained in oblivion if Simone de Beauvoir had not chosen to use a passage from his *De l'égalité des sexes* (Of the Equality of the Sexes, published in 1673) as an epigraph in *The Second Sex*: "Everything that has been written by men about women should be viewed with suspicion, because they are both judge and party." De Beauvoir mentions him again in the section she devotes to the ideological treatment of women in seventeenth-century France (Simone de Beauvoir, "History," in *The Second Sex* [New York: Alfred A. Knopf], 123–124, 152).

2. QUEENS AND QUEERS: THE THEATER OF GENDER IN "AMERICA"

1. Articles, portraits, and interviews appeared in *Libération*, *Paris-Match*, and *Le Nouvel Observateur*, to mention only a few press notices from fall 2007.

2. *Translator's note*: An Anglicism of fairly recent vintage used to designate a female performer, *performeuse* can have a somewhat pejorative connotation.

3. See Jacques Lacan, "The Signification of the Phallus," in *Écrits: The First Complete Edition in English*, trans. Bruce Fink with Héloïse Fink and Russell Grigg (New York: W. W. Norton & Co., 2006), 575.

4. Commenting on Judith Butler's "Melancholy Gender/Refused Identification," the American psychoanalyst Adam Phillips makes a very similar remark, which I discovered only after writing these lines. But he attributes the "paternity" of this "Platonism" to Freud himself, not to Lacan:

> If, as Freud suggests, character is constituted by identification—the ego likening itself to what it once loved—then character is close to caricature, an imitation of an imitation. Like the artists Plato wanted to ban, we are making copies of copies, but unlike Plato's artists we have no original, only an infinite succession of likenesses to someone who, to all intents and purposes,

does not exist. Freud's notion of character is a parody of a Platonic work of art; his theory of character makes a mockery of character as in any way substantive. The ego is always dressing up for somewhere to go. Insofar as being is being like, there can be no place for True selves or core gender identities. (Adam Phillips, "Keeping It Moving," in *The Psychic Life of Power*, ed. Judith Butler, 151–152 [Stanford, Calif.: Stanford University Press, 1997].)

5. Marjorie B. Garber, *Vested Interests: Cross-Dressing and Cultural Anxiety* (New York: Routledge, 1997), 165–185.

6. Let us note, however, that we are seeing an effort to *pass her language off* as English: The doubled "t" in "li*tt*erature" betrays its French origin.

7. The French LGBT community, which came together a decade or so ago and which borrows its codes and axioms as well as its label from a certain American cultural scene, has found still another way to transpose this translinguistic idiom: to mark, in "French," the non-coincidence of the American "femmes" with women (*femmes*) (or *some* women [*des femmes*]), even while flaunting the citational recuperation of the Anglo-(Franco)-American pairing "butch/femme," this community has adopted the word "*fem*," which makes the "femme" identifiable, thereby making trouble in and for the French language. This unprecedented *franglais* term, mixing Anglo-Saxon phonetics and French lexicology, is in favor with those Marie-Hélène Bourcier subtly characterizes as "identitarian/post-identitarian lesbians."

8. See Judith Butler, "Imitation and Gender Insubordination," in *The Lesbian and Gay Studies Reader*, ed. Henry Abelove, Michéle Aina Barale, and David M. Halperin, 307–320 (New York: Routledge, 1993).

9. Judith Butler, who is interested in the subversive potential of certain parodic "gender performances," offers her own warning in the second preface to the new edition of *Gender Trouble* (New York: Routledge, 1999, xxi–xxiii):

Just as metaphors lose their metaphoricity as they congeal through time into concepts, so subversive performances always run the risk of becoming deadening clichés through their repetition and, most importantly, through their repetition within commodity culture where 'subversion' carries market value.

10. See Robert Stoller, *Presentations of Gender* (New Haven, Conn.: Yale University Press, 1985). On gender as "presentation" or "(re)presentation "of the "self," see also the analyses of the sociologist of gender Erving Goffman, another of Stoller's American contemporaries, discussed in chapter 3 of this work.

11. In France, until very recently, the terms *gay* and *lesbienne* were rarely used to designate male and female homosexuals; the term *homosexuel(le)* sufficed, in its axiological and cultural neutrality. The widespread use of the borrowed labels today attests to a sort of spectacular "coming out" on the part of the French homosexual scene. The word *lesbienne* designates more than sexual orientation and

identity. Like *gay*, it indexes both a historical and cultural type *and* a role, in the theatrical sense of the term.

12. N. B. I include psychoanalytic hermeneutics in what I am calling "philosophy."

13. The term appeared for the first time accompanied by a first definition in John Money, "Hermaphroditism, Gender and Precocity in Hyperadrenocorticism: Psychologic Findings," *Bulletin of the Johns Hopkins Hospital* 96 (1955): 253–264.

14. The earliest formulations of "gender theory" are usually attributed to Stoller rather than to Money. Nevertheless, we owe to Money the first proto-theoretical definitions of "gender." But while both played an important role in formalizing the distinction between "sex" and "gender," and both sought to sort out the effects of biological mechanisms and sociocultural influences, each challenged in his own way the opposition between "nature" and "nurture," reformulated by feminist theory as an opposition between "essentialism" and "constructivism." In his writings, Money always tried to show how biological and sociological dimensions are intertwined, each inflecting the other in their interactions. He critiqued the sharp separation between (biological) sex and (cultural) gender that his writings had helped establish, based on considerations involving brain function. As for Stoller, trained in Freudian psychoanalysis, he set off on complex paths that have been little explored by the advocates and practitioners of gender studies. He distinguished, in effect, between anatomy and biology. Under the term "sex" he designates not so much a complex system of biological and anatomical markers as the coincidence between anatomy (visible morphology) and symbolic assignment to a sex. And if the adoption of a "gender" is for him an effect of the neonatal environment (especially the mother-child relationship) rather than an effect of biological characteristics (which are not determining factors in this area, according to Stoller), gender identity is no less foundational: neither incidental nor malleable, for him it constitutes the "kernel" of the self.

15. John Money, *Gendermaps: Social Constructionism, Feminism, and Sexosophical History* (New York: Continuum, 1995).

16. "By the term, gender role, we mean all those things that a person says or does to disclose himself or herself as having the status of boy or man, girl or woman, respectively. It includes, but is not restricted to sexuality in the sense of eroticism." See John Money, J. G. Hampson, and J. L. Hampson, "An Examination of Some Basic Sexual Concepts: The Evidence of Human Hermaphroditism," *Bulletin of the Johns Hopkins Hospital* 97, no. 4 (1955): 301–319.

17. In *Gendermaps*, Money explains that he "discovered" the notion of "gender identity," which was being forged around the same time in certain circles of pediatricians or sexologists that included Hooker and Stoller, in the early 1960s.

18. John Money and Anke Ehrhardt, *Man & Woman, Boy & Girl: The Differentiation and Dimorphism of Gender Identity from Conception to Maturity* (Northwale/London: Jason Aronson Inc., 1996 [1972]), 284.

19. On this topic, see the remarkable essay by Adeline Rother published online on the site of Cornell University's interdisciplinary French Studies program, *sans papier*: "La coupure implicite: circoncision médicale en Amérique," September 2009 (http://frenchstudies.einaudi.cornell.edu/files/sanspapier/ARother_sanspapier _sept2009.pdf; accessed April 14, 2012).

20. See the excellent chronological bibliography by Pierre-Henri Castel on the history of American transsexualism (as a phenomenon and as a concept): "Chronologie et bibliographie représentative du transsexualisme et des pathologies de l'identité sexuelle de 1910 à 1998," http://pierrehenri.castel.free.fr/pageanglaise.htm. An updated version is included in Pierre-Henri Castel, *La métamorphose impensable: essai sur le transsexualisme et l'identité personnelle* (Paris: Gallimard, 2003).

21. Stoller is one of the few doctors who have offered a very interesting psychological interpretation of this dissymmetry. Relying both on the biology of the embryo and on a psychoanalytic examination of the primary mother-child identification, Stoller offered the hypothesis that at the outset all little boys are "girls," thus taking the opposite tack from Freud. The male transsexual is then someone who not only failed to separate from his mother but also failed to "disidentify" with her. See Robert J. Stoller, "Facts and Fancies: An Examination of Freud's Concept of Bisexuality," in *Women & Analysis*, ed. Jean Strouse (New York: Grossman Publishers, 1974), 343–364.

22. Here, too, Stoller is one of the few doctors who based the assessment of the appropriateness of surgical intervention, which he supported, on an analysis of the "unconscious" meaning of the transsexual demand.

23. American racialist ideology and practices obviously constitute the inverse if not the repressed side of this credo.

24. Eric Fassin, who proposes a political genealogy of the notion of gender in the United States, notes on this subject: "Whereas state homophobia ran rampant under McCarthyism, when transsexuality became autonomous it escaped the homosexual stigma" (Eric Fassin, *Le sexe politique: genre et sexualité au miroir transatlantique* [Paris: EHESS, 2009], 48).

25. The "natural" body is literally (and some would add "is nothing but") the body received at birth, in conformity with the word "nature" and its derivatives (*natura* in Latin comes from the verb *nascor, natus sum*, which means "to be born"; "nature" is first of all "the fact or 'given' of birth").

26. "It can be said that one *is* a sex and one *does* gender," Diamond writes, in a formula that harmonizes with Butler's discourse (Milton Diamond, "Sex and Gender are Different: Sexual Identity and Gender Identity are Different," *Clinical Child Psychology & Psychiatry* 7, no. 3 (July 2002): http://www.hawaii.edu/PCSS/biblio/ articles/2000to2004/2002-sex-and-gender.html (p. 3; emphasis added).

It would nevertheless be a mistake to see in Diamond's statement merely a reformulation of Butler's propositions. The idea that gender is a matter of acts and not identity goes back at least to the work of West and Zimmerman in this area (see Candace West and Don H. Zimmerman, "Doing Gender" [1977], reprinted in *Gender and Society* 1, no. 2 [June 1987]: 125–151). It is because Butler's non-American readers are generally unaware of the American psychosociological tradition that they do not see what Butler herself owes, consciously or unconsciously, to that tradition. (On this subject, see chapter 3 of this work.)

27. This practice was condemned by the Puritans under Cromwell's regime and was abandoned in England at the end of the seventeenth century.

28. On the relation between the "oblique" and the "queer" intellectual and aesthetic undertaking, see, for example, Eve Kosofsky Sedgwick's textual and critical "performance" in "Queer and Now" (*Tendencies* [Durham, N.C.: Duke University Press, 2005], 1–20).

29. I should nevertheless point out the pioneering work in this field by the lesbian novelist Marijane Meaker: In 1955, under the name Ann Aldrich, she published a semi-ethnographic and semi-analytic study of the "lesbian type" titled *We Walk Alone*; written for a general audience, it was very successful. See the epilogue.

30. While transvestites in general are not necessarily homosexuals, as has often been pointed out, the use of the label "drag queen" is firmly linked, historically and culturally, to a certain homosexual performance.

31. See Esther Newton, *Margaret Mead Made Me Gay: Personal Essays, Public Ideas* (Durham, N.C.: Duke University Press, 2000), 65.

32. "When this maybe sweet but colorless person burst onto the stage as a towering dynamo of a sex goddess, the old thrill . . . shot through me. . . . We were both still laughing and it was perfect, all that art or ritual should be and do in front of a queer crowd plugging right into the spectacle of a metafemme and a meta-butch making it" ("My Butch Career," in *Margaret Mead Made Me Gay*, 211–212).

33. This is also true of traditional Japanese theater, Noh and Kabuki.

34. I am using the word "production" in its general sense but also in its restricted Anglo-American sense of "realization of a particular spectacle."

35. John Simpson and Edmund Weiner, eds., *Oxford English Dictionary*, 20 vols. (Oxford: Oxford University Press, 1989).

36. Here is what she writes in "Dick(less) Tracy":

In my view there have been two major themes of gay male sensibility and political action: one is drag queen-centered camp that highlights theatricality and humor, and the other is an egalitarian anarchism that foregrounds authenticity and realism. . . . [Camp style] has always centered around the figure of the queen; as such, it is not easily appropriated by lesbians. (65)

37. The emergence of a homosexual political movement in the United States is usually dated from the so-called Stonewall riots that took place in June 1969 in New York and other major cities. A sort of storming of the Bastille on the gay side,

these spontaneous riots followed a forceful police raid on the Stonewall Inn, a gay bar in Greenwich Village.

38. A rephallicization that thus entails the renunciation of an inextricably "abjected" and idealized femininity.

39. In this sense, the ethnographic work Newton undertook is marked by nostalgia. Recording the features of a vanishing culture has ethical and political urgency in the dominant tradition of Western anthropology.

40. Drag queens essentially set out to (re)play gender as a binary structure, according to Newton. As she writes in *Mother Camp*, in the chapter titled "Role Models" (reprinted in *Margaret Mead Made Me Gay*, 22): "Both the drag queen and the camp are expressive performing roles, and both specialize in transformation. But the drag queen is concerned with masculine-feminine transformation."

41. Near the end of "Dick(less) Tracy," Newton describes the attempt by certain gay theorists, male and female, to do away with genders and gender play as "a hopeless project": "Both camp and butch-femme do tend to dislodge gender from biology, but the purpose and effect is not to eliminate gender—a hopeless project, in any case—but rather to multiply and elaborate gender's meanings" (87). The multiplicity and complexity of the significations of gender to which Newton refers differ in this sense from the non-binary "proliferation" of the genders evoked and advocated by some of the female theorists who deal with these questions.

42. In his description of the *fort-da* game, Freud stresses both the compulsive character of the play—a compulsion manifested in the repetition, and *as* repetition—and the benefit of mastery that the child gains, thus transforming into action—in the double sense of "acting" and "enactment"—a situation (the mother's appearances and disappearances) that is experienced passively. The transformation of the passive experience into an active one happens through its scenographic transposition: With the *fort-da* game, the child finds a way to *figure* (and *figure out*) the drama he is living through, by producing both its trope and its representation. All this, of course, remains unconscious, including the aspect Freud characterizes as the operation of mastery.

43. Jennie Livingston's film *Paris Is Burning*, which came out in the early 1990s, follows the adventures of a certain number of African American and Latina drag queens of Harlem. These drag queens, organized in rival "houses," appear on stage during "balls" or "performance" contests. The film gave rise to commentaries and polemics in the fields of gender theory, black feminism, and queer theory, which was just emerging at the time.

44. Toward Derrida, Butler practices homage and more or less acknowledged borrowing.

45. Judith Butler, "Performative Acts and Gender Constitution: An Essay in Phenomenology and Feminist Theory," *Theatre Journal* 40 (1988): 538n32.

46. Butler, "Critically Queer," in *Bodies That Matter: On the Discursive Limits of "Sex"* (New York and London: Routledge, 1993), 312–313.

47. Butler, "Performative Acts and Gender Constitution," 526–527.

48. The dictionary notes that the familiar use of "to perform" as an absolute construction in the sense of "to make love" is blended today with its other use as an absolute construction: "to perform" in the sense of putting on a spectacle ("to put on a play, sing, dance, etc."). But the dictionary does not give a basis for this possible confusion of meanings. In both cases, the "act" (sexual or theatrical) is stressed. Finally, even if the dictionary cites a text from 1979 in which sexual "performance" is attributed to a woman (more precisely, to a bordello owner), the verb "to perform" used in this sense is usually associated with a masculine agent of the sex act; the action and activity connoted by this term are viewed as characteristics, or prerogatives, of masculine sexuality.

49. About the reversing reappropriation of the word "queer" by those, male and female, who claim this pejorative label for themselves, henceforth citing it to their advantage, Butler has this to say: "This kind of citation will emerge as *theatrical* to the extent that it *mimes and renders hyperbolic* the discursive convention that it also *reverses*" ("Critically Queer," 232).

50. "Heterosexuality offers normative sexual positions that are intrinsically impossible to embody, and the persistent failure to identify fully and without incoherence with these positions reveals heterosexuality itself not only as a compulsory law, but as an inevitable comedy. Indeed, I would offer this insight into heterosexuality as both a compulsory system and an intrinsic comedy, a constant parody of itself, as an alternative gay/lesbian perspective" (Butler, *Gender Trouble*, 165–166).

51. Here again, it is worth seeing what Butler wrote on the subject in "Critically Queer": "In so far as heterosexual gender norms produce inapproximable ideals, heterosexuality can be said to operate through the regulated production of *hyperbolic versions of 'man' and 'woman'*" (236; emphasis added). And a little further on: "*As an allegory that works through the hyperbolic, drag brings into relief* what is, after all, determined only in relation to the hyperbolic: *the understated, taken-for-granted quality of heterosexual performativity*" (237; emphasis added).

52. In the final analysis, everything depends on the context of reception: In the context of a "homosexual" or "transsexual" complicity of the audience with the stage, the drag queen's performance is experienced as magnifying, thus potentially magnificent, as is the case with the gay performances in Cherry Grove, or the performances of the Latina and African American drag queens filmed by Jennie Livingston in *Paris Is Burning*. Livingston's film came out the same year as *Gender Trouble*: Butler discusses it in *Bodies that Matter*. In the case of an ideological and phantasmatic split between the stage and the audience, it is the ironic (non-identificatory and possibly unsympathetic) reading of a spectacle perceived as burlesque that risks carrying the day.

53. I am thinking, for example, of the description, hyperbolic to an extreme, of the masculinity of the grooms of the Princesse de Guermantes in *Un amour de Swann*.

54. Preface to the second edition of Butler, *Gender Trouble*, xxvi.

55. Let us note nevertheless that certain *queer* theorists of gender performance as a deliberate and subversive parody willingly endorse this perspective.

56. Jacques Derrida, "Signature Event Context," in *Margins of Philosophy*, trans. Alan Bass (Chicago: University of Chicago Press, 1986), 307–330.

57. Butler, "Critically Queer," 234.

58. See J. L. Austin, *How to Do Things with Words: The William James Lectures Delivered at Harvard University in 1955*, ed. J. O. Urmson (Oxford: Clarendon Press, 1962). Austin himself acknowledges more than once, during his twelve lectures on the subject, that the distinctions he proposes are neither absolutely rigorous nor assured.

59. Derrida, "Signature Event Context," 316.

60. Ibid., 321.

61. Ibid., 323.

62. Ibid., 326.

63. Ibid., 324.

64. See Judith Butler, *Excitable Speech: A Politics of the Performative* (New York: Routledge, 1997). In her preface to the 1999 re-edition of *Gender Trouble*, Butler describes her project in *Excitable Speech* in the following terms: "In *Excitable Speech*, I sought to show that the speech act is at once performed (and thus theatrical, presented to an audience, subject to interpretation), and linguistic, inducing a set of effects through its implied relation to linguistic conventions. If one wonders how a linguistic theory of the speech act relates to bodily gestures, one need only consider that speech itself is a bodily act with specific linguistic consequences. Thus speech belongs exclusively neither to corporeal presentation nor to language, and its status as word and deed is necessarily ambiguous" (Butler, *Gender Trouble*, xxvii).

65. Judith Butler, *The Psychic Life of Power: Theories in Subjection* (Stanford, Calif.: Stanford University Press, 1997). If the lexicon of performance is redeployed on a massive scale in this collection, the notion of "performative"—qualified by Butler herself as "linguistic" in its Austinian-Derridean sense—is mobilized exactly twice, in the essay devoted to the Althusserian problematic of interpellation. See "'Conscience Doth Make Subjects of Us All': Althusser's Subjection," *Psychic Life*, 110, 114.

66. "Such acts, gestures, enactments, generally construed, are performative in the sense that the essence or identity that they otherwise purport to express are *fabrications* manufactured and sustained through corporeal signs and other discursive means" (*Gender Trouble*, 185).

67. Michel Foucault, *Discipline and Punish: The Birth of the Prison*, trans. Alan Sheridan (New York: Pantheon Books, 1977).

68. "*Discipline and Punish* can be read as Foucault's effort to rewrite Nietzsche's doctrine of internalization . . . . In the context of prisoners, Foucault writes, the strategy has not been to enforce a repression of their desires but to compel their bodies to signify the prohibitive law as their very essence, style, and necessity. *That law is not literally internalized, but incorporated* . . ." (Butler, *Gender Trouble*, 183; emphasis added).

69. Let us note that, for Abraham and Torok, the notion of "incorporation" includes a theatrical dimension. Because "incorporation" is a process of *phantasmatic* internalization and not a process of "actual" absorption of the object within the ego (a process that Abraham and Torok call "introjection"), it manifests itself in behaviors that externalize the phantasmatic scenario by staging it. In the wake of Abraham and Torok, Butler characterizes melancholic identification and consequently gender identity as a process of embodiment, theatrical *because it is phantasmatic*, of the gender of the loved/disavowed object. Melancholic identification takes the form of a corporeal and discursive mimetics; in other words, it is akin to what is ordinarily designated in French as *incarnation*, in the sense in which one "incarnates" or embodies a character.

70. "We succeeded in explaining the painful disorder of melancholia by supposing that [in those suffering from it] an object which was lost has been set up again inside the ego . . . At that time, however, we did not appreciate the full significance of this process and did not know how common and how typical it is. Since then we have come to understand that this kind of substitution has a great share in determining the form taken by the ego and that it makes an essential contribution towards building up what is called its 'character'" (Sigmund Freud, *The Ego and the Id*, in *The Standard Edition of the Complete Psychological Works of Sigmund Freud*, ed. and trans. James Strachey, in collaboration with Anna Freud, assisted by Alix Strachey and Alan Tyson (London: Hogarth Press, 1953–1974), vol. 19, p. 28.

71. Relying for her own part, too, on a certain reading of Freud, Irigaray had already described the process through which a little girl becomes a "woman" as a melancholic process based on "renunciation" of the maternal love object, in Luce Irigaray, "The Blind Spot of an Old Dream of Symmetry," *Speculum of the Other Woman*, trans. Gillian C. Gill (Ithaca, N.Y.: Cornell University Press, 1974), 68–73.

72. "The heterosexual logic that requires that identification and desire be mutually exclusive is one of the most reductive of heterosexism's psychological instruments: if one identifies *as* a given gender one must desire a different gender. On the one hand, there is no one femininity with which to identify . . . On the other hand, it is hardly descriptive of the complex dynamic exchanges of lesbian and gay rela-

tionships to presume that homosexual identifications 'mirror' or replicate one another. The vocabulary for describing the difficult play, crossing, and destabilization of masculine and feminine identifications within homosexuality has only begun to emerge within theoretical language" ("Critically Queer," 239).

73. Judith Butler, "Gender Is Burning: Questions of Appropriation and Subversion," in *Bodies That Matter*, 121–140.

74. Ibid., 129.

75. "Psychoanalysis argues . . . that what is exteriorized or performed can only be understood through reference to what is barred from the signifiers and from the domain of corporeal legibility" (Butler, "Gender Is Burning," 234).

76. Butler, "Gender Is Burning," 234.

77. In "The End of Sexual Difference?," Butler extends her analysis of the "unperformable," understood as that which escapes or resists, and at the same time conditions, the performance of gender, to the entire set of speech acts and bodily acts: "In my view, performativity is not just about speech acts. It is also about bodily acts. . . . *There is always a dimension of bodily life that cannot be fully represented, even as it works as the condition and activating condition of language*" (*Undoing Gender* [New York: Routledge, 2004], 198; emphasis added). It is here, where the Butlerian performative act draws its force and its intelligibility not first of all from what it "institutes" or "produces" but from what it excludes from its performance, that it differs most radically from the so-called "linguistic" conception of performativity (Austin revisited by Derrida). As Monique David-Ménard accurately notes in "L'institution des corps vivants selon Judith Butler," if "in linguistics, . . . the performative has as its meaning that which it accomplishes, . . . it is nowhere indicated that this speech act forecloses other aspects of meaning in order to be achieved" (Monique David-Ménard, *Sexualités, genres et mélancolie: s'entretenir avec Judith Butler* [Paris: Campagne première, 2009], 209). For Butler, on the contrary, the performative act has not only an "instituting power, thus it "has as its meaning" not only "that which it accomplishes"; it always creates both a field of intelligibility of the thing performed *and* a field constituted by what turns out to be excluded from the performance. What is excluded from and by the performance—the "unperformable"—thus turns out to be excluded from the thinkable and from the livable, in such a way that the powers of the "performative" and of the "normative" also come to coincide, as David-Ménard goes on to note (210). But, as is often the case in Butler's logic, this field of "the unperformable" traced by its absence in performance is sometimes considered as an effect (both residual and irreducible) of the latter, and sometimes as its "condition of activation."

78. Butler recalls in her introduction that Foucault is "notoriously taciturn on the topic of the psyche" (*Psychic Life*, 18).

79. Butler, *Psychic Life*, 19.

80. Ibid., 21.

81. Judith Butler, "Melancholy Gender / Refused Identification," in *Psychic Life*, 132–150.

82. Ibid., 146.

83. Butler, *Psychic Life*, 148. In the paragraph that follows this statement, Butler is particularly concerned with warning against the effects of identitary rigidity that result, paradoxically, from the melancholic fixation of certain homosexual persons on a heterosexuality that is all the more affirmed in its excluding unity to the extent that it is explicitly disavowed.

84. On the question of the gender/sexuality chiasmus in Butler, and on the relevance and limitations of this model for understanding sexuality, see the excellent article by Alain Lemosof, "Roc de *queer*," in *Sexualités, genres et mélancolie*, ed. Monique David-Ménard, 99–122.

85. Butler evokes "the *critical promise* of drag" in "Critically Queer," 237.

86. Let us recall that the French word *sortie*, translated by "exit" or "way out," provides the title of Hélène Cixous's "Sorties: Out and Out: Attacks/Ways Out/ Forays," in *The Newly-Born Woman*, ed. Hélène Cixous and Catherine Clément, trans. Betsy Wing, introduction by Sandra M. Gilbert (Minneapolis: University of Minnesota Press, 1986).

87. Butler, "Gender Is Burning," 124.

88. Ibid., 137.

89. See especially the conclusion of "The Lesbian Phallus and the Morphological Imaginary," in *Bodies That Matter*, 88–91.

90. Some of the drag queens who "perform their gender" in these productions are "in transition" (i.e., going through a sex change).

91. Butler, "Gender Is Burning," 137.

92. "The critical promise of drag," Butler writes in "Critically Queer," "does not have to do with the proliferation of genders, as if a sheer increase in numbers would do the job, but rather with the exposure or [*sic*] the failure of heterosexual regimes ever fully to legislate or contain their own ideals" (237). In so doing, Butler takes a stand once more against a certain queer celebration of the proliferating multitude of genders, as soon as sexual identity is no longer constrained or limited by the binary structure of sexual difference.

93. The "bear" gender, a relatively recent invention, combines masculinity in an original way with a form of motherliness, the two merging in the figure of a big teddy bear.

94. Esther Newton, "The Mythic Mannish Lesbian," in *Margaret Mead Made Me Gay*, 176–188.

95. On the invention of modern sexualities in Europe and particularly in France, see the work of the American intellectual historian Carolyn Dean, especially *Sexuality and Modern Western Culture* (New York: Twayne, 1996) and *The Frail*

Social Body: Pornography, Homosexuality and Other Fantasies in Interwar France (Berkeley: University of California Press, 2000).

96. Newton, "The Mythic Mannish Lesbian," 180.

97. Ibid., 181.

98. Freud, "Femininity," 131.

99. Newton, "The Mythic Mannish Lesbian," 182.

100. Ibid., 187.

101. Ibid.

102. "The vocabulary for describing the difficult play, crossing, and destabilization of masculine and feminine identifications within homosexuality has only begun to emerge within theoretical language.... The thought of sexual difference *within* homosexuality has yet to be theorized in its complexity" (Butler, "Critically Queer," 239).

103. "The idea that butch and femme are in some sense 'replicas' or 'copies' of heterosexual exchange underestimates the erotic significance of these identities as internally dissonant and complex in their resignification of the hegemonic categories by which they are enabled" (Butler, *Gender Trouble*, 168).

104. "If this is the production of the black transsexual for an exoticizing white gaze, is it not also the transsexualization of lesbian desire?" (Butler, "Gender Is Burning," 135).

105. Judith Butler, "Against Proper Objects," *differences* 6.2–3 (1994), reprinted in *Feminism Meets Queer Theory*, ed. Naomi Schor and Elizabeth Weed (Bloomington: Indiana University Press, 1997), 1–30.

106. See, respectively, Gayle Rubin, "The Traffic in Women: Notes on the 'Political Economy' of Sex," in *Toward an Anthropology of Women*, ed. Rayna Reiter, 157–210 (New York: Monthly Review Press, 1975), and "Thinking Sex: Notes for a Radical Theory of the Politics of Sexuality," in *The Lesbian and Gay Studies Reader*, 3–44.

107. Butler devotes several pages of *Gender Trouble* (98–102) to the analyses of Lévi-Strauss, Lacan, and Freud that Rubin offers in "The Traffic in Women." She salutes Rubin's "extraordinary work" again in the preface to the second edition of her book (1999). Finally, she reiterates her debt to Rubin at some length in "Sexual Traffic": "what interested me in 'The Traffic in Women' was that you, by using a term that comes from American sociological discourse—"gender"—by using that term, you actually made gender less fixed ... So I think that what you produced was an amalgamation of positions which I very much appreciated, and it became one of the reasons I went with gender myself in *Gender Trouble*" (Rubin with Butler, "Sexual Traffic: An Interview with Judith Butler," *Feminism Meets Queer Theory*, 73–74.

108. In Claude Lévi-Strauss, *The View from Afar*, trans. Joachim Neugroschel and Phoebe Hoss (New York: Basic Books, 1985), 39–62. The essay on families dates from 1956.

109. The graphic emphasis on the definite article "The" on the cover of the reader (*The Lesbian and Gay Studies Reader*) clearly indicates that the anthology claims a position of authority on the question from the outset.

110. Rubin, "Thinking Sex," 32).

111. In particular, Rubin denounces the objective collusion of the anti-pornography campaign led by Catharine MacKinnon and Andrea Dworkin, two important figures of American feminism, with the defense of the moral order orchestrated by the advocates of American Puritanism.

112. "In the English language, the word 'sex' has two very different meanings. It means gender and gender identity, as in 'the female sex' or 'the male sex'. But it also refers to sexual activity, lust, intercourse, and arousal, as in 'to have sex'. This semantic merging reflects a cultural assumption that sexuality is reducible to sexual intercourse and that it is a function of the relations between women and men. The cultural fusion of gender with sexuality has given rise to the idea that a theory of sexuality may be derived directly out of a theory of gender" (Rubin, "Thinking Sex," 32).

113. "Feminist conceptual tools were developed to detect and analyze gender-based hierarchies. To the extent that these overlap with erotic stratifications, feminist theory has some explanatory power. But as issues become less those of gender and more those of sexuality, feminist analysis becomes misleading and often irrelevant. . . . In the long run, feminism's critique of gender hierarchy must be incorporated into a radical theory of sex, and the critique of sexual oppression should enrich feminism. But an autonomous theory and politics specific to sexuality must be developed" (Rubin, "Thinking Sex," 34)

114. "Lesbian feminist ideology has mostly analyzed the oppression of lesbians in terms of the oppression of women. However, lesbians are also oppressed as queers and perverts, by the operation of sexual, not gender, stratification. Although it pains many lesbians to think about it, the fact is that lesbians have shared many of the sociological features and suffered from many of the same social penalties as have gay men, sadomasochists, transvestites, and prostitutes" (Rubin, "Thinking Sex," 33).

115. See Rubin, "The Traffic in Women": "Ultimately, a thoroughgoing feminist revolution would liberate more than women. It would liberate forms of sexual expression, and it would liberate human personality from the straightjacket [*sic*] of gender" (200); "I personally feel that the feminist movement must dream of even more than the elimination of the oppression of women. It must dream of the elimination of obligatory sexualities and sex roles" (204).

116. On several occasions, Rubin speaks out against this attempt to "make sense" of the variety of sexual practices. "Making sense" of "sexual practices" is, of course, the goal, or at least one of the aims, of psychoanalysis. In "Thinking Sex," she deplores the fact that sexual acts are "burdened with an excess of significance" (11). Elsewhere, she rejects the psychoanalytic interpretation of fetishism in favor of an analysis of its material and historical conditions of emergence in the West

(see Rubin with Butler, "Sexual Traffic": Interview with Judith Butler," in *Feminism Meets Queer Theory*, 85; see also my comments in chapters 4 and 5 of this work.

117. See Biddy Martin, "Extraordinary Homosexuals and Fear of Being Ordinary," published in the same volume and reprinted in *Femininity Played Straight: The Significance of Being Lesbian* (New York: Routledge, 1996), 45–70.

118. Judith Butler, "Against Proper Objects," in *Feminism Meets Queer Theory*, 23. Butler is alluding here to Luce Irigaray's book *Ce sexe qui n'en est pas un*, translated in English by Catherine Porter under the title *This Sex Which Is Not One*.

119. See chapter 4 of this work.

120. The term "gay male leather community" designates the "leather" and "SM" gay subculture in San Francisco. The French word for leather, *cuir*, is an approximate homonym of "queer."

121. Rubin with Butler, "Sexual Traffic," 102–104; emphasis added.

122. Ibid., 104.

123. In her article on the "visual stagings" of the bisexual "community," Catherine Deschamps uses the metaphor of a fishhook to evoke the iconic role and the power of attraction of "drag Queens" in gay pride demonstrations and other public displays: "especially in France, bisexual activists do not know how to play on the derision and inversion of stigmata. . . . There is no striking visual promotional tool such as drag Queens . . . to *snag the gaze* of the media; no *hook* that would bring attention to discourses produced by bisexuals themselves" ("Mises en scène visuelles et rapports de pouvoir: le cas des bisexuels," *Journal des Anthropologues* 82–83 [2000]: 251–263; cited from online version, http://jda.revues.org/3381, p. 6; emphasis added).

124. See Sue-Ellen Case, ed., *Feminist Critical Theory and Theater* (Baltimore: Johns Hopkins University Press, 1990).

125. See Kim Michasiw, "Camp, Masculinity, Masquerade," in *Feminism Meets Queer Theory*, 157–186, and Carole-Ann Tyler, "Passing: Narcissism, Identity and Difference," in the same volume, 227–265.

126. In Butler's language, "morphological ideals" are connected with the image of the bodily ego.

127. A *lure*—the word is a true false cognate of the French *leurre*—both seduces and traps.

128. "We know that the unconscious castration complex functions as a knot:. . . in regulating the development that gives its *ratio* to this first role: namely, the instating in the subject of an unconscious position without which he could not identify with the ideal type of his sex or even answer the needs of his partner in sexual relations without grave risk, much less appropriately meet the needs of the child who may be produced thereby" (Lacan, "The Signification of the Phallus," 575).

129. Lacan, "The Signification of the Phallus," 582.

130. Ibid.

131. "The reader may now ask how I define womanliness or where I draw the line between genuine womanliness and the 'masquerade.' My suggestion is not, however, that there is any such difference; whether radical or superficial, they are the same thing" (Joan Rivière, "Womanliness as Masquerade," in *Formations of Fantasy*, ed. Victor Burgin, James Donald, and Cora Kaplan [London: Methuen, 1986], 38). Rivière's article was first published in *The International Journal of Psychoanalysis* in 1929.

132. "With their entry into the phallic phase the differences between the sexes are completely eclipsed by their agreements. We are now obliged to recognize that the little girl is a little man" (Sigmund Freud, "Femininity," in *New Introductory Lectures on Psycho-Analysis*, in Sigmund Freud, *Standard Edition*, vol. 22, p. 118).

133. Lacan, "The Signification of the Phallus," 583.

134. Ibid., 581; emphasis added. From this standpoint, Lemosof is quite right to point out Butler's misreading in the section of the second chapter of *Gender Trouble* titled "Lacan, Rivière, and the Strategies of Masquerade." Commenting on what Lacan says about the projection in comedy of the relation between the "sexes," in the wake of the "subjection" of the "sexes" to the "phallic function," Butler attributes the operation that substitutes "appearing" for "having" to the feminine position alone, perhaps because she has not identified and understood the play on "sides" that is substituted for the play of grammatical genders at the end of Lacan's sentence: "Lacan appears to refer to the appearance of the 'reality' of the masculine subject as well as to the 'unreality' of heterosexuality. He also appears to refer to the position of women (my interruption is within brackets): 'This follows from the intervention of an "appearing" which gets substituted for the "having" [a substitution is required, no doubt, because women are said not 'to have'] *so as to protect it on one side and to mask its lack on the other*.' Although there is no grammatical gender here, it seems that Lacan is describing the position of women for whom 'lack' is characteristic, and hence, in need of masking and who are in some unspecified sense in need of protection" (Butler, *Gender Trouble*, 63; emphasis added). In so doing, Butler misses the distance marked by Lacan here with respect to Rivière's analyses, if not with respect to Freud himself. (See Alain Lemosof, "Roc de *queer*," in *Sexualités, genres et mélancolie*, 116n1.)

Laura Hughes, one of my students in the Centre d'études féminines et d'études de genre at Paris 8, has rightly noted that, in this essay, Lacan is hardly speaking about "men" and "women" but rather about "sexes," or even, as he does here, about "sides," in such a way that one can never be sure what "side" is at issue.

135. Lacan, "The Signification of the Phallus," 581.

136. Ibid., 584.

137. In *Vested Interests*, Marjorie Garber also focuses on the question of masculine masquerade. In "Spare Parts: The Surgical Construction of Gender," a chapter she devotes more precisely to the contemporary forms of transsexuality, she raises ques-

tions about the meaning of this "virile feminine display." Recalling that transsexualism was first considered—and was first manifested—as a phenomenon affecting beings of the male sex wanting to wear female masks, she attributes this dissymmetry to the so-called naturalness of masculinity, the latter being construed as a primary sexual and subjective disposition: The adoption of a "masculine" identity (by men or by women dreaming of becoming "men") is not perceived as akin to a masquerade or a disguise, as long as "[t]here remains some desire to see men as not constructed but 'natural' or essential—hence, again, the 'naturalness' of women's desire to be more like men" ("Spare Parts," 102). For Garber, it would be necessary on the contrary to bring out the equally "fabricated" character of male identity, which the development of a female to male transsexuality and its greater visibility today would help bring to light. If it turns out that male identity belongs, like female identity, to the order of a certain role play, and if it is a matter, as the English expression goes, of "playing a part" ("part" signifying both "role" and "fragment" or "piece," as we have seen), then this male part or script would invalidate the well-established idea that only "men" are "fully" subjects and as such are in relationship with the "whole," whereas women, as "parts," remain "not all" (on the question of "man" as "part," thus as participant in the masquerade, see Garber, "Spare Parts," 94).

138. "Although a number of theorists have suggested that lesbian sexuality is outside the economy of phallogocentrism, that position has been critically countered by the notion that lesbian sexuality is *as* constructed as any other form of sexuality within contemporary sexual regimes" ("The Lesbian Phallus and the Morphological Imaginary," in *Bodies That Matter*, 85).

139. "The Signification of the Phallus," 581; emphasis added.

140. Jacques Lacan, *The Four Fundamental Concepts of Psycho-Analysis*, ed. Jacques-Alain Miller, trans. Alan Sheridan (New York. W. W. Norton, 1981 [first American edition 1978]), session 14, "The Partial Drive and Its Circuit," 83; emphasis added.

141. Ibid., session 15, "From Love to the Libido," 193.

142. Ibid.

143. Ibid., session 9, "What Is a Picture," 107. "In the case of display, usually on the part of the male animal, or in the case of grimacing swelling by which the animal enters the play of combat in the form of intimidation, the being gives of himself, or receives from the other, something that is like a mask . . . Only the subject—the human subject, the subject of the desire that is the essence of man—is not, unlike the animal, entirely caught up in this imaginary capture."

144. Ibid., session 9, "What Is a Picture," 106.

145. Ibid., session 9, "What Is a Picture," 107.

146. Ibid.; emphasis added.

147. See Jacques Derrida, *The Animal That Therefore I Am*, trans. David Wills (New York: Fordham University Press, 2008).

148. Lacan, *The Four Fundamental Concepts*, 107.

149. The absence of a marker of coordination or a copula in the original French text ("C'est par l'intermédiaire des masques que *le masculin, le féminin*, se rencontrent") suggests subtly that there is no obligatory copulation between the two terms. See Lacan, *The Four Fundamental Concepts*, 107.

150. "The vocabulary for describing the difficult play, crossing, and destabilization of masculine and feminine identifications within homosexuality has only begun to emerge within theoretical language.... *The thought of sexual difference within homosexuality has yet to be theorized in its complexity*," Butler writes in "Critically Queer" (239; emphasis added). And in "The End of Sexual Difference?": "The human, it seems, must become strange to itself, even monstrous, to reachieve the human on another plane. This human will not be 'one,' indeed, will have no ultimate form, but it will be one that is constantly negotiating sexual difference in a way that has no natural or necessary consequences for the social organization of sexuality" (Butler, *Undoing Gender*, 191).

151. Jacques Lacan, *On a Discourse that Might Not Be a Semblance*, trans. Cormac Gallagher from unedited French manuscripts (London: Karnac Books, 2000). Published in French as *D'un discours qui ne serait pas du semblant, Séminaire XVIII*, ed. J.-A. Miller (Paris: Seuil, 2006).

152. Lacan, *On a Discourse*, session II, 20 Jan. 1971, p. 12.

153. "[A] very great number of insights that we can have very, very far into the animal phylum ... [show] the essential character, in the sexual relationship, of something that should be clearly limited to the level at which we touch it, that has nothing to do either with a cellular level, whether it is chromosomic or not, nor with an organic level, whether it is a matter or not of the ambiguity of one or other tract involving the gonad, namely, an ethological level which is properly one of a semblance" (Lacan, *On a Discourse*, session II, 20 Jan. 1971, pp. 11–12).

154. "[In] adult age, what is at stake is to be-a-man [a doing-man] (*de faire-homme*) ... this is what constitutes the relation to the other party ..." (Lacan, *On a Discourse*, session II, 20 Jan. 1971, p. 13).

155. Robert Stoller, *Sex and Gender*, 2 vols. (New York: J. Aronson, 1974–1976).

156. "[I]t is in [that] light, ... starting from something that constitutes a fundamental relation, that there is questioned everything that in the behaviour of the child can be interpreted as being oriented towards this being-a-man [doing-man], for example, and that one of the essential correlates of this being-a-man [doing-man], is to indicate to the girl that one is so ..." (Lacan, *On a Discourse*, session II, 20 Jan. 1971, p. 13).

157. See Patrick Garlinger, "Homo-ness and the Fear of Femininity," *Diacritics* 29, no. 1 (1999): 65n14.

158. For a more fully developed commentary on this distinction, see chapter 3 of this work.

159. Arthur Rimbaud, "Royalty," in *Rimbaud: Complete Works, Selected Letters: A Bilingual Edition*, trans. Wallace Fowlie, rev. Seth Whidden (Chicago: University of Chicago Press, 2005), 321.

160. "The bakla in fact often seem to assimilate their identity to a language of visibility and hypervisibility, frequently talking about their charismatic power to seduce as 'exposing ourselves' " (Fenella Cannell, *Power and Intimacy in the Christian Philippines* [Cambridge: Cambridge University Press, 1999], 216).

161. "Bicolano beauty-contestants . . . become the temporary bodily '*lodging places for potency*' which are felt to originate from somewhere 'outside' of one's own culture. *The bakla epitomize these recapturings of power*, not literally through possession, but through a wrapping of the body in symbols of protective status, and a transformation of the persona by *proximity to the power it imitates*, which are in many ways akin to it" (Cannell, *Power and Intimacy in the Christian Philippines*, 223; emphasis added).

162. "The audience's recognition that they are like women—or even better—is terribly important to the bakla. . . . The experience was always one of happiness . . . *But the reason for this happiness was not just that you felt like a woman, but that you felt like a star*" (Cannell, *Power and Intimacy in the Christian Philippines*, 219; emphasis added).

163. Lacan, *On a Discourse that Might Not Be a Semblance*.

164. With the help of writing, one fabricates rules but also their obverse, dreams.

165. See Butler, "Critically Queer," 235.

166. Newton, "My Butch Career: A Memoir," in *Margaret Mead Made Me Gay*, 207 (1996).

167. Newton, "The Misunderstanding," in *Margaret Mead Made Me Gay*, 172.

168. Butler, *Gender Trouble*, 169; emphasis added.

169. See, for example, statements like these: "[T]he sexual might be continuous with something other than sex itself—something like politics"; or "sexual difference [is] a function of sexual dominance"; or "[t]he next question concerns [sexuality's] relation to gender asymmetry and to gender as a division of power." Catharine A. MacKinnon, "Sexuality," in *Toward a Feminist Theory of the State* (Cambridge, Mass.: Harvard University Press, 1989), 439; reprinted in *Feminist Theory: A Reader*, ed. Wendy Kolmar and Frances Bartkowski (Mountain View, Calif.: Mayfield Publishing Company, 2000), 437–448.

170. Brown's essay, titled "Power," with the subtitle "Power without Logic without Marx," begins like this: "It seems to me that contemporary left intellectuals— Marxists, post-Marxists, democratic socialists, critical race theorists, and feminist theorists—are often uncertain about how to think about the nature of power even as they are preoccupied by power's effects." After recalling the main conceptions of power that are contending for primacy on the terrain of left-wing political thought

today, she adds: "[M]ost leftists have been influenced, tacitly or explicitly, by post-Marxist accounts of power and can be described as working rather awkwardly between mutually contradictory conceptions of power" (Wendy Brown, "Power: Power without Logic without Marx," in *Politics Out of History* [Princeton, N.J.: Princeton University Press, 2001], 62).

171. Karlene Faith, "Resistance: Lessons from Foucault and Feminism," in *Power/Gender: Social Relations in Theory and Practice*, ed. H. Lorraine Radtke and Henderikus J. Stam (London: Sage, 1994), 36–66.

172. Butler, "Critically Queer," 224; emphasis added.

173. See Émile Benveniste, *Le vocabulaire des institutions indo-européennes* (Paris: Minuit, 1969), vol. 1, "L'hospitalité," 87–101. Jacques Derrida returned to Benveniste's analysis in his unpublished seminar on hospitality.

174. "I continue to hope for a coalition of sexual minorities . . . I would hope that such a coalition would be based on the irreducible complexity of sexuality and its implications in various dynamics of discursive and institutional power, and that no one will be too quick to reduce power to hierarchy and to refuse its productive political dimensions" (Butler, preface, *Gender Trouble*, xxvii).

175. In "The Signification of the Phallus," Lacan sets the power of the mask in relation to the status of "fetish" that the mask acquires in its function as it fends off castration. Thanks to his disguise and his stage performance, the masked subject would proceed to the phantasmatic restoration of the ideal image of his/her "self," an image that was damaged or torn under the threat of castration. Castration would, in fact, injure narcissism by compromising the integrity of the bodily image as an image of the ideal ego. To become a "queen" would thus mean to heal one's wound by presenting to others the fetishized (or fetishist) image of one's ideal ego.

176. Joan Scott, "Gender: A Useful Category of Historical Analysis," *American Historical Review* 91, no. 5 (1986): 1053–1075. This article, translated into French by Eleni Varikas, was published in an issue of *Cahiers du GRIF* edited by Michèle Riot-Sarcy, Christine Planté, and Eleni Varikas and devoted to "the gender of history": See *Cahiers du GRIF* 37–38 (1988): 125–153.

177. See chapter 4 of this work.

178. Scott, "Gender: A Useful Category of Historical Analysis," 1069.

179. Ibid.

180. "My 1986 essay was . . . for me a way of posing questions that I associated with the influence of Michel Foucault, about how the certain knowledge of 'natural' sexual difference was established, and about how and when one 'regime of truth' was replaced by another" (Scott, "Gender: Still a Useful Category of Analysis?," 9).

181. See the final section of Scott, "Gender: A Useful Category of Historical Analysis," 1070–1075.

182. On the subject of the effects, in the realm of gender relations, of the "dematerialization" of forms of "power" in the era of global capitalism and the reign of financial "speculation," see Pheng Cheah, "Female Subjects of Globalization" in *Genre et postcolonialismes*, ed. Anne Emmanuelle Berger and Eleni Varikas (Paris: Archives Contemporaines, 2011), 215–227.

183. Sedgwick, "Queer and Now," 20.

184. In his famous article "Is the Rectum a Grave?," Leo Bersani says just the opposite: "If you are out to make someone you turn off the camp" (*Is the Rectum a Grave? and Other Essays* [Chicago: University of Chicago Press, 2010], 14). But it is possible to think, as a number of his commentators do, that Bersani's manifest horror of "camp" has to do, above all, with his horror of femininity. What Bersani finds anti-erotic is the "feminine" performance of the drag queen. But what if a "drag king" put on a show for him? Would he be equally "turned off"? Or would he succumb to the charm of this masculine performance the way Newton succumbed to the feminine power of seduction of a drag queen?

185. Butler, *Gender Trouble*, 165.

186. On the importance of "play" in the erotic scene, see, for example, what Foucault says about the "S/M game" in "Sex, Power, and the Politics of Identity," an interview from June 1982 published in *Ethics: Subjectivity and Truth*, ed. Paul Rabinow, trans. Robert Hurley et al. (New York: The New Press, 1997): "[T]he S&M game is very interesting because it is a strategic relation, but it is always fluid. Of course, there are roles, but everybody knows very well that those roles can be reversed. . . . This strategic game as a source of bodily pleasure is very interesting. But I wouldn't say that it is a reproduction, inside the erotic relationship, of the structures of power. It is an acting-out of power structures by a strategic game that is able to give sexual pleasure or bodily pleasure" (169).

187. "But what of those cafés that *do* cater to the gay Parisian? . . . The one I visited in 1954 was located in the rather unpretentious Trocadero Quarter. Downstairs in a somewhat dark cellar, it was lit by candlelight. There was no band and no jukebox, only the very soft music made by a small, dark-haired accordionist seated in a corner of a large white-walled room. . . . young girls and older women whom I saw there were little inclined to brand themselves as specific fems or butches. While several of them wore pants, these pants were more like slacks than like trousers . . . Most of these slack-clad lesbians also wore lipstick and perfume and powder. . . . Those women in that cellar who were not wearing slacks looked quite like women one would see anywhere in 'nice' society. There was none of the harsh, whorish quality about them that some feminine lesbians who frequent homosexual dives have. They seemed to possess mild natures, posed countenances, and pleasant dispositions. There was less ostentatiousness evidenced in their choice of wardrobe, fewer bright colors and bold, dramatic design. They seemed to play everything down" (Ann Aldrich, *We Walk Alone* [New York: Feminist Press at the City University of New York, 2006], 64–65).

188. "The flowing Greek robes worn by habituées of Natalie Barney's Temple à l'Amitié, and the cult of Sappho and all things Greek fostered by Barney's set, offered an alternative sartorial mode, a mode of 'feminine' elegance that declared itself as artistic, aristocratic and sexually free-spirited (rather than monogamous). . . . The lesbianism of Paris, in short, was neither exclusively 'male' nor exclusively 'female'" (Garber, *Vested Interests*, 146).

189. Since the publication of *Queer zones: politique des identités sexuelles, des représentations et des savoirs* (Paris: Balland, 2001), *Queer zones 2: sexpolitiques* (Paris: La Fabrique, 2005), and *Queer zones 3: identités, cultures et politiques* (Paris: Éditions Amsterdam, 2011), Marie-Hélène Bourcier has become known both as the introducer and the most important representative of a certain queer thought in France. She translated *Théorie queer et cultures populaires: de Foucault à Cronenberg* (Paris: La Dispute, 2007), a collection of essays by Teresa de Lauretis, and thereby helped launch a queer version of "cultural studies" in France. A postfeminist lesbian, Bourcier challenges Judith Butler's attachment to the problematics of feminism. She is also a *"performeuse."* As for Béatriz Preciado, a philosopher of Spanish origin living in France, she, too, made her appearance on the queer theoretical scene and in the media in the early 2000s. She published *Le manifeste contra-sexuel* (Paris: Balland) in 2000, in a translation by Marie-Hélène Bourcier; she also plays a role in the cultural theater of queer metamorphoses, on the "king's" side of the stage.

190. An anthology of works by Donna Haraway, including her "Cyborg Manifesto," was published in France in 2007 (*Manifeste cyborg et autres essais: sciences-fiction-féminisme*, ed. Laurence Allard, Delphine Gardey, and Nathalie Magnan [Paris: Exils]). Another work by Teresa de Lauretis, *Freud's Drive: Psychoanalysis, Literature and Film* (New York: Palgrave Macmillan, 2008), appeared in French translation in 2010.

191. Jean Baudrillard, "We Are All Transsexuals Now," in *Screened Out*, trans. Chris Turner (London: Verso: 2002), 9–20.

192. See my analysis of this passage by Gayle Rubin in chapter 5 of this work.

193. For a summary of her theses, see "Thinking Sex," 17–18 and 24–25.

194. Baudrillard, "We Are All Transsexuals Now," 11 (emphasis added): "We no longer have the time to seek out an identity in the historical record, in memory, in a past, nor indeed in a project or a future. We have to have an instant memory which we can plug in to immediately, *a kind of promotional identity which can be verified at every moment.* What we look for today, where the body is concerned, is not so much health, which is a state of organic equilibrium, but fitness, which is an ephemeral, hygienic, promotional radiance of the body—*much more a performance than an ideal state*—which turns sickness into failure. In terms of fashion and appearance, we no longer pursue beauty or seductiveness, but the 'look.'"

3. PARADOXES OF VISIBILITY IN / AND CONTEMPORARY IDENTITY POLITICS

1. Faith, "Resistance: Lessons from Foucault and Feminism," 37.

2. The same can be said of a certain East. This division of the spheres, on which Aristotle based his theory in *Politics*, dates from a pre-Christian and even pre-monotheistic period in which the division between West and East had no meaning, or at least not the meaning it is given today.

3. On this topic, see Anne Emmanuelle Berger, "Comment peut-on être Persane?," *Contretemps* 2/3, special issue, *Voiles* (1997): 77–95.

4. Arthur Rimbaud, "Parisian Orgy or Paris is Repopulated," in Rimbaud, *Complete Works: A Bilingual Edition*, trans. Wallace Fowlie, rev. Seth Widden (Chicago: University of Chicago Press, 2005), 89.

5. The clamorous poor are anything but mute; they are not "without voice," except in the narrow sense that the phrase evokes in politics. It is obviously important that the right to vote in Western democracies should be conceived as a right to "have one's voice heard," since, according to the most common catachresis in French in this domain, one gives or refuses one's "voice" in voting; in elections, "voices" are counted. Western democracy is phonocentric in its foundations; see in this connection Rousseau's *Essay on the Origin of Languages* (in *Essay on the Origin of Languages and Writings Related to Music* [Hanover, N.H.: University Press of New England, 1998]) and Derrida's reading of Rousseau's text (*Of Grammatology*, trans. Gayatri Chakravorty Spivak [Baltimore: Johns Hopkins University Press, 1997]). From this standpoint, does the contemporary shift to an oculocentric regime of political practice not signal, if not a crisis, at least a transformation, not only of democratic practice but of the very notion of democracy?

6. More recently, Joy Sorman, a self-proclaimed French "feminist" writer, declared in an interview in *Le Monde*: "The history of feminism is first of all the history of women's accession to visibility, their irruption onto the public stage" (July 15, 2011). She thus explicitly conflates women's becoming "visible" with their access to the public sphere.

7. Butler, "Critically Queer," 233.

8. Ibid.; emphasis added.

9. See Jamison Green, "Look! No, Don't! The Visibility Dilemma for Transsexual Men," in *The Transgender Studies Reader*, ed. Susan Stryker and Stephen Whittle (New York: Routledge, 2006), 499–508.

10. For the particular way in which I am using this epithet, see the glossary.

11. On this topic, see the end of the interview between Gayle Rubin and Judith Butler titled "Sexual Traffic": After accounting for her abandonment of the category of gender as a political and analytical tool for grasping the variety of sexual types and practices, Rubin concludes her remarks with a detailed evocation of the

various "styles" of practitioners of S/M eroticism. Now, these styles are based on an invocation of "masculine" and "feminine" imagery that reintroduces both the binarity of gender and its double connection with a problematics of the image and a problematics of theatrical performance (see my comments on the subject in chapter 2 of this work). Similarly, in the chapter in *Homos* titled "The Gay Daddy," Leo Bersani seeks to demonstrate the conventional character of a certain S/M phantasmagoria in the queer milieu that would replay power relations—without displacing them—through "its costumes, its roles, its rituals, its theatricalized dialogue" (*Homos* [Cambridge, Mass.: Harvard University Press, 1995], 91).

12. See Jacques Derrida, "Ants," trans. Eric Prenowitz, *Oxford Literary Review* 24 (2002): 36.

13. See Martin Jay, *Downcast Eyes: The Denigration of Vision in Twentieth-Century French Thought* (Berkeley: University of California Press, 1994).

14. From this standpoint, I subscribe wholly to the methodological and political caveats articulated by Eric Fassin in the introduction to his book on gender and sexuality "in the trans-Atlantic mirror" (*Le sexe politique: genre et sexualité au miroir transatlantique*).

15. See Catherine Deschamps, "Mises en scène visuelles et rapports de pouvoir: le cas des bisexuels": http://jda.revues.org/381; and *Le miroir bisexuel: une socioanthropologie de l'invisible* (Paris: Balland, 2002).

16. Joan Scott, "The Evidence of Experience," *Critical Inquiry* 17 (Summer 1991): 773–797.

17. Ibid., 778.

18. Ibid., 779.

19. Samuel Delany, *The Motion of Light in Water: Sex and Science Fiction in the East Village.* New York: Arbor House/W. Morrow, 1988.

20. Delany, *The Motion of Light in Water*, 174; emphasis added. Unlike the French word *sexe*, "sex" in English can designate both a category to which one belongs—male, female, or "transsexual"—and the practice of some form of sexuality.

21. "As I read it, a metaphor of visibility as literal transparency is crucial to his project. The blue light illuminates a scene he has participated in before (in darkened trucks parked along the docks under the West Side Highway, in men's rooms in subway stations), but understood only in a fragmented way. 'No one got to *see* its whole' (*The Motion of Light in Water*, 174; emphasis added). He attributes the impact of the bathhouse scene to its visibility: 'You could *see* what was going on throughout the dorm' (*The Motion of Light in Water*, 173; emphasis added)" (Scott, "The Evidence of Experience," 779).

22. A change in idiom marks the new awareness of identity that follows the "vision" in the passage cited previously: Delany no longer "sees" "individual *homosexuals*" (isolated individuals who are homosexual), but rather "millions of *gay men*": The revelation of the socio-political existence of a male homosexual com-

munity can be read through the transformation of a nosographic category into a sociocultural category indexed by the term "gay."

23. In the context of the political battle waged on the terrain of projected images, one can also point to the many video recordings produced by AIDS patients or their companions with the earliest video cameras. A few of these recordings, which followed the progress of the patient and his disease up to the moment of death, and which thus offered a picture of homosexual life and love in the time of AIDS, made it to the television screen on channels targeting specific audiences (television being the main audiovisual medium at the time). In France, the writer Hervé Guibert filmed his own death struggle this way. Thus even before a certain type of "performance" combining exhibition and autofiction had become widespread, before the creation of the Internet and well before YouTube, male homosexuals had invented a genre of demonstration that was inseparably aesthetic and political, taking advantage of the new technologies of visibilization.

24. Ralph Ellison, *The Invisible Man* (New York: Vintage Books, 1980), xv; emphasis added.

25. The novel's prologue includes a remarkable formula that combines the synecdoche of abstraction with a device resembling hypallage: "Before that I lived in the darkness into which I was chased, but now I see. *I've illuminated the blackness of my invisibility*—and vice versa" (Ellison, *The Invisible Man*, 13; emphasis added).

26. Erving Goffman, *The Presentation of Self in Everyday Life* (Garden City, N.Y.: Doubleday, 1959).

27. Erving Goffman, "The Arrangement between the Sexes," excerpted in *The Goffman Reader*, ed. Charles Lemert and Ann Branaman (Malden, Mass.: Blackwell, 1997), 206.

28. Erving Goffman, *Goffman Reader*, "Gender Display," in *Gender Advertisements: Studies in the Anthropology of Visual Communication* (Cambridge, Mass.: Harvard University Press, 1979), 214.

29. Ibid., 226.

30. "What the human nature of males and females really consists of, then, is a capacity to learn to provide and to read depictions of masculinity and femininity and a willingness to adhere to a schedule for presenting these pictures, and this capacity they have by virtue of being persons, not females or males. One might just as well say there is no gender identity. There is only a schedule for the portrayal of gender" (Goffman, "Gender Display," 214). Thus "human nature" is fundamentally not "natural": it is social, that is, theatrical. To be a human being is to be a "person," in other words, as the etymology of the word indicates, a mask (Latin *persona*). To be a human being, rather than merely a living being, is to be capable of "personifying," thus of embodying genders by adopting one system of representation or another.

31. Ibid. To this question of the origins and sources of masculine and feminine "styles," Goffman responds, as we have seen, with the definitive imprinting of family structure, a hypothesis already formulated by Simone de Beauvoir in *The Second Sex*. However, he fails to explain either why or how the parental power that is exercised over children and that will become the model for relationships between men and women is reduced to paternal power.

32. "The expression of subordination and domination through this swarm of situational means is more than a mere tracing or symbol or ritualistic affirmation of the social hierarchy. These expressions considerably constitute the hierarchy; they are the shadow *and* the substance. And here gender styles qualify. For these behavioral styles can be employed in any social situation" (ibid., 220).

33. On contrary uses of the word "style" in contemporary language, see chapter 2 of this work.

34. "And behavioral style itself? Not very stylish. A means of making assumptions about life palpable in social situations. At the same time a choreography through which participants present their alignments to situated activities in progress" (Goffman, "Gender Display," 214).

35. "One can say that female behavioral style 'expresses' femininity in the sense of providing an incidental, gratuitous portrait. But Durkheim recommends that such expression is a political ceremony, in this case affirming the place that persons of the female sex-class have in the social structure, in other words, holding them to it. And ethnologists recommend that feminine expression is an indication of the alignment a person of the female sex-class proposes to take (or accept) . . . —an alignment which does not merely express subordination but in part constitutes it" (ibid., 224).

36. In *The Presentation of Self in Everyday Life*, Goffman cites a lengthy passage from Simone de Beauvoir's *The Second Sex*, evidence that his interest in the construction of gender and the formation of ideals of gender is long-standing and plays a fundamental role in his overall view of social interaction (see *Goffman Reader*, 102–103).

37. See Judith Butler, "Performative Acts and Gender Constitution," 528: "As opposed to a view such as Erving Goffman's which posits a self which assumes and exchanges various 'roles' within the complex social expectations of the 'game' of modern life, I am suggesting that this self is not only irretrievably 'outside,' constituted in social discourse, but that the ascription of interiority is itself a publically regulated and sanctioned form of essence fabrication."

38. See Butler, *Gender Trouble*, 2nd ed., 45, 190–191.

39. There are complex reasons for this which I sought to analyze in chapter 2 of this work.

40. Jacques Derrida and Christie V. McDonald, "Choreographies," interview translated by Christie V. McDonald, *Diacritics* 12, no. 2 (Summer 1982): 75.

41. See Derrida, "Ants," 17–42.

42. Derrida, "Ants," 18–19; original emphasis in italics; emphasis added in bold.

43. "*I observed the progress of the weaving, to be sure, but without seeing anything, in sum. . . . this extraordinary process remained at bottom invisible . . . It was not impossible, to be sure, to distinguish between a head and a tail . . . But it was impossible to discern a sex. . . . I was drinking it in with my eyes. But without seeing anything, at bottom. I was observing the invisible progress of the weaving . . .*" And so on (ibid., 82–83; emphasis original).

44. "One never goes from *seeing* to *reading* without an absolute leap" (ibid., 36).

45. Ibid., 21. The conference in which Derrida participated, organized by the Centre d'études féminines at Paris 8 in collaboration with the Collège de philosophie, was titled "Lectures de la différence sexuelle" (Readings of Sexual Difference).

46. Ibid., 36; emphasis original.

47. See Anne Emmanuelle Berger, "Sexing Differances," in *differences: A Journal of Feminist Cultural Theory* 16, no. 3 (2005): 52–67, and chapter 4 of this work.

48. Garlinger, "Homo-ness and the Fear of Femininity," 65; emphasis added.

49. Here is what Derrida says about his reading of Nietzsche in "Choreographies": "In *Spurs/Éperons*, I have tried to formalize the movements and typical moments of the scene Nietzsche creates throughout a very broad and diverse body of texts. I have done this up to a certain limit, one that I also indicate, where the decision to formalize fails for reasons that are absolutely structural. Since these typical features are and must be unstable, sometimes contradictory, and finally 'undecidable,' any break in the movement of the reading would settle in a counter-meaning, in *the meaning* which becomes counter-meaning" (Derrida and McDonald, "Choreographies," 69; emphasis original).

50. Jacques Derrida, *Dissemination*, trans. Barbara Johnson (Chicago: University of Chicago Press, 1981), 63; emphasis added.

51. On the relation between identification (or visual spotting) and the neo-Hegelian problematics of recognition, see the work of the German philosopher and sociologist Axel Honneth, especially *La lutte pour la reconnaissance* (Paris: Cerf, 2000), and "Visibility and Invisibility," in *Revue du Mauss*, special issue, *De la reconnaissance*, no. 24 (2004): 136–150. See also the work of the Swiss sociologist Olivier Voirol, especially "Visibilité et invisibilité: une introduction," *Réseaux* 1, nos. 129–130 (2005): 9–36.

52. Linda Alcoff, a contemporary American theorist of race-based and gender-based identity politics, defines the features of race and gender as attributes of the self, and moreover of what one could call, following Freud, the "bodily ego," that is, the physical image of the self as the basis for the self: "Race and gender are forms of social identity that share at least two features: they are fundamental rather than peripheral to the self . . . and they operate through visual markers on the body" (Linda Alcoff, *Visible Identities: Race, Gender and the Self* [New York: Oxford

University Press, 2006], 5). On the notion of "bodily ego" in Freud, see *The Ego and the Id, Standard Edition*, vol. 19.

53. Alcoff, *Visible Identities*, 8.

54. For an analysis of the relation between display or exhibition and power effect, see chapter 2 of this work. In certain respects, my observations converge here, in a contemporary register, with the thinking that historians, anthropologists, and theorists of political power and sovereignty have been devoting for a long time to the relations between "dramaturgy" and "power" (see, for example, Georges Balandier, *Le pouvoir sur scènes* [Paris: Fayard, 1985]).

55. Deschamps, "Mises en scène visuelles et rapports de pouvoir: le cas des bisexuels," paragraph 15.

56. Ibid., paragraph 14.

57. Ibid., paragraphs 18–19.

58. Cf. Bersani, *Homos*: "This . . . is what Freud appears to be moving toward as a definition of the sexual: an aptitude for the defeat of power by pleasure, the human subject's potential for a jouissance in which the subject is momentarily undone" (100). "Psychoanalysis has justifiably been considered an enemy of anti-identitarian politics, but it also proposes a concept of the sexual that might be a powerful weapon in the struggle against the disciplinarian constraints of identity. Furthermore, . . . self-shattering is intrinsic to the homo-ness in homosexuality. Homoness is an anti-identitarian identity" (101). "Indeed, the person disappears in his or her desire, a desire that seeks more of the same, partially dissolving subjects by extending them into a communal homo-ness" (149).

59. On the relation between the scene of the political and its "others," see Derrida and McDonald, "Choreographies."

60. I am referring here to a well-known passage from Foucault's *History of Sexuality*: "It is the agency of sex that we must break away from, if we aim— through a tactical reversal of the various mechanisms of sexuality—to counter the grips of power with the claims of bodies, pleasures, and knowledges, in their multiplicity and their possibility of resistance. The rallying point for the counterattack against the deployment of sexuality ought not to be sex-desire, but bodies and pleasures" (*History of Sexuality*, vol. 1: *An Introduction*, trans. Robert Hurley [New York: Vintage Books, 1990], 157).

4. THE ENDS OF AN IDIOM, OR SEXUAL DIFFERENCE IN TRANSLATION

The first version of this essay, "Les fins de la 'différence sexuelle,'" appeared in *Traduction, Traductions*, a special issue of the journal *Théorie Littérature Enseignement* published by the Presses Universitaires de Vincennes (2008, 153–164). The article was reproduced in October 2008 in the online journal *Les Rencontres de*

Bellepierre, no. 3: http://www.lrdb.fr/articles.php?lng=fr&pg=1062 (accessed April 14, 2012).

1. The interview first appeared in the journal *differences* (*A Journal of Feminist Cultural Studies*), in a special issue devoted to the complex "encounter" between feminism and queer theory; it was later republished in *Feminism Meets Queer Theory*, ed. Elizabeth Weed and Naomi Schor (Bloomington: Indiana University Press, 1997), 68–108.

2. Rubin with Butler, "Sexual Traffic," 173.

3. Ibid., 82–83; emphasis added.

4. "Progressives who would be ashamed to display cultural chauvinism in other areas routinely exhibit it towards *sexual differences*" (Rubin, "Thinking Sex," 15; emphasis added).

5. Fraisse refuses to subscribe to the nature/culture or body/psyche opposition that underlies, in France, the ongoing grievance of "constructionists" against those they accuse of "essentialism."

6. See, for example, Fraisse's remarks in a conversation with Frédérique Ildefonse and Sabine Prokhoris, published in an issue of the electronic journal *Vacarme* devoted to "minorities in the feminine plural" (04/05, fall 1997): "I insist on using the expression 'difference between the sexes,' which, unlike 'sexual difference,' offers no set content. It is an empty concept, and that is good. I am not proposing a theory of difference, but I am concerned with the conditions of epistemological thinking about difference." And again, in "La contradiction comme lieu du féminisme," a compilation of earlier articles posted online in November 2008 by Arnaud Sabatier, editor of the electronic journal *Les Rencontres de Bellepierre* published in La Réunion (http://www.lrdb.fr/articles.php?lng=fr&pg=1074; accessed April 14, 2012): "I have decided to stick with one category, that of the difference between the sexes (*Geschlechtdifferenz*, as the German language aptly puts it, since *Geschlecht* is both sex and gender), which in this case is a category devoid of content."

7. According to Paola Marrati, who uses the notions of "sexual difference" and "difference between the sexes" interchangeably in her discussion of Butler's work, the notion of "sexual difference" functions on the contrary as a Kantian transcendental category for a number of French thinkers (she mentions Lacan, Irigaray, and Kristeva). As such, "sexual difference" does not put into play "any idea of substance or natural or social identity." It is not an experiential fact (natural or cultural), for Marrati, but rather "the condition of possibility for all experience." This is also why, like Kant's categories, it is "*devoid of content*, but [it is rather] that without which no content could be given" ("La vie et les normes," in *Sexualités, genres et mélancolie: s'entretenir avec Judith Butler*, ed. Monique David-Ménard [Paris: Campagne première, 2008], 190–191; emphasis added).

8. See the chapter "Empiricité et monnaie" in her book *La différence des sexes* (Paris: Presses Universitaires de France, 1996), 45: " 'Sexual difference' is a

philosophical position proper to French thought, especially to that of Hélène Cixous and Luce Irigaray; sexual difference is already a definition of the difference between the sexes, the ontological or psychological assertion of a difference, the point of departure of a philosophy of the feminine."

9. Translator's note: The more literal "difference between the sexes" has been maintained throughout this chapter to translate *la différence des sexes*.

10. "The language problems remain to be highlighted, and they are worthy of interest: [S]*exual difference* has biological connotations in English, hence the need to create 'gender' in the hope of escaping a determinist representation" (Fraisse, *La différence des sexes*, 46).

11. I want to emphasize the "quasi" and the kind of thinking about (la "pensée" in Derrida's view cannot be conflated with "la théorie") "quasi" we have inherited from Derrida.

12. See Simon Watney, "The Banality of Gender," *The Oxford Literary Review* 8, nos. 1–2 (July 1986): 14: "It should at once be noted that the sense of sexual difference which informs these overlapping institutions [and Watney is hereby referring to law and the state, but also to sociology, anthropology, cultural studies, and psychoanalysis as institutional disciplines] involves a taken-for-granted distinction between male and female, a sense of opposition which constitutes the bed-rock of their understanding of 'difference.' At the same time, however, each reveals its own sexual unconscious in the degree to which it acknowledges, handles, disavows, or entirely represses the other major axis of sexual difference—that which Freud explores in the name of the object-choice, and to which Foucault gives the word 'sexuality.'"

13. See Geneviève Fraisse, "La contradiction comme lieu du féminisme," and Jean Laplanche, "Psychanalyse et sexualité," conversation with Francis Martens (in *Psychanalyse: que reste-t-il de nos amours?*, ed. F. Martens (Paris: Complexe, 2000), 188.

14. Sigmund Freud, "Femininity," *New Introductory Lectures on Psychoanalysis*, in Sigmund Freud, *Standard Edition*, vol. 22, p. 121.

15. The difference between *Zwiegeschlechtigkeit* and *Bisexualität* is lost in the English translation of this passage: "[Science] regards their occurrence as indications of *bisexuality*, as though an individual is not merely a man or a woman but always both" (Freud, "Femininity," 114).

16. On the subject of the exclusion of "biology," as a matter of principle, from women's studies and the gender studies that came after, an exclusion that restricts the field of investigation and the scope of relevance of these studies in advance, see the excellent contribution to the volume *Feminist Consequences* by Biddy Martin (ed. Elisabeth Bronfen and Misha Kavka [New York: Columbia University Press, 2001]), an important figure in the American dialogue between feminist theory and queer theory ("Success and its Failures," 353–380). Catherine Malabou also works

in a relevant way to move biological thinking (that is, both thinking about biology and the thinking that biology is helping to forge and to inform) away from its "essentializing" reading. In "Woman's Possibility, Philosophy's Impossibility," she relies on the latest work in this domain to show that the notion of "cerebral plasticity" goes against fixed conceptions of identity construction. "As the current incredible growth in epigenetics proves, biology is not essentialist," she writes toward the end of this essay. And she adds, "The space between 'bio' and 'trans' is perhaps already, in itself, a biological phenomenon . . ." (Catherine Malabou, *Changing Difference: The Feminine and the Question of Philosophy*, trans. Carolyn P. T. Shread [Cambridge, UK: Polity, 2011], 138–139).

17. Let us note that in contemporary German, the word *Weib* is rarely used to designate women. Etymologically close to the English "wife," it has the same connotations. The *weibliche* destiny of the bisexual child Freud discusses in his lecture on "femininity" is thus indeed, in this sense, the *domestic* destiny (as spouse or prostitute, according to the different meanings of "wifery") of the female child in the phallocratic regime, something that the notion of "femininity," more general and more polyvalent in French and in English, does not imply as clearly.

18. *Se* is a personal pronoun used in particular with reflexive verbs: *se toucher* = to touch oneself/one another.

19. Hélène Cixous, "Tales of Sexual Difference," in *The Portable Cixous*, trans. Eric Prenowitz, ed. Marta Segarra (New York: Columbia University Press, 2010), 57.

20. On the inevitability and the "responsibility" of "inheritance," and on the necessity of problematizing it, see, for example, what Derrida says in a filmed conversation with Bernard Stiegler: "Only when the assignations are multiple and contradictory is there inheritance, only when they are secret enough to challenge interpretation, to call for the limitless risk of active interpretation. Only then is there a decision and a responsibility to be taken or made." And, further on: "If to inherit is to reaffirm an injunction," then we are only what we inherit. "And we inherit language, which we use to bear witness to the fact that we are what we inherit. It is a paradoxical circle within which we must struggle and settle things by decisions which at one and the same time inherit and invent—necessarily in the absence of stable norms, of programs—their own norms. To say that inheritance is not a good that we receive, to remember that we are inheritors through and through is, therefore, in no way traditionalist or backward-looking" (Jacques Derrida and Bernard Stiegler, *Echographies of Television: Filmed Interviews*, trans. Jennifer Bajorek [Cambridge, UK: Polity, 2002], 26).

21. See Watney, "Banality of Gender," 17: "It is of course impossible to reconcile any sense of this unitary stabilising factor which gender theory finds behind individual identity, with the uneven, unstable nature of subjectivity disclosed by Freud"; and p. 20: "To be gay for Foucault was a state always waiting to be achieved. He believed passionately in the innovative potential of gay culture to contest disciplinary

regimes of power organised in the body, and to construct totally new social, cultural and psychological forms. It was the image of diversity which he shared with Freud."

22. By putting the emphasis on the "sex/gender system," "The Traffic in Women" laid the groundwork for the strategic and epistemological shift from "woman" to "gender" and therefore from women's studies to gender studies programs in the late 1980s.

23. Rubin, "The Traffic in Women," 199–200.

24. Rubin, "Thinking Sex" [1984], 12; emphasis added.

25. On this point, see Elizabeth Grosz's reflection on the different uses of the term "difference" in contemporary thought, and, in particular, on Derrida's handling of the term. In the Fall 2005 issue of *differences*, dedicated to Derrida, Grosz stresses the philosopher's contribution to feminist theory: "It is Derrida who demonstrated that difference exceeds opposition, dichotomy, or dualism and can never be adequately captured in any notion of identity or diversity (which is the proliferation of sameness or identity and by no means its overcoming or difference)" ("Derrida and Feminism: A Remembrance," *differences* 16.3 [2005]: 90).

26. "My title is intended as a citation of a skeptical question, one that is often posed to theorists who work on gender or sexuality, a challenge I wish both to understand and to which I propose a response" (Butler, "The End of Sexual Difference?," 176).

27. A reference to Luce Irigaray, *This Sex Which Is Not One*, trans. Catherine Porter (Ithaca, N.Y.: Cornell University Press, 1985); cf. the heading of the second section in this chapter (Sexual Difference Is Not One).

28. Butler, "The End of Sexual Difference?" [2001], 432.

29. Ibid., 425.

30. Joan Scott, whose theoretical alliances with Butler are long-standing, formulates a similar proposition in a recent article titled "Gender: Still a Useful Category of Analysis?" (*Diogenes* 57, no. 1 [2010]: 7–14), with reference to her well-known earlier essay, "Gender: A Useful Category of Historical Analysis" (*American Historical Review* 91, no. 5 [1986]: 1053–1075). Reflecting on the more or less "critical" uses of the notion of "gender" made by its feminist promoters since her 1986 article appeared, Scott proposes to return to the question of "sexual difference" as it is articulated by psychoanalysis. Not, of course, in order to abandon the feminist problematic of "gender" but on the contrary in order to reenergize it and give it a new inflection. For Scott, it is henceforth a matter of showing that gender is a useful category of analysis precisely because it asks us to "historicize" the way sex and sexual difference have been conceived. At the end of her recapitulation, we thus read: "Perhaps it is sexual difference that now needs to be problematized so that gender can be freed to do its critical work. For this I've found it useful to turn to psychoanalytic theory, not to its conservative articulations (which have, among

other things, been used to shore up the heterosexual family as the key to normal psyches and stable cultures), but to the places where it addresses the difficulties associated with establishing the boundaries and meanings of sexed identities. On the one hand, 'the psychic knowledge of sexual difference . . . is something one cannot not know' . . . On the other hand, there is no certain knowledge of what it means" (Scott, "Gender: Still a Useful Category of Analysis?," 12).

31. "'Traffic in Women' had its origins in early second-wave feminism when many of us who were involved in the late 1960's were trying to figure out how to think about and articulate the oppression of women. The dominant political context at that time was the New Left, particularly the anti-war movement and the opposition to militarized U.S. imperialism. The dominant paradigm among progressive intellectuals was Marxism, in various forms" (Rubin with Butler, "Sexual Traffic," 69).

32. The notion of "second-wave feminism" arose in the United States in tandem with the development of feminist studies and gender theory. The term points to feminist thinking as it evolved in the wake of the various movements of the 1960s. Second-wave feminism is characterized by a strongly theoretical tenor, a focus on sexuality, reflection on the way the hierarchical opposition of the sexes has been constituted, and an attempt to provide the instruments and tools necessary for reading the historical oppression of women.

33. In an effort to justify, theoretically and politically, the decriminalization of "sex workers" and the "sex business" (pornographic publications, films, accessories, and so on), Gayle Rubin protests in the name of Marx against the relegation of the "sex business" to the outskirts of the ordinary marketplace for manufactured objects and service providers, to an ambiguous zone where authorized and clandestine exchanges mingle dangerously: "Marx himself considered the capitalist market a revolutionary, if limited, force. He argued that capitalism was progressive in its dissolution of pre-capitalist superstition, prejudice, and the bonds of traditional modes of life. 'Hence the great civilizing influence of capital, its production of a state of society compared with which all earlier stages appear to be merely local progress and idolatry of nature.' Keeping sex from realizing the positive effects of the market economy hardly makes it socialist" ("Thinking Sex," 20). Is it an "American" paradox? Marx, whose *Introduction to the Critique of Political Economy* (known by its German name *Grundrisse*) Rubin cites here, is *the* major and positive reference of a discourse based on a "liberal" logic with both the political (progressive) *and* economic (capitalist) meanings that the term has long held in American public discourse. (On this topic, see chapter 5 of this work.)

34. Butler, "The End of Sexual Difference?," 201.

35. Ibid.

36. Ibid.

37. See the article "sexe" in the *Dictionnaire historique de la langue française*, ed. Alain Rey [Paris: Dictionnaires Le Robert, 2000]. As we know, we owe to American

medicine the first formulations regarding transsexualism and thus the disjunction between "natural" anatomical sex and psychical gender.

38. As we know, Lacan likes to play with sexually charged signifiers and phonemes. That is because, as he says, "language thinks about nothing else" (*la langue ne pense qu'à ça*). Thus, in *On Feminine Sexuality*, he states: "As opposed to what Freud maintains it is man—I mean he who happens to be male without knowing what to do with it, all the while being a speaking being—who approaches woman, or who can believe that he approaches her, because on that score there is no dearth of convictions, the *con-victions* I spoke about last time" (Lacan, *On Feminine Sexuality: The Limits of Love and Knowledge*, trans. Bruce Fink, Book 20 of *The Seminar of Jacques Lacan*, ed. Jacques-Alain Miller [New York: W. W. Norton, 1998, 72). Here, he wants to be sure that we hear the "con" (English "cunt") that contributes to "con-vincing" us, hence his emphasis on the word. Elsewhere, he doesn't even insist, counting on his audience to catch the undertone.

39. Derrida, "Ants," 39.

40. Ibid.

41. In his study not of colonial languages but of the "language" of colonization in the Francophone world, Dubreuil distinguishes the notion of "discourse" from that of *parlure*, or sociolect. Unlike "discourse," which, in Foucaldian conceptual language, is a usually negatively "oriented" notion, "parlure" designates an "aggregate of language elements" or a combination of "phrases" going from isolated syntagma to complete utterances, which, to be sure, "impose themselves socially and politically as available speech," or even hegemonic speech, but nonetheless create a space for contradictory thinking through the ambiguity of their deployment. Dubreuil gives as an example of this (negatively) "oriented" use of the word "discourse," the notion of "Orientalist discourse" developed by Edward Said. See Laurent Dubreuil, *L'empire du langage: colonie et francophonie* (Paris: Hermann, 2008).

42. See Derrida and Stiegler, *Echographies of Television*, 26.

5. ROXANA'S LEGACY: FEMINISM AND CAPITALISM IN THE WEST

1. Marianne Hirsch and Evelyn Fox Keller, eds., *Conflicts in Feminism* (New York: Routledge, 1990), 2.

2. Interdisciplinarity, which refers to—and destabilizes—the organization of disciplines in institutions of higher education and research, must then be distinguished from "purely" epistemological border crossings. For the "critical" and "pan-epistemophilic" thinking of the Enlightenment already engaged in large-scale boundary-crossings between domains of knowledge and modes of thought, and even in reciprocal grafting.

3. See "What Is Theory?," chapter 1 in Jonathan Culler, *Literary Theory: A Very Short Introduction* (Oxford: Oxford University Press, 1997), 13–14. Because the term *theory* is historically dated and refers to a corpus characterized by several features presumed to be shared, the term "theory" has come to function almost as a proper noun.

4. Wendy Brown, "The Impossibility of Women's Studies," *differences* 9, no. 3 (Fall 1997): 79–101.

5. Ibid., 86. Even so, it must be said that the disaffection Brown notes in the American university context since the mid-1980s with regard to women's, feminist, or gender studies is largely limited to the faculty; student enrollment (men and women alike) in women's studies and queer studies courses has held steady. Faculty members (of both sexes) are less mobilized or less militant, either because they consider that the institutional battle has already been won, or because the field has lost the attraction of "novelty" in their eyes.

6. Wendy Brown, "Feminism Unbound: Revolution, Mourning, Politics," *Parallax* 9, no. 2 (2003): 3–16.

7. I am borrowing this double-edged expression from Laurent Dubreuil, who uses it to speak about the critical import of literature today, but also about the critical state in which it finds itself. See Laurent Dubreuil, *L'état critique de la littérature* (The Critical State of Literature) (Paris: Hermann, 2009).

8. "What does it mean for feminist scholars to be working in a time after revolution, after the loss of belief in the possibility and viability of a radical overthrow of existing social relations?" Wendy Brown wonders at the beginning of her essay ("Feminism Unbound," 4). And again: "What are the possible postrevolutionary modalities of radical and social transformation in our time?" (14).

9. Nancy Fraser, "Feminism, Capitalism, and the Cunning of History," *New Left Review* 56 (March-April 2009): 97–117.

10. Luc Boltanski and Eve Chiapello, *The New Spirit of Capitalism*, trans. Gregory Elliott (London: Verso, 2005).

11. Fraser, "Feminism," 109.

12. On the politics (singular or plural) of utopia, see Michèle Riot-Sarcey, ed., *L'utopie en questions* (Saint-Denis: Presses Universitaires de Vincennes, 2001).

13. Regarding the "pro-prostitution" positions of a number of queer thinkers, Fraisse writes: "The horizon proposed is that of the unionization of prostitutes, their social organization as salaried workers ... It is difficult ... to connect the theory of subversion of sexual norms with the non-utopian pragmatism of the social organization of sexualities. On the one hand, subversion; on the other, realism. Between the two, and this is my addition, the absence of utopia" (Geneviève Fraisse, *Du consentement* [Paris: Seuil, 2007], 117).

14. Drucilla Cornell, *Beyond Accommodation: Ethical Feminism, Deconstruction, and the Law* (New York: Routledge, 1991).

15. Butler, *Gender Trouble*, 4, 48.

16. "Obviously, the political task is not to refuse representational politics—as if we could. The juridical structures of language and politics constitute the contemporary field of power; hence, there is no position outside this field, but only a critical genealogy of its own legitimating practices. As such, the critical point of departure is *the historical present*, as Marx put it" (ibid., 7).

17. Rubin with Butler, "Sexual Traffic," 62–99; repr. in Elizabeth Weed, ed., *Feminism Meets Queer Theory* (Bloomington: Indiana University Press, 1997), 68–108. For a detailed discussion, see chapter 4 of this work.

18. Rubin, "The Traffic in Women," 157–210.

19. "It would be nice to be able to conclude here with the implications for feminism and gay liberation of the overlap between Freud and Lévi-Strauss. But I must suggest, tentatively, a next step on the agenda: a Marxian analysis of sex/gender systems. Sex/Gender systems are not ahistorical emanations of the human mind; they are products of historical human activity" (ibid., 204).

20. Cf. Luce Irigaray, "Women on the Market," in *This Sex Which Is Not One*, trans. Catherine Porter (Ithaca, N.Y.: Cornell University Press, 1985), 170–191.

21. Rubin with Butler, "Sexual Traffic," 97.

22. Rubin, "Thinking Sex," 3–44.

23. Ibid., 10.

24. Rubin with Butler, "Sexual Traffic," 85, 92.

25. "Ultimately, a thoroughgoing feminist revolution would liberate more than women" (Rubin, "The Traffic in Women," pp. 199–200); "I personally feel that the feminist movement must dream of even more than the elimination of the oppression of women. It must dream of the elimination of obligatory sexualities and sex roles" (p. 204).

26. Rubin, "Thinking Sex," 20.

27. Karl Marx, "Grundrisse," in *Selected Writings*, ed. David McLellan, 2nd ed. (Oxford: Oxford University Press, 2000), 398. Cited in Rubin, "Thinking Sex," 20.

28. Marx, "Grundrisse," 398.

29. "Hence the absurdity of considering free competition as being the final development of human liberty, and the negation of free competition as being the negation of individual liberty and of social production founded on individual liberty. It is only free development on a limited foundation—that of the dominion of capital. This kind of individual liberty is at the same time the most complete suppression of all individual liberty . . . The only rational answer to the deification of free competition by the middle-class prophets, or its diabolization by socialists, lies in its own development" (ibid., 407).

30. "The assertion that free competition is the final form of the development of productive forces, and thus of human freedom, means only that the domination of the middle class is the end of the world's history—of course quite a pleasant thought for yesterday's parvenus!" (ibid., 408).

31. See Foucault, *The History of Sexuality*, 154.

32. Rubin with Butler, "Sexual Traffic," 85.

33. Cf. ibid., 92: "There were so many things I loved about [Foucault's *History of Sexuality*]—the brilliance and descriptive richness of his writing, . . . the dazzling insights . . . He generated many wonderful phrases—such as the proliferation of perversions."

34. Alain Rey, ed., *Dictionnaire historique de la langue française*, 3 vols. (Paris: Le Robert, 2000).

35. Rubin, "Thinking Sex," 20.

36. Rubin with Butler, "Sexual Traffic," 74.

37. Ibid., 76.

38. Marcel Proust, *Swann's Way*, trans. Lydia Davis (New York: Viking Penguin, 2003), 396; emphasis added.

39. Émile Zola, *Nana*, trans. Douglas Parmée (Oxford: Oxford University Press, 1992), 89–90; emphasis added.

40. See Elsa Dorlin, "Les putes sont des hommes comme les autres," in *Raisons politiques* 11 (Aug. 2003): 117–132.

41. See Alain Corbin, *Women for Hire: Prostitution and Sexuality in France after 1850*, trans. Alan Sheridan (Cambridge, Mass.: Harvard University Press, 1990).

42. *Travail* is one of the four modern "Gospels" that Zola set out to write between 1898 and 1902, the year of his death. The other three were titled *Fécondité* (Fertility), *Vérité* (Truth), and *Justice* (Justice). He was unable to complete the last two volumes.

43. Karl Marx, *Karl Marx's Early Writings*, ed. Quintin Hoore, intro. Lucio Colletti, trans. Rodney Livingstone and Gregor Benton (New York: Random House/ Vintage Books, 1975), "Economic and Philosophical Manuscripts (1844), Third Manuscript, section 2, "Private Property and Communism," 350; cf. the original German: "Die Prostitution nur ein *besondrer* Ausdruck der *allgemeinen* Prostitution des *Arbeiters*, und da die Prostitution ein Verhältnis ist, worin nicht nur der Prostituierte, sondern auch der Prostituierende fällt—dessen Niedertracht noch größer ist—, so fällt auch der Kapitalist etc. in diese Kategorie." The French edition treats as a note by Marx the portion given here between dashes and at the end of the paragraph in the body of the original manuscript, after the words "*der durchgefürhte Humanismus der Natur.*" The German editors for their part have reproduced these passages in their *Lesarten* (editors' notes), indicating that the text was included between dashes in the body of the manuscript. See Ökonomisch-philosophische *Manuskripte aus dem Jahre 1844*, 3. Privateingentum und Kommunismus," 538, Lesarten A 58, Ebook Bibliothek Zeno.org.

44. Marx, *Karl Marx's Early Writings*, 346.

45. Ibid.

46. "Die Prostitution ein Verhältnis ist, worin nicht nur *der Prostituierte*, sondern auch *der Prostituierende* fällt" (cf. n. 41; emphasis added). It is noteworthy that Marx does not write *die Prostituierte* but *der Prostituierte*, using the masculine form here to include both sexes.

47. The reader should not see the order of presentation of Marx's theses adopted here as the reflection of a presumed chronology of their development or of their respective importance in my eyes; it is purely a matter of an order of exposition.

48. Karl Marx, *Wage-labor and Capital*, pref. Frederick Engels, trans. Harriet E. Lothrop (New York: New York Labor News Company, 1902), 22–23.

49. Karl Marx, *Capital: A Critique of Political Economy*, intro. Ernest Mandel, trans. Ben Fowkes (New York: Random House/Vintage Books, 1977), Book 1, Part One, Chapter 2, "The Process of Exchange," 179. Maritornes is a female character in Cervantes' *Don Quixote*. It is worth noting that both "commodity" and "merchandise" are translations of the German *Ware*, a feminine noun. Marx's prosopopeia clearly builds on this linguistic feature.

50. Here is the original German: "Geborner Leveller und Zyniker, steht [die Ware] daher stets auf dem Sprung, mit jeder andren Ware, sei selbe auch ausgestattet mit mehr Unannehmlichkeiten als Maritorne, *nicht nur die Seele, sondern den Leib* zu wechseln" (Karl Marx, *Das Kapital*, in Karl Marx and Friedrich Engels, *Werke* [Berlin: Dietz Verlag, 1962], 100; emphasis added).

51. Marx, *Capital*, 205.

52. Ibid.

53. Ibid., 271.

54. Marx, *Wage-labor and Capital*, 25.

55. Karl Marx, "Wages," in *Collected Works*, ed. Karl Marx and Frederick Engel (New York: International Publishers, 1976), vol. 6, p. 237.

56. Marx, *Capital*, 272.

57. Ibid., 272–273.

58. Marx, *Wage-labor and Capital*, 26.

59. Ibid., 25.

60. Ibid., 24–25.

61. "Money is the absolutely alienable commodity" (Marx, *Capital*, 205).

62. Gail Pheterson, *The Prostitution Prism* (Amsterdam: Amsterdam University Press, 1996), 10.

63. Ibid., 11; emphasis added.

64. "When asked whether they realized that sex work could be dangerous, prostitutes in Nairobi, for example, made it clear that they hadn't become prostitutes to be safe, but to make money and lead an independent life" (ibid., 18).

65. Pheterson, *The Prostitution Prism*, 87.

66. "*Red light district* et porno durable!" September 30, 2010; http://multitudes .samizdat.net

67. Cheah, "Female Subjects of Globalization," 221, 222.

68. Ibid., 222.

69. Right before the passage just cited on the oppression of women who hire themselves out as servants abroad, Pheng Cheah warns: "In the case of foreign domestic workers, it can be argued that what drives their temporary emigration is not only their ideological constitution as good wives, daughters, mothers or sisters, but . . . the crafting of their interests as subjects of needs by bio-power" (ibid., 221).

70. Georg Simmel, *The Philosophy of Money*, trans. Tom Bottomore and David Frisby (London: Routledge and Kegan Paul, 1978).

71. Ibid., chapter 4, "Individual Freedom," 297.

72. Ibid., 335.

73. Ibid., 337.

74. "One may characterize the effect of money as an atomization of the individual person, as an individualization that occurs within the person," Simmel writes (*Philosophy of Money*, 342) and he adds, further on: "Money brings about the differentiation of elements in society just as much as in the individual" (351).

75. Ibid., chapter 5, "The Money Equivalent of Personal Values," 376; emphasis added.

76. Ibid.

77. Balzac and Zola both see in the (an-)economy of prostitution the "upsetting" underside of the process of capitalist accumulation in the bourgeois regime. Here is what Balzac has to say, in *Splendeurs et misères des courtisanes*, about girls who live as if they have money to burn: "But for these little details, a decent citizen would be puzzled to conceive how a fortune melts in the hands of these women, whose social function, in Fourier's scheme, is perhaps to rectify the disasters caused by avarice and cupidity. Such squandering is, no doubt, to the social body what a prick of the lancet is to a plethoric subject" (Honoré de Balzac, *Scenes from a Courtesan's Life*, trans. James Waring [London: Society of English Bibliophilists, 1901]); Web (Project Gutenberg): http://www.gutenberg.org/catalog/world/readfile ?fk_files=1629390 (accessed July 10, 2012).

78. "Now I say that the human being, and in general every rational being, *exists* as end in itself, *not merely as means* to the discretionary use of this or that will, but in all its actions, those directed toward itself as well as those directed toward other rational beings, it must always *at the same time* be considered as an *end*. . . . rational beings, by contrast, are called *persons*, because their nature already marks them out as ends in themselves, i.e., as something that may not be used merely as means . . ." (Immanuel Kant, *Groundwork for the Metaphysics of Morals*, ed. and trans. Allen W. Wood [New Haven, Conn.: Yale University Press, 2002], 45–46).

79. "The same cultural process of differentiation that gives to the individual a special significance which renders him relatively unique and irreplaceable makes money the standard and equivalent of such a divergent range of objects that the

growing indifference and objectivity makes it increasingly less suitable as an equivalent of personal values" (Simmel, *Philosophy of Money*, 380).

80. *Le Monde*, Page débat, 6 January 2012.

81. See the entry *contrat* in the historical dictionary of the French language edited by Alain Rey.

82. Marx, *Capital*, 178.

83. Ibid., 178–179.

84. See Carole Pateman, *Sexual Contract* (Stanford, Calif.: Stanford University Press, 1988), 12.

85. Ibid., 17.

86. Ibid., 135.

87. "A (house)wife does not contract out her labour power to her husband. She is not paid a wage—there is no token of free exchange . . ." (ibid.).

88. Pateman, *Sexual Contract*, 168.

89. Ibid., 147.

90. As long as the wife was supported "for sexual services rendered," in Mauss's terms, the comparison was relevant. It is much less so today in the West, where a majority of women work and have independent incomes.

91. "The short-term prostitution contract cannot include the protection available in long-term relations. In this respect, *the prostitution contract mirrors the contractualist ideal. The* individual as owner will never commit himself far into the future . . ." (Pateman, *Sexual Contract*, 209; emphasis added).

92. See Jean-Jacques Rousseau, *Le contrat social* (first version), chapter 4, "En quoi consiste la souveraineté, et ce qui la rend inaliénable," *Ecrits politiques* III, ed. Robert Derathé (Paris: Gallimard, Pléiade, 1964), 294–297.

93. Marcel Hénaff, *The Price of Truth: Gift, Money, and Philosophy*, trans. Jean-Louis Morhange with Anne-Marie Feenberg-Dibon (Stanford, Calif.: Stanford University Press, 2010), 347.

94. Ibid.; emphasis added.

95. Hénaff, *The Price of Truth*, 347.

96. Ibid., 347n21.

97. Ibid., 360.

98. A prolific playwright and essayist of bourgeois origin committed to the rights of women and slaves, Olympe de Gouges was the author of a celebrated *Déclaration des droits de la femme et de la citoyenne* (1791), modeled on the 1789 *Déclaration des droits de l'homme*. Opposed to marriage and an advocate of divorce after her own unhappy marriage, she died on the scaffold in 1793, condemned for protesting against the "Montagnard dictatorship." She had written: "Woman has the right to mount the scaffold; she must also have the right to mount the [speaker's] platform." It took more than a century and a half in France for women to gain the right to "mount the platform."

99. The Marxist notion of "alienation," inherited from Hegel, no doubt leads back to the notion of "own" (*propre*), of "owning" in itself and of oneself, thus of the self as "self-owned"; without this, the notion is meaningless. At least where the word "alienation" translates in particular the German *Entfremdung,* rather than the word *Erausserung:* unfortunately, the two words are translated by the same single word in both the French and English versions of Hegel. In any case, as Derrida has shown, the opposition between "own" (*le propre*) and "foreign"—or external, *alien*—governs all modern philosophy of the subject in the West.

100. Pateman, *Sexual Contract,* 13–14.

101. Marx, "Grundrisse," 398.

102. Here I am thinking of the American postfeminist Janet Halley, who, in *Split Decisions: How and Why to Take a Break from Feminism,* bases a considerable part of her argument in favor of "moving beyond" feminism on the examination of what she calls the "costs" and "benefits" of such an intellectual and political "operation." See part 3, "The Costs and Benefits of Taking a Break from Feminism" (Princeton, N.J.: Princeton University Press, 2006), 283–363.

103. Daniel Defoe, *Roxana: The Fortunate Mistress,* ed. John Mullan (Oxford: Oxford University Press, 1996). Originally published as *The Fortunate Mistress: or, A History of the Life and Vast Variety of Fortunes of Mademoiselle de Beleau, Afterwards Call'd the Countess de Wintselsheim, in Germany. Being the Person Known by the Name of the Lady Roxana, in the Time of King Charles II* (London: T. Warner, 1724).

104. Just after mentioning the anti-marriage texts by Mary Astell and Lady Chudleigh, Pateman goes on: "A few years later, Daniel Defoe stated that he 'did not take the State of Matrimony to be designed as that of Apprentices who are bound to the Family, and that the Wife is to be us'd only as the upper Servant in the House.' And in 1792, in *A Vindication of the Rights of Woman,* Mary Wollstonecraft criticized the patriarchal claim that woman was 'created merely . . . to be the upper servant who provides [the man's] meals and takes care of his linen'" (Pateman, *Sexual Contract,* 125).

105. I have in mind, in particular, another of Defoe's novels, *Moll Flanders,* published two years before *Roxana;* Montesquieu's *Lettres persanes* (*Persian Letters*), published around the same time (it appeared without the author's name in 1721 and was published again in 1724, the same year as *Roxana,* under Montesquieu's name); and, finally, the Abbé Prévost's *Histoire d'une Grecque moderne* (*The Story of a Fair Greek of Yesteryear*), published in 1740. In *Les lettres persanes,* which may have inspired Defoe, another exotic Roxana speaks in revolutionary terms. Between Defoe's Roxana, the first explicitly feminist "businesswoman" who condemns marriage in favour of free-enterprise prostitution, and Montesquieu's Roxana, who dies on the altar of a different conception of intellectual and sexual freedom, two programs and two contradictory destinies of Western feminist thought are played out.

106. "As Necessity first debauch'd me, and Poverty made me a Whore at the Beginning; so excess of Avarice for getting Money, and excess of Vanity, continued me in the Crime, not being able to resist the Flatteries of Great Persons; being call'd the finest Woman in *France*; being caress'd by a Prince . . ." (Defoe, *Roxana*, 202).

107. As in English, where a prostitute is sometimes said to be "in the game."

108. Defoe, *Roxana*, 289; emphasis original.

109. Here is what Roxana says about her at a point toward the end of the novel when Amy seems to have disappeared inexplicably: "I was, for want of *Amy*, destitute; I had lost my Right-Hand. She was my Steward, gather'd all my Rents, *I mean my Interest-Money*, and kept my Accompts, and, *in a word*, did all my Business; and without her, *indeed*, I knew not how to go away, nor how to stay" (ibid., 318; emphasis original).

110. Corbin, *Women for Hire*, 114.

111. Ibid., 205.

112. See Jill Harsin, *Policing Prostitution in Nineteenth-Century Paris* (Princeton, N.J.: Princeton University Press, 1985).

113. Defoe, *Roxana*, 131.

114. "The thing Under our present Care was to shew not Gratitude only, but Charity and Affection too, to our kind Friend the QUAKER. . . . and the first word [my Husband] spoke of, was to settle a thousand Pounds upon her, *for her life, that is to say*, sixty Pounds a year; . . . I thought that a little too much too . . . ; so I told him, I thought if he gave her a Purse with a Hundred Guineas as a Present *first,* and then made her a Compliment of *40 l. per Annum* for her life, . . . it would be very handsome" (Defoe, *Roxana*, 250).

115. Defoe, *Roxana*, 131.

116. Ibid., 147.

WORKS CITED

Abelove, Henry, Michèle Aina Barale, and David M. Halperin, eds. *The Lesbian and Gay Studies Reader*. New York: Routledge, 1993.

Alcoff, Linda. *Visible Identities: Race, Gender, and the Self*. New York: Oxford University Press, 2006.

Aldrich, Ann. *We Walk Alone*. New York: Feminist Press at the City University of New York, 2006.

Astell, Mary. *Some Reflections upon Marriage*. London: John Nutt, 1700.

Austin, J. L. *How to Do Things with Words: The William James Lectures delivered at Harvard University in 1955*. Edited by J. O. Urmson. Oxford: Clarendon Press, 1962.

Balandier, Georges. *Le pouvoir sur scènes*. Paris: Fayard, 1985.

Balzac, Honoré de. *Scenes from a Courtesan's Life*. Translated by James Waring. London: Society of English Bibliophilists, 1901. Web (Project Gutenberg). http://www.gutenberg.org/catalog/world/readfile?fk_files=1629390 (accessed July 10, 2012).

Baudrillard, Jean. "We Are All Transsexuals Now." In *Screened Out*, translated by Chris Turner, 9–20. London: Verso, 2002.

Beauvoir, Simone de. *America Day by Day*. Translated by Carol Cosman. Foreword by Douglas Brinkley. Berkeley: University of California Press, 1999.

———. *The Second Sex*. Translated by Constance Borde and Sheila Malovany-Chevallier. Introduction by Judith Thurman. New York: Alfred A. Knopf, 2010.

Benveniste, Émile. "L'hospitalité." *Le vocabulaire des institutions indo-européennes*. Vol. l, 87–101. Paris: Minuit, 1969.

Berger, Anne Emmanuelle. "Comment peut-on être Persane?" *Contretemps* 2–3 (1997): 77–95.

———. "Les fins de la 'différence sexuelle.'" *Traduction, Traductions*, special issue, *Théorie Littérature Enseignement* (2008): 153–164. Reprinted in *Les Rencontres de Bellepierre*, no. 3 (Oct. 2008): http://www.lrdb.fr/articles.php?lng=fr&pg=1062 (accessed April 14, 2012).

———. "Les lieux et les moments." Introduction to *Genre et postcolonialismes: dialogues transcontinentaux*, ed. Anne Emmanuelle Berger and Eleni Varikas, 3–10. Paris: Éditions des Archives contemporaines, 2011.

———. "Sexing Differances." In *differences: A Journal of Cultural Feminist Studies*, special issue, *Derrida's Gift* 16, no. 3 (2005): 52–67.

———. "Traversées de frontières: postcolonialité et études de genre en Amérique." In *Faut-il être post-colonial?* Edited by Laurent Dubrueil. Special issue, *Labyrinthe* 24 (2006): 10–37.

Bersani, Leo. "The Gay Daddy." In *Homos*, 77–112. Cambridge, Mass.: Harvard University Press, 1995.

———. *Homos*. Cambridge, Mass.: Harvard University Press, 1995.

———. "Is the Rectum a Grave?" In *Is the Rectum a Grave? and Other Essays*, 3–31. Chicago: University of Chicago Press, 2010.

Boltanski, Luc, and Eve Chiapello. *The New Spirit of Capitalism*. Translated by Gregory Elliott. London: Verso, 2005.

Bourcier, Marie-Hélène. *Queer zones: politique des identités sexuelles, des représentations et des savoirs*. Paris: Balland, 2001.

———. *Queer zones 2: sexpolitiques*. Paris: La Fabrique, 2005.

———. *Queer zones 3: identités, cultures et politiques*. Paris: Éditions Amsterdam, 2011.

———. "*Red light district* et porno durable!" September 30, 2010, http://multitudes .samizdat.net.

Brown, Wendy. "Feminism Unbound: Revolution, Mourning, Politics." *Parallax* 9, no. 2 (2003): 3–16.

———. "The Impossibility of Women's Studies." *differences* 9, no. 3 (Fall 1997): 79–101.

———. "Power: Power without Logic without Marx." In *Politics Out of History*, 62–90. Princeton, N.J.: Princeton University Press, 2001.

Butler, Judith. "Against Proper Objects." *differences* 6, nos. 2–3 (1994): 1–26. Reprinted in *Feminism Meets Queer Theory*, edited by Elizabeth Weed and Naomi Schor, 1–30. Bloomington: Indiana University Press, 1997.

———. *Bodies That Matter: On the Discursive Limits of Sex*. New York: Routledge, 1993.

———. "'Conscience Doth Make Subjects of Us All': Althusser's Subjection." In *The Psychic Life of Power: Theories in Subjection*, 106–131. Stanford, Calif.: Stanford University Press, 1997.

———. "Critically Queer." In *Bodies That Matter: On the Discursive Limits of "Sex*," 223–242. New York: Routledge, 1993.

———. "The End of Sexual Difference?" In *Feminist Consequences: Theory for the New Century*, edited by Elisabeth Bronfen and Misha Kavka, 414–434. New York: Columbia University Press. Revised version in *Undoing Gender* (New York: Routledge, 2004), 174–203.

———. *Excitable Speech: A Politics of the Performative*. New York: Routledge, 1997.

———. "Gender Is Burning: Questions of Appropriation and Subversion." In *Bodies That Matter: On the Discursive Limits of "Sex,"* 121–140. New York: Routledge, 1993.

———. *Gender Trouble: Feminism and the Subversion of Identity*. New York: Routledge, 1999.

———. "The Lesbian Phallus and the Morphological Imaginary." In *Bodies That Matter: On the Discursive Limits of "Sex,"* 57–91. New York: Routledge, 1993.

———. "Melancholy Gender/Refused Identification." In *The Psychic Life of Power: Theories in Subjection*, 132–150. Stanford, Calif.: Stanford University Press, 1997.

———. "Performative Acts and Gender Constitution: An Essay in Phenomenology and Feminist Theory." *Theatre Journal* 40, no. 4 (Dec. 1988): 519–531.

———. *The Psychic Life of Power: Theories in Subjection*. Stanford, Calif.: Stanford University Press, 1997.

Caballero, Francis, and Sauveur Bourkris. Pages débat. *Le Monde*, January 6, 2012.

Cannell, Fenella. *Power and Intimacy in the Christian Philippines*. Cambridge: Cambridge University Press, 1999.

Case, Sue-Ellen, ed. *Feminist Critical Theory and Theater*. Baltimore: Johns Hopkins University Press, 1990.

Castel, Pierre-Henri. "Chronologie et bibliographie représentative du transsexualisme et des pathologies de l'identité sexuelle de 1910 à 1998." http://pierrehenri .castel.free.fr/pageanglaise.htm (accessed April 14, 2012).

———. *La métamorphose impensable: essai sur le transsexualisme et l'identité personnelle*. Paris: Gallimard, 2003.

Cheah, Pheng. "Female Subjects of Globalization." In *Genre et postcolonialismes*, edited by Anne Emmanuelle Berger and Eleni Varikas, 215–227. Paris: Archives Contemporaines, 2011.

Cixous, Hélène. "Tales of Sexual Difference." In *The Portable Cixous*, edited by Marta Segarra, 48–60. New York: Columbia University Press, 2010.

Cixous, Hélène, and Catherine Clément. "Sorties: Out and Out: Attacks/Ways Out/Forays." *The Newly Born Woman*, translated by Betsy Wing. Minneapolis: University of Minnesota Press, 1986.

Corbin, Alain. *Women for Hire: Prostitution and Sexuality in France after 1850*. Translated by Alan Sheridan. Cambridge, Mass.: Harvard University Press, 1990.

Cornell, Drucilla. *Beyond Accommodation: Ethical Feminism, Deconstruction, and the Law*. New York: Routledge, 1991. Repr. Lanham, Md.: Rowman and Littlefield, 1999.

Culler, Jonathan. *Literary Theory: A Very Short Introduction*. Oxford: Oxford University Press, 1997.

David-Ménard, Monique. "L'institution des corps vivants selon Judith Butler." In *Sexualités, genres et mélancolie: s'entretenir avec Judith Butler*, edited by Monique David-Ménard, 197–212. Paris: Campagne première, 2008.

———, ed. *Sexualités, genres et mélancolie: s'entretenir avec Judith Butler*. Paris: Campagne première, 2008.

Dean, Carolyn. *The Frail Social Body: Pornography, Homosexuality and Other Fantasies in Interwar France*. Berkeley: University of California Press, 2000.

———. *Sexuality and Modern Western Culture*. New York: Twayne, 1996.

Defoe, Daniel. *The Fortunes and Misfortunes of the Famous Moll Flanders &c. Written from her own memorandums*. London: T. Edlin, 1722.

———. *Roxana: The Fortunate Mistress*. Edited by John Mullan. Oxford: Oxford University Press, 1996. First published as *The Fortunate Mistress: or, A History of the Life and Vast Variety of Fortunes of Mademoiselle de Beleau, Afterwards Call'd the Countess de Wintselsheim, in Germany. Being the Person Known by the Name of the Lady Roxana, in the Time of King Charles II*. London: T. Warner, 1724.

Delany, Samuel. *The Motion of Light in Water: Sex and Science Fiction in the East Village*. New York: Arbor House/W. Morrow, 1988.

De Lauretis, Teresa. *Freud's Drive: Psychoanalysis, Literature and Film*. New York: Palgrave Macmillan, 2008.

———. *Théorie queer et cultures populaires: de Foucault à Cronenberg*. Translated by Marie-Hélène Bourcier. Paris: La Dispute, 2007.

———. *Queer Theory: Lesbian and Gay Sexualities*. Bloomington: Indiana University Press, 1991.

Derrida, Jacques. *The Animal that Therefore I Am*. Edited by Marie-Louise Mallet. Translated by David Wills. New York: Fordham University Press, 2008.

———. "Ants." Translated by Eric Prenowitz. *Oxford Literary Review* 24 (2002): 17–42.

———. *Dissemination*. Translated by Barbara Johnson. Chicago: University of Chicago Press, 1981.

———. *Of Grammatology*. Translated by Gayatri Chakravorty Spivak. Baltimore: Johns Hopkins University Press, 1997.

———. "Plato's Pharmacy." In *Dissemination*, translated by Barbara Johnson, 61–171. Chicago: University of Chicago Press, 1981.

———. "Signature Event Context." In *Margins of Philosophy*, translated by Alan Bass, 307–330. Chicago: University of Chicago Press, 1982.

Derrida, Jacques, and Christie V. McDonald. "Choreographies." Translated by Christie V. McDonald. *Diacritics* 12, no. 2 (Summer 1982): 66–76.

Derrida, Jacques, and Bernard Stiegler. *Echographies of Television: Filmed Interviews*. Translated by Jennifer Bajorek. Cambridge, UK: Polity, 2002.

Deschamps, Catherine. *Le miroir bisexuel: une socio-anthropologie de l'invisible*. Paris: Balland, 2002.

———. "Mises en scène visuelles et rapports de pouvoir: le cas des bisexuels." *Journal des Anthropologues: Anthropologie des sexualités*, ed. Laurent Bazin, Rommel

Mendès-Leite, and Catherine Quiminal 82–83 (2002): 251–263. http://jda.revues
.org/3381 (accessed March 30, 2012).

Diamond, Milton. "Sex and Gender Are Different: Sexual Identity and Gender
Identity Are Different." *Clinical Child Psychology & Psychiatry* 7, no. 3 (July
2002): 320–334. Web version cited: http://www.hawaii.edu/PCSS/biblio/articles
/2000to2004/2002-sex-and-gender.html (accessed March 30, 2012).

Dorlin, Elsa. "Les putes sont des hommes comme les autres." *Raisons politiques* 11
(Aug. 2003): 117–132.

Dubreuil, Laurent. *L'empire du langage: colonie et francophonie.* Paris: Hermann,
2008.

———. *L'état critique de la littérature.* Paris: Hermann, 2009.

———. "L'impossible généalogie du métissage." In *Genre et postcolonialismes*, edited by Anne E. Berger and Eleni Varikas, 165–174. Paris: Archives contemporaines, 2011.

Ellison, Ralph. *The Invisible Man.* New York: Vintage Books, 1981 [1952].

Engels, Friedrich. *The Origin of the Family, Private Property, and the State.* Introduction by Evelyn Reed. New York: Pathfinder, 1993.

Faith, Karlene. "Resistance: Lessons from Foucault and Feminism." In *Power/
Gender: Social Relations in Theory and Practice*, edited by H. Lorraine Radtke
and Henderikus J. Stam, 34–66. London: Sage, 1994.

Fassin, Eric. *Le sexe politique: genre et sexualité au miroir transatlantique.* Paris:
EHESS, 2009.

Foucault, Michel. *Discipline and Punish: The Birth of the Prison.* Translated by
Alan Sheridan. New York: Pantheon Books, 1977.

———. *History of Sexuality, vol. 1: An Introduction.* Translated by Robert Hurley.
New York Vintage Books, 1990 [c. 1978].

———. "Sex, Power, and the Politics of Identity." In *Ethics: Subjectivity and Truth*,
vol. 1, edited by Paul Rabinow, translated by Robert Hurley et al., 163–173. New
York: The New Press, 1997.

Fraisse, Geneviève. *Du consentement.* Paris: Seuil, 2007.

———. "Empiricité et monnaie." *La différence des sexes.* Paris: Presses Universitaires de France, 1996.

———. "J'ai vu les femmes avoir peur." Conversation with Frédérique Ildefonse
and Sabine Prokhoris. *Vacarme* 04/05 (Fall 1997). http://www.vacarme.org/
article1153.html.

———. "La contradiction comme lieu du féminisme."*Les Rencontres de Bellepierre.* http://www.lrdb.fr/articles.php?lng=fr&pg=1074 (accessed April 14,
2012).

———, ed. *L'exercice du savoir et la différence des sexes.* Paris: L'Harmattan, 1991.

Fraser, Nancy. "Feminism, Capitalism, and the Cunning of History." *New Left Review*
56 (Mar.–Apr. 2009): 97–117.

Freud, Sigmund. *Beyond the Pleasure Principle* [1920]. *The Standard Edition of the Complete Psychological Works of Sigmund Freud.* Edited by James Strachey. Vol. 18: *Beyond the Pleasure Principle, Group Psychology, and Other Works.* London: Hogarth, 1964, 7–64.

———. *The Ego and the Id* [1923]. *The Standard Edition of the Complete Psychological Works of Sigmund Freud.* Edited by James Strachey, 12–59. London: Hogarth, 1964. Vol. 19. *The Ego and the Id and Other Works.*

———. "Femininity" [1933]. *The Standard Edition of the Complete Psychological Works of Sigmund Freud.* Edited by James Strachey, 112–135. London: Hogarth, 1964. Vol. 22: *New Introductory Lectures on Psycho-Analysis and Other Works.*

———. "Mourning and Melancholia." *The Standard Edition of the Complete Psychological Works of Sigmund Freud.* Edited by James Strachey, 237–258. London: Hogarth, 1964. Vol. 14: *On the History of the Psycho-Analytic Movement, Papers on Metapsychology and Other Works.*

Gallop, Jane, Marianne Hirsch, and Nancy K. Miller. "Criticizing Feminist Criticism." In *Conflicts in Feminism,* edited by Marianne Hirsch and Evelyn Fox Keller, 349–369. New York: Routledge.

Garber, Marjorie. *Vested Interests: Cross-Dressing and Cultural Anxiety.* New York: Routledge, 1997.

Garlinger, Patrick. "Homo-ness and the Fear of Femininity." *Diacritics* 29, no. 1 (1999): 57–71.

Goffman, Erving. "The Arrangement between the Sexes." Excerpted in *The Goffman Reader,* edited by Charles Lemert and Ann Branaman. Malden, Mass.: Blackwell, 1997. First published in *Theory and Society* 4, no. 3 (1977): 301–331.

———. *Gender Advertisements: Studies in the Anthropology of Visual Communication.* Cambridge, Mass.: Harvard University Press, 1979.

———. *The Goffman Reader.* Edited by Charles Lemert and Ann Branaman. Malden, Mass.: Blackwell, 1997.

———. *The Presentation of Self in Everyday Life.* Garden City, N.Y.: Doubleday, 1959.

Green, Jamison. "Look! No, Don't! The Visibility Dilemma for Transsexual Men." In *The Transgender Studies Reader,* edited by Susan Stryker and Stephen Whittle, 499–508. New York: Routledge, 2006.

Grosz, Elizabeth. "Derrida and Feminism: A Remembrance." *differences* 16, no. 3 (Fall 2005): 88–94.

Halley, Janet, and Andrew Parker, eds. "After Sex: Writing After Queer Theory." Special issue. *South Atlantic Quarterly* 106 (Summer 2007).

Halley, Janet. *Split Decisions: How and Why to Take a Break from Feminism.* Princeton, N.J.: Princeton University Press, 2006.

Haraway, Donna. *Manifeste Cyborg et autres essais. Sciences-Fiction-Féminisme.* Edited by Laurence Allard, Delphine Gardey, and Nathalie Magnan. Paris: Editions Exils, 2007.

Harsin, Jill. *Policing Prostitution in Nineteenth-Century Paris*. Princeton, N.J.: Princeton University Press, 1985.

Hénaff, Marcel. *The Price of Truth: Gift, Money, and Philosophy*. Translated by Jean-Louis Morhange with Anne-Marie Feenberg-Dibon. Stanford, Calif.: Stanford University Press, 2010.

Hirsch, Marianne, and Evelyn Fox Keller, eds. *Conflicts in Feminism*. New York: Routledge, 1990.

Honneth, Axel. "Visibilité et invisibilité." In *Revue du Mauss*, special issue, *De la reconnaissance* 23 (2004): 136–150.

Irigaray, Luce. *Speculum of the Other Woman*. Translated by Gillian C. Gill. Ithaca, N.Y.: Cornell University Press, 1985.

———. *This Sex Which Is Not One*. Translated by Catherine Porter. Ithaca, N.Y.: Cornell University Press, 1985.

———. "Women on the Market." In *This Sex Which Is Not One*. Translated by Catherine Porter, 170–191. Ithaca, NY: Cornell University Press, 1985.

Jardine, Alice. *Gynesis: Configurations of Woman and Modernity*. Ithaca, N.Y.: Cornell University Press, 1985.

Jay, Martin. *Downcast Eyes. The Denigration of Vision in Twentieth-Century French Thought*. Berkeley: University of California Press, 1994.

Kamuf, Peggy. "Replacing Feminist Criticism." In *Conflicts in Feminism*, edited by Marianne Hirsch and Evelyn Fox Keller, 105–111. New York: Routledge, 1990.

Kant, Immanuel. *Groundwork for the Metaphysics of Morals*. Edited and translated by Allen W. Wood. New Haven, Conn.: Yale University Press, 2002.

King, Katie. "Producing Sex, Theory and Culture: Gay/Straight Remappings in Contemporary Feminism." In *Conflicts in Feminism*, edited by Marianne Hirsch and Evelyn Fox Keller, 82–101. New York: Routledge, 1990.

Lacan, Jacques. *The Four Fundamental Concepts of Psycho-Analysis*. Edited by Jacques-Alain Miller. Translated by Alan Sheridan (New York. W. W. Norton, 1981 [first American edition 1978].

———. *On a Discourse that Might Not Be a Semblance 1971*. Translated by Cormac Gallagher. London: Karnac Books, 2000.

———. *On Feminine Sexuality: The Limits of Love and Knowledge*. Translated by Bruce Fink. *The Seminar of Jacques Lacan*, edited by Jacques-Alain Miller, Book 20. New York: W. W. Norton, 1998.

———. "The Signification of the Phallus." *Écrits: The First Complete Edition in English*. Translated by Bruce Fink with Héloïse Fink and Russell Grigg, 575–584. New York: W. W. Norton & Co., 2006.

Laplanche, Jean. "Psychanalyse et sexualité." Conversation with Francis Martens in *Psychanalyse: que reste-t-il de nos amours?*, edited by Francis Martens, 187–191. Paris: Complexe, 2000.

Lemosof, Alain. "Roc de *queer.*" In *Sexualités, genres et mélancolie: s'entretenir avec Judith Butler*, edited by Monique David-Ménard, 99–122. Paris: Campagne première, 2008.

Lévi-Strauss, Claude. *The Elementary Structures of Kinship.* Translated by James Harle Bell, John Richard von Sturmer, and Rodney Needham, editor. Boston: Beacon Press, 1969.

———. "The Family." In *The View from Afar*, translated by Joachim Neugroschel and Phoebe Hoss, 39–62. New York: Basic Books, 1985.

Longino, Helen, and Evelynn Hammonds. "Conflicts and Tensions in the Feminist Study of Gender and Science." In *Conflicts in Feminism*, edited by Marianne Hirsch and Evelyn Fox Keller, 264–283. New York: Routledge, 1990.

MacKinnon, Catharine. "Sexuality." In *Toward a Feminist Theory of the State*, 126–154. Cambridge, Mass.: Harvard University Press, 1989. Reprinted in *Feminist Theory: A Reader*, edited by Wendy Kolmar and Frances Bartkowski, 437–448. Mountain View, Calif.: Mayfield Publishing Company, 2000.

Malabou, Catherine. *Changing Difference: The Feminine and the Question of Philosophy.* Translated by Carolyn P. T. Shread. Cambridge, UK: Polity, 2011.

Marks, Elaine, and Isabelle de Courtivron, eds. *New French Feminisms.* Amherst: University of Massachusetts Press, 1980.

Marrati, Paola. "La vie et les normes." In *Sexualités, genres et mélancolie: S'entretenir avec Judith Butler*, edited by Monique David-Ménard, 183–193. Paris: Campagne première.

Martens, Francis, ed. *Psychanalyse: que reste-t-il de nos amours?* Paris: Complexe, 2000.

Martin, Biddy. "Extraordinary Homosexuals and the Fear of Being Ordinary." In *Femininity Played Straight: The Significance of Being Lesbian*, 45–70. New York: Routledge, 1996.

———. "Success and Its Failures." In *Feminist Consequences: Theory for the New Century*, edited by Elisabeth Bronfen and Misha Kavka, 353–380. New York: Columbia University Press, 2001.

Marx, Karl. *Capital: A Critique of Political Economy.* Translated by Ben Fowkes. New York: Random House/Vintage Books, 1977.

———. *A Contribution to the Critique of Political Economy.* Translated from the 2nd edition by N. I. Stone. Chicago: Charles H. Kerr, 1904.

———. *Das Kapital.* In Karl Marx and Friedrich Engels, *Werke.* Vol. 23. Berlin: Dietz Verlag, 1962.

———. *Karl Marx's Early Writings.* Introduction by Lucio Colletti. Translated by Rodney Livingstone and Gregor Benton. New York: Random House/Vintage Books, 1975.

———. *Ökonomisch-philosophische Manuskripte aus dem Jahre 1844.* Berlin: Dietz Verlag, 1968.

———. "Wages." Translated by Barbara Ruhemann. In Karl Marx and Frederick Engels, *Collected Works*, vol. 6, 215–237. New York: International Publishers, 1976.

———. "Grundrisse." In *Selected Writings*, edited by David McLellan, 2nd edition, 379–423. Oxford: Oxford University Press, 2000.

———. *Wage-labor and Capital*. Prefaced by Frederick Engels. Translated by Harriet E. Lothrop. New York: New York Labor News Company, 1902.

Michasiw, Kim. "Camp, Masculinity, Masquerade." In *Feminism Meets Queer Theory*, edited by Elizabeth Weed and Naomi Schor, 57–86. Bloomington: Indiana University Press, 1997.

Money, John. *Gendermaps: Social Constructionism, Feminism, and Sexosophical History*. New York: Continuum, 1995.

———. "Hermaphroditism, Gender and Precocity in Hyperadrenocorticism: Psychologic Findings." *Bulletin of the Johns Hopkins Hospital* 96 (1955): 253–264.

Money, John, and Anke Ehrhardt. *Man & Woman, Boy & Girl: The Differentiation and Dimorphism of Gender Identity from Conception to Maturity*. Northwale/London: Jason Aronson Inc., 1996 [1972].

Money, John, J. G. Hampson, and J. L. Hampson. "An Examination of Some Basic Sexual Concepts: The Evidence of Human Hermaphroditism." *Bulletin of the Johns Hopkins Hospital* 97, no. 4 (1955): 301–319.

Montesquieu, Charles de Secondat. *Persian Letters*. Translated by Margaret Mauldon. Oxford: Oxford University Press, 2008.

Newton, Esther. "Dick(less) Tracy and the Homecoming Queen: Lesbian Power and Representation in Gay Male Cherry Grove" (1996). In *Margaret Mead Made Me Gay: Personal Essays, Public Ideas*, 63–89. Durham, N.C.: Duke University Press, 2000.

———. "Imitation and Gender Insubordination." In *The Lesbian and Gay Studies Reader*, edited by Henry Abelove, Michèle Aina Barale, and David M. Halperin, 307–320. New York: Routledge, 1993.

———. *Margaret Mead Made Me Gay: Personal Essays, Public Ideas*. Durham, N.C.: Duke University Press, 2000.

———. *Mother Camp: Female Impersonators in America*. Englewood Cliffs, N.J.: Prentice-Hall, 1972.

———. "My Butch Career." In *Margaret Mead Made Me Gay: Personal Essays, Public Ideas*, 195–212. Durham, N.C.: Duke University Press, 2000.

———. "The Mythic Mannish Lesbian: Radclyffe Hall and the New Woman." In *Margaret Mead Made Me Gay: Personal Essays, Public Ideas*, 176–188. Durham, N.C.: Duke University Press, 2000.

———. "Role Models." In *Margaret Mead Made Me Gay: Personal Essays, Public Ideas*, 14–29. Durham, N.C.: Duke University Press, 2000.

Pateman, Carole. *Sexual Contract*. Stanford, Calif.: Stanford University Press, 1988.

Pheterson, Gail. *The Prostitution Prism*. Amsterdam: Amsterdam University Press, 1996.

Phillips, Adam. "Keeping It Moving." In *The Psychic Life of Power*, edited by Judith Butler, 151–159. Stanford, Calif.: Stanford University Press, 1997.

Preciado, Béatriz. *Le manifeste contra-sexuel*. Translated by Marie-Hélène Bourcier. Paris: Balland, 2000.

Prévost, Abbé. *The Story of a Fair Greek of Yesteryear*. Edited and translated by James F. Jones Jr. Potomac, Md.: Scripta Humanistica, 1984.

Proust, Marcel. *Swann's Way*. Translated by Lydia Davis. New York: Viking Penguin, 2003.

Rey, Alain, ed. *Dictionnaire historique de la langue française*. Paris: Dictionnaires Le Robert, 2000.

Rimbaud, Arthur. "Parisian Orgy or Paris is Repopulated." In *Rimbaud: Complete Works, Selected Letters: A Bilingual Edition*, translated by Wallace Fowlie, revised by Seth Whidden, 85–89. Chicago: University of Chicago Press, 2005.

———. "Royalty." In *Rimbaud: Complete Works, Selected Letters: A Bilingual Edition*, translated by Wallace Fowlie, revised by Seth Whidden, 321. Chicago: University of Chicago Press, 2005.

———. "Story." In *Rimbaud: Complete Works, Selected Letters: A Bilingual Edition*, translated by Wallace Fowlie, revised by Seth Whidden, 313–315. Chicago: University of Chicago Press, 2005.

Riot-Sarcey, Michèle, ed. *L'utopie en questions*. Saint-Denis: Presses Universitaires de Vincennes, 2001.

Rivière, Joan. "Womanliness as Masquerade." In *Formations of Fantasy*, edited by Victor Burgin, James Donald, and Cora Kaplan, 35–44. London: Methuen, 1986. First published in *International Journal of Psychoanalysis*, 1929.

Rother, Adeline. "La coupure implicite: circoncision médicale en Amérique." *sans papier*. http://frenchstudies.einaudi.cornell.edu/files/sanspapier/ARother_sanspapier_sept2009.pdf (accessed April 14, 2012).

Rousseau, Jean-Jacques. *Essay on the Origin of Languages and Writings Related to Music*. Hanover, N.H.: University Press of New England, 1998.

———. *Le contrat social* (first version). In *Écrits politiques* III, edited by Robert Derathé. Paris: Gallimard, Pléiade, 1964.

Rubin, Gayle. "Thinking Sex: Notes for a Radical Theory of the Politics of Sexuality." *The Lesbian and Gay Studies Reader*, edited by Henry Abelove, Michèle Aina Barale, and David M. Halperin, 3–44. New York: Routledge, 1993.

———. "The Traffic in Women: Notes on the 'Political Economy' of Sex." In *Toward an Anthropology of Women*, edited by Rayna Reiter, 158–210. New York: Monthly Review Press, 1975.

Rubin, Gayle, with Judith Butler. "Sexual Traffic: An Interview with Judith Butler." *differences: A Journal of Feminist Cultural Studies* 6, nos. 2–3 (Summer 1994): 62–99. Reprinted in *Feminism Meets Queer Theory*, edited by Elizabeth Weed and Naomi Schor, 68–108. Bloomington: Indiana University Press, 1997.

Schaffauser, Thierry. "La majorité des travailleurs du sexe ne sont pas victimes de la traite des êtres humains." Pages débat, *Le Monde*. January 5, 2012.

Scott, Joan. "The Evidence of Experience." *Critical Inquiry* 17, no. 4 (1991): 773–797.

———. "Gender: Still a Useful Category of Analysis?" *Diogenes* 57, no. 1 (2010): 7–14.

———. "Gender: A Useful Category of Historical Analysis." *American Historical Review* 91, no. 5 (1986): 1053–1075.

Sedgwick, Eve Kosofsky. *Epistemology of the Closet*. Berkeley: University of California Press, 2008.

———. "Queer and Now." In *Tendencies*, 1–20. Durham, N.C.: Duke University Press, 1993.

Simmel, Georg. *The Philosophy of Money*. Translated by Tom Bottomore and David Frisby. London: Routledge and Kegan Paul, 1978.

Simpson, John, and Edmund Weiner, eds. *Oxford English Dictionary*, 20 vols. Oxford: Oxford University Press, 1989.

Stoller, Robert J. "Facts and Fancies: An Examination of Freud's Concept of Bisexuality." In *Women & Analysis*, edited by Jean Strouse, 343–364. New York: Grossman Publishers, 1974. Originally published as "Faits et hypothèses: un examen du concept freudien de bisexualité." Translated by Claude Monod. In *Nouvelle revue de Psychanalyse* 7 (Spring 1973): 135–155. Repr. in *Bisexualité et différence des sexes*, edited by Jean-Bertrand Pontalis et al., 135–155.

———. *Presentations of Gender*. New Haven, Conn.: Yale University Press, 1985.

———. *Sex and Gender*. 2 vols. New York: J. Aronson, 1974–1976.

Tyler, Carole-Ann. "Passing: Narcissism, Identity and Difference." In *Feminism Meets Queer Theory*, edited by Elizabeth Weed and Naomi Schor, 227–265. Bloomington: Indiana University Press, 1997.

Voirol, Olivier. "Visibilité et invisibilité: une introduction."*Réseaux* 1, nos. 129–130 (2005): 9–36.

Watney, Simon. "The Banality of Gender." *The Oxford Literary Review* 8, nos. 1–2. Special issue, *Sexual Difference*, 13–21.

Weed, Elizabeth, ed. *Feminism Meets Queer Theory*. Bloomington: Indiana University Press, 1997.

West, Candace, and Don H. Zimmerman. "Doing Gender" (1977). *Gender and Society* 1, no. 2 (June 1987): 125–151.

Wollstonecraft, Mary. *A Vindication of the Rights of Woman*. Edited by Miriam Brody. London: Penguin Books, 2004.

Zola, Émile. *Labor* = Travail. New York: Harper & Brothers, 1901.

———. *Nana*. Translated by Douglas Parmée. Oxford: Oxford University Press, 1992.

INDEX

Freud, Sigmund: concept of sexual difference, 102, 111–14; on fetishism, 133; on melancholic identification and gender, 37–38, 41–42
"Freud and the Melancholia of Gender" (Butler), 38

Garber, Marjorie, 12, 78, 184–85n137
La Garçonne (Margueritte), 47
Garlinger, Patrick Paul, 64, 101–2
gay and lesbian politics, 85–86
gay genders, 48
gender: Butler's concept of, 26–30, 97, 121–22; distinction from sex/sexuality and sexual difference, 49–56, 64–65, 72, 107–10, 172n14; identification systems and, 93–94; as mask/masquerade, 56, 60–64, 65, 66–67; not a focus of lesbian/gay studies, 52–53; prostitutes and the rules of, 137–38; relationship to power, 65–75; as role in the performance of Wendy Delorme, 13–15; Rubin's concept of, 50, 117, 118–19
Gender Advertisements (Goffman), 93, 94–97
"Gender as a Useful Category of Historical Analysis" (Scott), 72–73
gender difference, 80. *See also* sexual difference(s)
"gender disfunction," 17–19
gender hierarchies, 94–95
gender ideals, 12, 29–30, 57, 60–61
gender identity: Erving Goffman on, 93–97; John Money on, 16–17; Milton Diamond on, 19; politics of visibility/invisibility and, 86–88; transsexualism and, 17–19
Gender-Identity/role (G-I/R), 17
gender incorporation, 36–44
"Gender Is Burning" (Butler), 40, 44, 45–46
Gendermaps (Money), 16
gender melancholia, 37–43
gender oppression, 49–50
gender performance: gender incorporation / melancholia in, 36–44; gender as performance, 26–30; Lacan's "masquerade" as prototype for, 65; linguistic model of, 30–36; Wendy Delorme and, 13–15
gender reassignment, 17–19
gender roles: Esther Newton on, 21–22, 23; John Money on, 15–17; Milton Diamond on, 19
gender solidarity and lesbianism, 136–37
gender studies: in America, 1–4; in France, 1–4, 79; *versus* lesbian/gay studies, 52–53

gender style, 96–97
gender theory: as "crisis state" of feminist theory, 127–28; emergence of feminist gender theory, 20; Erving Goffman's impact on in America, 96–97; as a Franco-American invention, 2–4; performance theory and, 14–15; relationship to queer theory, 14–15, 76–77; *théorie(s) du genre* and, 9; Wendy Delorme and, 11–15
Gender Trouble (Butler), 30–31, 36–37, 41, 68, 76, 97, 127, 129–30
Goffman, Erving, 92–97, 99–100
Green, Jamison, 86
Grundrisse (Marx), 132, 160
Gynesis: Configurations of Woman and Modernity (Jardine), 3

Hall, Radclyffe, 47
Halley, Janet, 1
Hénaff, Marcel, 157–58
heterosexuality, 75–76, 176n50
heterosexual melancholia, 42
Hirsch, Marianne, 126
"history of difference," 88–89
The History of Sexuality (Foucault), 106, 112, 131, 167–68n5
"Homo-ness and the Fear of Femininity" (Garlinger), 101–2
Homos (Bersani), 103
homosexuality: Esther Newton's definition of, 21–22; transsexualism and, 18
Hooker, Evelyn, 16
human trafficking, 148
hyperbole, 29–30

ideal ego, 56–57
"ideality" of gender, 12. *See also* gender ideals
identification, 37–43, 56–57, 102
identification systems, 93–94
identity politics, 103–6
idiom: defined, 111; sexual difference as (*see* sexual difference(s))
image effects, 95
imitation, 13, 27
"Imitation and Gender Insubordination" (Butler), 13, 27
impersonation, 27, 37
"The Impossibility of Women's Studies" (Brown), 128
incorporation, 37, 178n69
individual freedom, 150, 151–52. *See also* freedom
individual owners, 155–56, 158–59

individuals: constituted by monetary exchange, 150–54; market contracts and, 154–60
intersexuals, 19
invisibility. *See* visibility/invisibility
Invisible Man (Ellison), 91–92
Irigaray, Luce, 38, 45
iteration/iterability, 33–35

Jardine, Alice, 2–3
Jay, Martin, 87–88

Keller, Evelyn Fox, 126
"kept women," 153
kitsch, 80–81

labor. *See* wage labor
Lacan, Jacques, 56–64, 65, 66–67, 188n175
"leather" communities, 54
The Lesbian and Gay Studies Reader, 50–51, 52
lesbian continuum, 136
lesbian/gay studies: focus on sexuality rather than gender, 52–53; importance of "Thinking Sex" to, 50–51
lesbian gender play, 25–26
lesbianism: Ann Aldrich's study of, 77–78; Esther Newton on genealogy of, 47–48; gender solidarity and, 136–37; prostitutes and, 138–39
lesbian mimeticism, 24
lesbiennes "lipstick," lipstick lesbians, 13
Lévi-Strauss, Claude, 50
"lipstick lesbians." *See lesbiennes "lipstick"*
Livingston, Jennie, 40, 49
location/dislocation: cultural history and, 110–11; idiom of sexual difference and, 123–25

MacKinnon, Catharine, 69
"mannish lesbian," 47
Margaret Mead Made Me Gay (Newton), 21
Margueritte, Victor, 47
market contracts, 154–60
marriage "contract," 156
Marx, Karl: analysis of wage labor, 140–46, 147, 150; on capitalism and "nature," 160; influence on Rubin's thought, 130–32; on market contracts, 155; Georg Simmel's reading of, 151–52
Marxism, 122, 130–31
masculinity: butches and, 13; as mask/masquerade, 60–64, 184–85n137. *See also* gender ideals; sexual difference(s)

masquerade/masks: femininity as, 22, 58–59, 60–64; gender as, 56, 60–64, 65, 66–67; gender style and, 97; masculinity as, 60–64, 184–85n137
Mauss, Marcel, 150
McDonald, Christie, 97
melancholia, 37–43, 178n70
"Melancholy Gender / Refused Identifications" (Butler), 41–42, 43
"mirror stage," 56–57
"The Misunderstanding: Toward a More Precise Sexual Vocabulary" (Newton), 68
money: in Marx's analysis of wage labor, 142–43; Georg Simmel's analysis of, 150–54
Money, John, 15–17, 19, 172n14
Montesquieu, 83–84
morphological ideals, 39–40
Mother Camp (Newton), 20, 21, 27
The Motion of Light in Water (Delany), 90–92
Mourning and Melancholia (Freud), 37
"My Butch Career" (Newton), 22, 68
"Mythic Mannish Lesbian: Radclyffe Hall and the New Woman" (Newton), 47–48

Newton, Esther: analysis of drag queens and butches, 20–26; Butler's debt to, 26–27; genealogy of lesbianism, 47–48; on power and gender, 68
"new women," 47

On Discourse that Might Not Be a Semblance (Lacan), 63

"paper tigers," 66
Parent-Duchâtelet, Alexandre, 138
Paris Is Burning (documentary), 40, 175n43
Parker, Andrew, 1
Pateman, Carole, 155–57, 158, 159, 160–61
penumbra, 97–98
performance/performatives, 28–29, 31–36, 179n77. *See also* gender performance
performance theory, 14–15
"Performative Acts and Gender Constitution" (Butler), 28
Persian Letters (Montesquieu), 83–84
persons: constituted by monetary exchange, 150–54; market contracts and, 154–60
perversion, 108–9
phallus/phallocentrism, 56, 57–59
Pheterson, Gail, 147–48, 149, 162
Philippines: queer beauty contests in, 65–67
Phillips, Adam, 170–71n4

COMMONALITIES
Timothy C. Campbell, series editor

Roberto Esposito, *Terms of the Political: Community, Immunity, Biopolitics.* Translated by Rhiannon Noel Welch. Introduction by Vanessa Lemm.

Maurizio Ferraris, *Documentality: Why It Is Necessary to Leave Traces.* Translated by Richard Davies.

Dimitris Vardoulakis, *Sovereignty and Its Other: Toward the Dejustification of Violence.*

Anne Emmanuelle Berger, *The Queer Turn in Feminism: Identities, Sexualities, and the Theater of Gender.* Translated by Catherine Porter.

James D. Lilley, *Common Things: Romance and the Aesthetics of Belonging in Atlantic Modernity.*

www.ingramcontent.com/pod-product-compliance
Lightning Source LLC
Chambersburg PA
CBHW032132020426
42334CB00016B/1133